The *Twilight* Mystique

CRITICAL EXPLORATIONS IN SCIENCE FICTION AND FANTASY
(a series edited by Donald E. Palumbo and C.W. Sullivan III)

1 *Worlds Apart? Dualism and Transgression in Contemporary Female Dystopias* (Dunja M. Mohr, 2005)

2 *Tolkien and Shakespeare: Essays on Shared Themes and Language* (ed. Janet Brennan Croft, 2007)

3 *Culture, Identities and Technology in the* Star Wars *Films: Essays on the Two Trilogies* (ed. Carl Silvio, Tony M. Vinci, 2007)

4 *The Influence of* Star Trek *on Television, Film and Culture* (ed. Lincoln Geraghty, 2008)

5 *Hugo Gernsback and the Century of Science Fiction* (Gary Westfahl, 2007)

6 *One Earth, One People: The Mythopoeic Fantasy Series of Ursula K. Le Guin, Lloyd Alexander, Madeleine L'Engle and Orson Scott Card* (Marek Oziewicz, 2008)

7 *The Evolution of Tolkien's Mythology: A Study of the History of Middle-earth* (Elizabeth A. Whittingham, 2008)

8 *H. Beam Piper: A Biography* (John F. Carr, 2008)

9 *Dreams and Nightmares: Science and Technology in Myth and Fiction* (Mordecai Roshwald, 2008)

10 Lilith *in a New Light: Essays on the George MacDonald Fantasy Novel* (ed. Lucas H. Harriman, 2008)

11 *Feminist Narrative and the Supernatural: The Function of Fantastic Devices in Seven Recent Novels* (Katherine J. Weese, 2008)

12 *The Science of Fiction and the Fiction of Science: Collected Essays on SF Storytelling and the Gnostic Imagination* (Frank McConnell, ed. Gary Westfahl, 2009)

13 *Kim Stanley Robinson Maps the Unimaginable: Critical Essays* (ed. William J. Burling, 2009)

14 *The Inter-Galactic Playground: A Critical Study of Children's and Teens' Science Fiction* (Farah Mendlesohn, 2009)

15 *Science Fiction from Québec: A Postcolonial Study* (Amy J. Ransom, 2009)

16 *Science Fiction and the Two Cultures: Essays on Bridging the Gap Between the Sciences and the Humanities* (ed. Gary Westfahl, George Slusser, 2009)

17 *Stephen R. Donaldson and the Modern Epic Vision: A Critical Study of the "Chronicles of Thomas Covenant" Novels* (Christine Barkley, 2009)

18 *Ursula K. Le Guin's Journey to Post-Feminism* (Amy M. Clarke, 2010)

19 *Portals of Power: Magical Agency and Transformation in Literary Fantasy* (Lori M. Campbell, 2010)

20 *The Animal Fable in Science Fiction and Fantasy* (Bruce Shaw, 2010)

21 *Illuminating Torchwood: Essays on Narrative, Character and Sexuality in the BBC Series* (ed. Andrew Ireland, 2010)

22 *Comics as a Nexus of Cultures: Essays on the Interplay of Media, Disciplines and International Perspectives* (ed. Mark Berninger, Jochen Ecke, Gideon Haberkorn, 2010)

23 *The Anatomy of Utopia: Narration, Estrangement and Ambiguity in More, Wells, Huxley and Clarke* (Károly Pintér, 2010)

24 *The Anticipation Novelists of 1950s French Science Fiction* (Bradford Lyau, 2010)

25 *The* Twilight *Mystique: Critical Essays on the Novels and Films* (ed. Amy M. Clarke, Marijane Osborn, 2010)

26 *The Mythic Fantasy of Robert Holdstock: Critical Essays on the Fiction* (ed. Donald E. Morse, Kálmán Matolcsy, 2011)

27 *Science Fiction and the Prediction of the Future: Essays on Foresight and Fallacy* (ed. Gary Westfahl, Wong Kin Yuen, Amy Kit-sze Chan, 2011)

28 *Apocalypse in Australian Fiction and Film: A Critical Study* (Roslyn Weaver, 2011)

29 *British Science Fiction Film and Television: Critical Essays.* (ed. Tobias Hochscherf, James Leggott, 2011)

30 *Cult Telefantasy Series: A Critical Analysis of The Prisoner, Twin Peaks, The X-Files, Buffy the Vampire Slayer, Lost, Heroes, Doctor Who and Star Trek* (Sue Short, 2011)

The *Twilight* Mystique

Critical Essays on the Novels and Films

Edited by Amy M. Clarke *and* Marijane Osborn

Critical Explorations in Science Fiction and Fantasy, 25

Donald E. Palumbo *and* C.W. Sullivan III, *series editors*

McFarland & Company, Inc., Publishers
Jefferson, North Carolina, and London

Amy M. Clarke is also the author of
Ursula K. Le Guin's Journey to Post-Feminism (McFarland, 2010)

LIBRARY OF CONGRESS CATALOGUING-IN-PUBLICATION DATA

The Twilight mystique : critical essays on the novels and films / edited by Amy M. Clarke and Marijane Osborn.
[Donald Palumbo and C.W. Sullivan III, series editors]
p. cm. — (Critical explorations in science fiction and fantasy ; 25)
Includes bibliographical references and index.

ISBN 978-0-7864-4998-9
softcover : 50# alkaline paper ∞

1. Meyer, Stephenie, 1973– Twilight saga series. 2. Young adult fiction, American — History and criticism. 3. Meyer, Stephenie, 1973– — Film and video adaptations. I. Clarke, Amy M., 1961– II. Osborn, Marijane.
PS3613.E979Z595 2010
813'.6 — dc22 2010029367

British Library cataloguing data are available

Manufactured in the United States of America

McFarland & Company, Inc., Publishers
Box 611, Jefferson, North Carolina 28640
www.mcfarlandpub.com

For
Harry and John
perfect pieces of my forever
and
Marie Ohlsen, Alia and Kyra
gleawe ond ælfscýnu each one

Table of Contents

Preface and Acknowledgments

This collection was born in the summer of 2008, when Amanda Price, of the University of California at Davis, anticipated a heightened media interest in Stephenie Meyer's series due to the impending release of the first *Twilight* film. Amanda enlisted UC Davis faculty working on young adult and fantasy literature to serve as press contacts; among them was Amy Clarke. Thus began for Amy a curious season of interviews with various news outlets, including one with the *Washington Post* in which she was portrayed as rabidly anti–*Twilight*.

That interview caused a short-lived barrage of anti–Amy postings on *Twilight* blogs which should have hurt her feelings but instead piqued her interest. Since the most common question interviewers asked Amy was whether she thought *Twilight* was anti-feminist, fan reaction to her (misrepresented) views struck her as a sign of female empowerment. These fans had opinions to voice, and their defense of Meyer and her books was always impassioned and sometimes quite well argued. They also voted with their pocketbooks, making the series and its female author incredibly successful. Amy soon found herself answering emails from students looking for as-then-nonexistent scholarly sources on the *Twilight* phenomenon. So she called on her old friend and mentor, Marijane Osborn, an emeritus professor of English, to help her find an answer to the question: what makes *Twilight* so popular? This collection represents an attempt to explore that question, looking at it from a variety of viewpoints.

Friends, family, and colleagues have all made this work possible.

Amy would like to thank the Teaching Resources Center at the University of California Davis for sponsoring a freshman seminar on the *Twilight* phenomenon; the students in that course responded to several of the essays in this collection and also supplied their own astute observations about the series. Amy would also like to thank Vanessa Goh, Lillian Whithaus and Eileen Rendahl for sharing their perspectives on the series. She is especially grateful to her husband Larry and sons Harrison and John Greer, who patiently walked around piles of books on vampires and werewolves and made very few comments about her bringing *Twilight* into their house. They are especially to be commended for never asking her, "Team Jacob or Team Edward?"

Marijane is similarly grateful to her family, three people especially: First, she would like to thank her niece Alia Stone for conversations so intense and lively that her befuddled brother Rem once fell asleep exhausted on the couch and woke up some hours later to grumble, "Are you two still talking about that stuff?" Second and third, she is grateful to Fay and Camby for rarely grumbling about the project and never phasing in public. She also wants to thank her friend June Gulyassy for introducing her to Hisa Kumagai because of a shared interest in *Twilight*. Hisa is a Japanese-American intellectual over eighty who was transfixed by the books and films because of, she explains, the social dynamics portrayed in them. Another woman friend to whom Marijane sent a copy of *Twilight* for Christmas devoured it and wrote back tersely, "Now I get it!"

Don Palumbo, co-editor of the *Critical Explorations* series, eased the process of getting this book published. Above all others, we are grateful to our contributors, who worked so quickly and so well to bring this book to life and to forge a path for future Meyer scholars.

Introduction: Approaching Twilight

AMY M. CLARKE

To say that Stephenie Meyer's *Twilight* series[1] and its attendant films and fan-world represent a cultural phenomenon is to risk considerable understatement. The first novel in the series, *Twilight*, appeared in 2005, with three following quickly on its heels: *New Moon* (2006), *Eclipse* (2007) and *Breaking Dawn* (2008).[2] By early 2010, these novels had sold a staggering 85 million copies and translation rights for fifty countries[3]; the first *Twilight* film had debuted to the highest opening day profits for any film directed by a woman[4]; graphic novels based on the series were set to debut[5]; and *Twilight* merchandise, from action figures to underwear, abounded.[6] The internet, in the meantime, hosted hundreds of *Twilight*-inspired multimedia websites from around the world, replete with fan-made videos and illustrations, spin-off fiction, and endless commentary from the series' vocal acolytes. While readers were initially teen and preteen girls, their mothers were soon sharing their dog-eared copies; eventually even some reluctant boyfriends and grown men fell under the glamour of the series.[7]

Certainly the escalation of all things *Twilight* was fueled in part by the success of the Harry Potter franchise. J.K. Rowling's equally thorough domination of the world's cultural commons both primed the pump for the marketing of Meyer's books and, after the publication of the final book in the Potter series, left a void, a need for another shared narrative. Like the Potter books, the *Twilight* series features an engaging main character, a fantastic world coexisting with our own mundane one, and the mystery of how the author will bring her story to an end in the final volume. There are of course many other similarities, not the least being the rags-to-riches legends of the Potter and Twilight authors, both young mothers at the time, and neither of whom had published a word before the first novels in their series took to the printed page. And although her massive success has caused us mostly to forget this, Rowling's first few novels were not greeted with overwhelming critical acclaim.[8] Like

Meyer, Rowling was also criticized by feminists, in her case because she featured a male protagonist.[9] But none of this fully accounts for why Isabella Swan, *Twilight's* awkward but relatable narrator, became the heir to Harry Potter's throne. After all, given the success of the Potter books, publishers were claiming that each new young adult fantasy series would be "the next Harry Potter."[10] Why was Bella's story the one that so completely captured the public imagination?

The series' very popularity meant that it would undergo intense scrutiny, first by fans and members of the media then by academics. Religious groups concerned with a story about a girl who risks her soul to become a vampire soon joined the fray. Debate within and between these groups has been, as it was with the Potter series, remarkably vehement, engaging a wide array of issues. How does the *Twilight* series rank as literature? How does Meyer draw from Romance novels, the Gothic, Quileute tradition and vampire lore? Is Bella a bad role model for girls? Is the series, like its author, Mormon? Why are fans so engaged with this story, to the point of making pilgrimages to Forks, WA?

This collection begins to answer these questions. As the articles took shape, we watched in amazement as the contributors went deeper and further in their analyses than we would have suspected possible. Taken together, these essays illustrate that the series is far more complex than a casual first reading would suggest. Out of her original and audacious imagination, Stephenie Meyer has brought forth a narrative that offers multiple layers of appeal to readers, much of that appeal operating on a subconscious level. The contributors to this volume have attempted to delve into some of those layers, to enrich the experience of reading the novels as well as to help answer the driving question: What is it about the books themselves and about the cultural moment they inhabit that has led the *Twilight* series to its phenomenal international success?

To meet the needs of scholars at varying levels, we encouraged contributors to explore a range of voice and style. Similarly, since discussion of the *Twilight* series is so often polarized, we have included essays that represent differing reactions to the Twilight phenomenon, particularly where it involves Bella and the question of her suitability as a role model for girls. Readers should be aware that, even in this introduction, we discuss the entire series using detail but without providing spoiler alerts.

Assessing Stephenie

In the early days of the *Twilight* phenomenon, Meyer-bashing seemed to be a popular sport. In newspaper articles and blogs alike, she was frequently ridiculed for her (purported lack of) writing skill, for her characterization of Bella, and even for the excesses of her avid fan base.[11] The intensity of some of this criticism seemed to be proportionate to her extraordinary success. In these assessments, mainly on blogs and listservs but also in such venerable newspapers as *The Washington Post*, frequent mention was made of the vampire Edward Cullen as a stalker,[12] Bella as a hapless victim, and the author herself as a hopeless writer. The general feeling could be summed up in Stephen King's much quoted statement that Meyer "can't write worth a darn. She's not very good."[13] Yet many "Twi-haters," as vocal critics of all things Meyer are sometimes known, did not read past the first book, some had not finished the first book, and a good many had not read the books at all but still pronounced upon the series with abandon.[14]

Judging the series or indeed the author on the first book alone misses the growth of both Bella and Edward, who change considerably over the course of some 2300 pages, and indeed of the author, who becomes more skilled with each new novel. Granted, these books will never be held up as models of perfect writing. In *Twilight*, for example, we hear too often about Edward's god-like beauty, and he spends an inordinate amount of time touching Bella's face. But such distractions—which some editors would have removed prior to publication—grow less frequent over the course of Meyer's novels. The truth is that few first novels are published, let alone read by millions; Stephen King, for instance, wrote a good deal before his wife fished a draft of *Carrie* out of a trash can and suggested he develop it further.[15] Writing a novel is no ordinary feat, and most writers complete two or three novels (which often go unpublished), before they really master their craft. Meyer's creation story—a housewife with three young children had a dream one night, wrote a novel around that dream and became rich and famous[16]—reminds us that the novel *Twilight* is the work of a new writer. Even so, in her first novel, Meyer tells an engaging story, establishing voice, setting and narrative tension from the very first page, and she builds on these elements in the successive novels.

New Moon extends the narrative by developing Jacob Black as a competitor for Bella's love and introducing the Quileute wolf pack, thus thickening the atmosphere of the texts. Second published novels are notoriously less artistically successful than the first, probably because authors use up their best material in the first book,[17] and *New Moon* does have some structural problems. The Volturi, for example, make a sudden and rushed appearance at the end of the novel,[18] and indeed Edward's disappearance seems contrived to allow the story of Bella and Jacob to evolve. Evidently marketing forces had a hand here, as Meyer's editor encouraged her to extend a story that was originally told in a single book.[19] Nonetheless, the prose improves, depending less on telling and more on nuances of showing, and characters continue to evolve. By *Eclipse*, arguably the best of the four novels in terms of the writing, the author has returned to her narrative stride, balancing the conflict of Bella's choice between Edward and Jacob with the tension of Victoria's vendetta against her.[20] In *Breaking Dawn*, Bella moves on in her progression toward adulthood, marrying Edward and—finally—consummating their relationship. *Breaking Dawn* can be a perplexing novel, switching voices as it does midway, and then switching back again. Certainly, Bella's death and resurrection as a vampire had to be described by a witness rather than narrated in the first person, but the effect of telling that portion of the story in Jacob's voice and of describing Bella's pregnancy from his point of view invites extended analysis.

Despite this interruption in Bella's narrative voice, the four books of the series tell a single cohesive story, that of Bella's maturation from a seventeen-year-old girl, a loner from a broken home, into a married woman, a mother and a member of an extended, loving family. The *Twilight* series is a classic *Bildungsroman*, the story of the education of a young woman. The novels similarly illustrate the growth of their author who, like Bella, matures before our eyes. Nowhere is this better illustrated than in the last chapters of *Breaking Dawn*, where Meyer's prose takes on more energy and force, keeping pace with Bella's changed condition, and telegraphing Bella's excitement over the fruition of her relationship with Edward, the birth of their daughter, and the development of her once-latent powers of shielding. Meyer also resists ending her series in an epic battle in the manner of Homer, Tolkien, Lewis, Rowling and countless other writers of fantasy.[21] Instead of bloodshed, mental acuity of various sorts allows the newly extended Cullen–Wolf Pack clan to walk away the victors. We see a similar unexpected resolution in Meyer's novel *The Host*, further evidence of the author's ability to depart from expectations and to attend to her own sense of narrative.[22]

Twilight*'s Literary Heritage*

Clearly Meyer can sustain readers' attention over the course of a very long narrative. But the *Twilight* books have more to them than page-turning plotting or a tempestuous love story. Meyer borrows eclectically from various traditions, weaving them together in new ways. Marijane Osborn, this collection's co-editor, explores one of Meyer's innovations, the diamond-like shine of the vampires' skin,[23] looking for possible antecedents in the literary tradition. In "Luminous and Liminal: Why Edward Shines," she finds links to the classic fantasies of J.R.R. Tolkien and C.S. Lewis as well as to Beauty and the Beast, among other sources. Meyer has spoken frequently about her love of literature and about her use of some classics of western literature to structure her stories. Yvette Kisor, in her essay, "Narrative Layering and 'High Culture' Romance," expands on the significance of references in the *Twilight* novels to such works as *Wuthering Heights, Pride and Prejudice, Romeo and Juliet* and *The Merchant of Venice.* Not only do these texts anchor Meyer's stories, Dr. Kisor argues, they also subtly create a complex layer of subtext.

Two essays here specifically consider the *Twilight* series in relationship to the Gothic, a genre which arose in response to the Enlightenment's emphasis on reason over religion and which is typically associated with haunted castles, damsels in distress and looming threats from supernatural beings. In "Carlisle's Cross: Locating the Post-Secular Gothic," Lori Branch argues that the Gothic can easily be seen in *Twilight*—in its forest setting, its damsel Bella and the supernatural threat the vampires represent. *Twilight* is so popular, Dr. Branch believes, because our world is again responding to a lack of spirituality, this time as a result of the materialism and displacement of the family that characterized the late twentieth century. Despite the novels' seeming ambivalence about whether redemption is possible for vampires, Carlisle's cross is a reminder of the possibility of salvation. James and Emma Catherine Mc Elroy similarly locate *Twilight* in the Gothic. Like Dr. Branch, they consider setting to be a determining factor in categorizing the series in that genre, but their emphasis in "Eco-Gothics for the Twenty-First Century" is more directly on the locations themselves and on Meyer's porous sense of species boundaries. Their discussion focuses on unique shifts in species relations, interspecies confrontation, and cooperation within an eco-system possible only in the postmodern Gothic.

Kristian Jensen discusses the complicated relationship between Meyer and the Quileute tradition she borrows from and sometimes alters. In his essay "Noble Werewolves or Native Shape-Shifers?" Jensen investigates actual Quileute traditions, comparing them with Meyer's retellings and questioning whether the author has, in the wolf pack and particularly in the person of Jacob, created another version of the "Noble Savage," rendering Native Americans in a stereotypic, artificial light. At the same time, he addresses the issue of whether these wolves should more accurately be described not as werewolves in the European sense, but as shapeshifters.

Abstention and Mormonism: Twilight and Religion

Having described herself from the beginning as an "active member" of the Church of Jesus Christ of Latter-day Saints, Meyer has easily become one of the most famous living Mormons. Though such self-identification would be unlikely to attract as much attention if she said she was Catholic or Jewish, her Mormonism has led many critics to wonder if the books reflect Meyer's religious beliefs or even house a Mormon agenda. Because Bella and Edward, and indeed Bella and Jacob, refrain from sexual activity apart from some quite passionate kissing, and due to the Cullens' refusal to kill humans to satisfy their need for blood, the books have been considered from early on as promoting abstinence. In "Abstinence, American Style" Ann V. Bliss links the abstentions less directly to Mormonism and more to an American tradition of abstention which equally has its roots in religion, particularly Protestantism. The essay that follows this, "Is *Twilight* Mormon?," engages the title question quite directly; in it Sarah

Schwartzman outlines the various ways in which the books conform to Church of Jesus Christ of Latter-day Saints doctrine and norms of behavior, ultimately determining that Meyer's Mormonism is clearly visible in the series but that the books are not meant to be Mormon per se. She also discusses the manner in which religious leaders have struggled to reconcile Bella's consorting with monsters and her desire to become a vampire with a spiritual agenda. In some quarters, this has led to an outright campaign against the books. Conversely, among members of the discernment movement, who attempt to find a spiritual lesson in media popular with the young, the series is seen as having the potential to teach religious lessons.[24]

Is Bella Bad for Girls?

Probably the most debated question about the series is whether Bella is a good role model for the multitude of teenage girls who read and reread these books so avidly. Readers seem to identify with Bella in the same way they do with Jane Eyre or Harry Potter: she is an outlier, introverted and intelligent but lacking in both self-confidence and self-awareness. This identification, however, has led feminists to question a series that from start to finish emphasizes a young woman's relationship to the opposite sex, shows her being physically and emotionally pushed around, and has her marry and bear a child at eighteen. Do the books depict a reactionary sense of female potential?

Susan Jeffers, like Meyer an active member of the Church of Jesus Christ of Latter-day Saints, finds in the books a story of female empowerment. In "Bella and the Choice Made in Eden" she explains the Mormon understanding of Eve's story with its emphasis on Eve's agency and central role in human salvation. When read in this light, Bella can be seen not as a passive victim but instead as a powerful character exercising her choices, and indeed through those choices she both creates and saves her family. Keri Wolf, in "Bella and Boundaries, Crossed and Redeployed," does not address the question of Bella's agency as directly as Jeffers does; instead, she closely analyses the dynamics of Bella's spatial awareness, including her singular ability to move between mundane reality and the treaty-controlled spheres of influence of the Cullens and the Quileute. She argues that in *Twilight* Meyer lays the groundwork—perhaps unwittingly when she wrote that first novel—for the climax of *Breaking Dawn*, where Bella's spatial awareness becomes an aspect of her gift of shielding, a power which ultimately saves her family from the Volturi. Janice Hawes believes instead that the series *does* send girls the wrong message. In analyzing Meyer's use of fairy tales, in particular of "Sleeping Beauty," Dr. Hawes argues that Bella does not confront the difficulties of life as a seventeen-year-old but desires instead to skip them by being changed into a vampire. Though hers is the most directly critical essay in the collection, concerns about various aspects of the series—

Bella's agency or her lack of agency, the Cullens' ecologically questionable use of wealth, the emphasis on beauty and seeming fear of aging, among other things— appear in various forms throughout the collection.

Vampires, Fans, and Film

Despite the fact that Meyer claims she knew that Edward was a vampire from the time of that now-famous dream, she also has been clear from the beginning that the novels are about the experience of first love and not about vampirism per se. Couples in timeless love stories— think of Romeo and Juliet, Mr. Darcy and Elizabeth Bennet, Jane Eyre and Edward Rochester — must face a complication, a barrier that intensifies the lovers' yearning and increases the drama of the climax. Edward's vampirism supplies such a barrier, but Meyer cleverly uses this complication to expand the possibilities of the story, including of course the threats to Bella's life provided by James, Victoria and the Volturi. The author also arrives at her Quileute storyline as a result of the Cullens' presence in Forks (a real place next to a real reservation), thus leading to what many readers consider her most delicious complication to Edward and Bella's story, the young "werewolf" Jacob. But of course the draw that pulls readers through the 2379 pages is the question: Will Bella change? Will she become a vampire herself? Since Alice's visions are subjective and Edward is so opposed to Bella's turning, we cannot be sure, again intensifying the narrative tension.

Some critics of Meyer's work have decried her neglect of the "facts" about vampires.[25] Like most such creatures, Meyer's vampires need blood, are virtually immortal, and are physically and mentally superior to humans. But the author felt no need to follow the "rules" of vampirism as established early on by such writers as Polidori and elaborated upon in the two centuries of vampire stories that have followed. As Stephanie Dowdle writes in "Why We Like Our Vampires Sexy," however, the "historical" vampire not only literally does not exist but the lore of the vampire has never been specifically fixed. Meyer's vampires don't sleep in coffins (or at all), don't have fangs, and can't be destroyed by sunlight; the author has said she was creating her own world and didn't see any reason to abide by anyone else's rules. But this independent attitude may partly account for why Meyer has so captured our attention: she is telling a story authentic to her imagination, making it as "true" a story as possible. As Professor Dowdle makes clear, that story rings so true to some readers that they have made an enormous emotional investment in the *Twilight* phenomenon.

Whether the draw is the possibility of seeing vampires or shirtless Quileute boys or to simply be in the place of the story itself, fans of the series have made pilgrimages to Forks, Washington, and the nearby Quileute reservation part of the *Twilight* experience. In "Forks, Washington: From Farms to Forests to Fans," Christine M. Mitchell writes about the way fan activity in that small Washington town has transformed its economy. Professor Mitchell, who splits her year between winters in a Louisiana college town and summers in Forks, brings a light-hearted approach to her essay but nonetheless plumbs the depths of the fan phenomenon by showing to what lengths— geographically speaking, often quite great lengths—fans will go to extend the *Twilight* experience. How and why fans so avidly engage with the series is also the subject of Pamela H. Demory's "The Pleasures of Adapting: Reading, Viewing, Logging On." Considering the various media in which *Twilight* now appears, including the unfathomable depths of the webworld of fan fiction, Dr. Demory looks at the ways in which books, films, and internet texts interrelate and create for fans both a shared experience and an intensely private one.

The Future of Meyer Studies

It is inevitable that popular interest in Meyer's series will wane; no phenomenon can sustain such a level of fervor. Meyer herself, however, seems to be in the early stages of a long career as a popular writer. Her first science fiction novel, *The Host*, written for an adult audience, debuted in the number one spot on the *New York Times* bestseller list.[26] Doubtless its immediate success was guaranteed by Meyer's fanbase, but the novel is a very respectable first entry in the genre of science fiction and a clear indication that Meyer is not limited to the *Twilight* storyline. Nevertheless, one can begin to predict here: like many venerated fantasy series, *Twilight* will certainly enjoy a long history, though it will resonate differently with future generations, and its influence will reach beyond the scope of the novels themselves. Just as the Potter books did, *Twilight* has already had an immediate effect on the marketing of related books, films, and auxiliary materials, not to mention influencing the content of young adult fiction. Scholarly activity, which began even before this book's gathered essays, will also help Meyer's reputation to endure, since academic interest tends to keep books on class reading lists, extending their shelf life.[27]

We believe the scholarship in this volume will deepen and expand the conversation about the *Twilight* phenomenon, but ours is only a first step, and further avenues for investigation are sure to open up. There are a number of immediately interesting topics we do little more than touch on here. For example, how does Meyer's habit of listening to popular music while writing affect her creative process, and how have her published soundtracks for the books affected the music industry?[28] The series also offers an interesting example for studying how engagement with fans shapes the writing process and, along the same lines, how the *Twilight* films have also been shaped around fan reaction and the growing awareness of studios of the mostly untapped economic clout of female viewers.[29] Meyer, like Rowling, similarly exemplifies a trend in publishing toward massive financial returns on female writers; this, along with Oprah Winfrey and her choices for book clubs, invites investigation into the general influence of women on trends in the arts. Kristian Jensen's article on "Noble Werewolves" opens up more economic and even ethical questions about profiting from use of Native American traditions, but it also invites more discussion about werewolves, shapeshifters and the series' wolf packs. More analysis of Jacob's role in the novels, and of less central characters like Charlie Swan or Leah Clearwater are certainly warranted, as is a consideration of how the films extend the characterization of all concerned. What face, for example, do we now "see" as we read these novels? The first *Twilight* graphic novel, which appeared just on the eve of our finishing this collection, suggests yet another forum for analyzing the role of not only this retelling of the story but of spin-offs in general, both sanctioned and fan-made.[30] While a number of writers here consider Meyer in relationship to fairy tales and some fantasy, there is room for scholarship on how her work relates to science fiction and other forms of fantasy, including comic books.[31] She claims, for example, the Mormon science fiction writer Orson Scott Card as among her favorites. How has she engaged with his work in her own?

All in all, the essays collected here establish a starting place for deeper consideration of Meyer's series and the cultural phenomenon that has risen around it. Both Marijane Osborn and I began the study of *Twilight* with some wonder about why we had been drawn into a young adult story so quickly and easily. The simple answer is because Stephenie Meyer *can* "write worth a darn." Far more is going on in the *Twilight* series than anyone could have guessed, as is evidenced by the riches the scholars who contributed to this volume have unearthed.

Notes

1. Throughout this text, except where our authors use "saga" to add variety, we favor "series," as saga implies a more epic, multigenerational narrative.

2. All books in the series are published by Little, Brown and Company, New York, NY.

3. These figures are taken from the press release for the graphic novel version of *Twilight* posted on stepheniemeyer.com. This release, from Yen Press, was dated January 20, 2010.

4. "All-Time Box Office: U.S.A.," *The Internet Movie Database*, http://www.imdb.com/boxoffice/alltimegross.

5. See note 3 about the press release describing the first volume of this graphic novel series.

6. Stephanie Dowdle discusses *Twilight* marketing in "Why We Like our Vampires Sexy."

7. This hidden culture of boy readers is spoofed in the collegehumor.com video in which two high school boys mock their girlfriends for being obsessed with *Twilight* while revealing their own extensive knowledge of the series, http://www.collegehumor.com/video:1926101. In "Real Men Read (and Love) *Twilight*— Really" author Brad Meltzer admits to his deep fascination with the books, http://www.npr.org/templates/story/story.php?storyId=104347311.

8. Columnist William Safire, in "Besotted with Potter" an opinion piece for the *New York Times*, said about the early Potter books, "Prizeworthy culture it ain't; more than a little is a waste of adult time," 27 January 2000, http://www.nytimes.com/library/opinion/safire/

012700safi.html. Author A. S. Byatt, in the same publication, later contributed an editorial opinion piece describing Rowling's magical world as a "secondary secondary world, made up of intelligently patchworked derivative motifs from all sorts of children's literature," "Harry Potter and the Childish Adult," July 7, 2003, http://www.nytimes.com/2003/07/07/opinion/harry-potter-and-the-childish-adult.html?pagewanted=1. *The New York Times* had a particular stake in determining the literary worth of the Potter books; Rowling's novels so thoroughly dominated its best seller list that a new category was eventually created for children's novels, and Rowling was dispatched to it.

9. For overviews of feminist opinion on Potter see Eliza T. Dresang, "Hermione Granger and the Heritage of Gender," in *The Ivory Tower and Harry Potter: Perspectives on a Literary Phenomenon,* ed. Laura Whited (Columbia, MO: University of Missouri Press, 2002), 211–242; and Sarah Zettel, "Harry Potter and the Charge of Sexism," in *Mapping the World of Harry Potter*, ed. Mercedes Lackey (Dallas: Benbella, 2005), 83–99.

10. A few of the series marketed as the "next Harry Potter" include *Tunnels* (by Roderick Gordon and Brian Williams), *The 39 Clues* (Scholastic: written by a corporate author), *Incarceron* (by Catherine Fisher) and the Percy Jackson books (by Rick Riordan).

11. From early on, while reporting on Meyer's rapid rise to fame and fortune, the news media focused on the series' fan base, the author's writing skills, and the role model Bella presents. This reporting often seemed designed to entertain rather than enlighten, and to entertain particularly at the expense of the author and her fans. My own experience with *The Washington Post* exemplifies this. When asked whether I thought Bella was a bad role model for girls, I expressed ambivalence since *Breaking Dawn* had not yet been published and Bella's story was incomplete. I said that I was not yet sure if she was the kind of female whose story "we really wanted our daughters reading" or if she was a new type of post-feminist hero. The reporter, Laura Yao, only printed the first half of my sentence and included enough other carefully culled statements to make me sound dismissive of Meyer, her writing, and her heroine, in "Bitten and Smitten: Readers Crave Stephenie Meyer's 'Twilight' Tales of Vampire Love," *The Washington Post,* August 1, 2008, C01.

12. The assertion that Edward is an abusive stalker should be taken quite seriously, but it has not yet been discussed at length in an academic essay. While a number of contributors to this collection touch on Edward's behavior, Janice Hawes is the most openly critical of the representation of gender dynamics in the series. Note should be taken that Jacob's behavior toward Bella in *Eclipse* is similarly coercive and sometimes physically so, particularly when he forces a kiss on her. I am I indebted to the novelist Eileen Rendahl for sharing with me her views on Edward.

13. Stephen King made his oft-cited statement about Meyer's writing in an interview with *USA Today*, http://www.usatoday.com/life/books/news/2009–08–03-twilight-series_N.htm.

14. Academics are trained not to judge what they have not seen firsthand. In July 2009, I posted a call for papers for this volume on an academic listserv for members of the Science Fiction Research Association. This call set off a flurry of postings in response, some from scholars who demeaned the series even without having read it. One writer, "Concetta," who saw the movie but admits she had not read the books, nonetheless called the plot of the books "nonsensical." Later in her message she says, "I'm especially turned off by the fact that the main werewolf turns out to be a pedophile (yes, yes, call it 'imprinting' all you want, I'm still not interested)," sfra-l-bounces@wiz.cath.vt.edu.

15. Stephen King, *On Writing: A Memoir of the Craft* (New York: Scribner 2000), 76–77.

16. A description of her dream can be found at http://www.stepheniemeyer.com/twilight.html.

17. I am grateful to Larry Greer for this explanation.

18. In an interview with Oprah Winfrey, Meyer said that her mother read *New Moon* in draft form and suggested that the ending needed more action. Meyer therefore introduced the Volturi, who were already slated to make an appearance in a later volume, into the final

chapters of *New Moon*, November 13, 2009, http://www.mtv.com/movies/news/articles/1626296/story.jhtml.

19. The draft of *Twilight* that Meyer sent to publisher Megan Tingley ended with Edward and Bella's marriage, Lev Grossman, "It's Twilight in American," *Time Magazine*, November 23, 2009, *www.time.com/time/magazine/*article/0,9171,1938712,00.html.

20. In response to *Eclipse*, fan debate raged over which boy Bella should choose, and readers lined up on the sides of "Team Edward" and "Team Jacob." Once trailers for the movie of *New Moon* appeared, with their frequent shirtless shots of the actor Taylor Lautner who portrays Jacob, Team Jacob's side grew considerably.

21. I am grateful to Marijane Osborn for this observation, which bears further analysis.

22. Stephenie Meyer, *The Host* (New York: Little, Brown and Company, 2008).

23. Marijane Osborn notes that Anne Rice's Vampire Lestat describes himself as having "extremely white and highly reflective skin," *The Vampire Lestat* (New York: Alfred A. Knopf, 1985, 3. His skin does not seem to be diamond-hard and *twinkling*, however.

24. Henry Jenkins, in his article "Why Heather Can Write," discusses religious opposition and the discernment movement relative to the Potter series. His ideas can be applied to *Twilight* as well, *Digital Renaissance*, February 6, 2004, http://www.southernct.edu/~hochman/Whyheathercanwrite.htm.

25. To offer one example, in the same online discussion mentioned above in note 14, Mark Finn writes, "I cannot stand this revisionist view of vampires."

26. *The Host* debuted at number one on the *New York Times* Best Seller list, http://www.stepheniemeyer.com/thehost.html.

27. Twilight scholarship is growing, and it already includes a range of approaches and levels of difficulty, from the easy to read and minimally footnoted *A New Dawn: Your Favorite Authors on Stephenie Meyer's* Twilight *Series*, ed. Ellen Hopkins (Borders, 2008; completed before the publication of *Breaking Dawn*), to the somewhat more erudite but still lay-friendly Twilight *and Philosophy*, eds. Rebecca Housel, and J. Jeremy Wisnewski (Hoboken, NJ: John Wiley and Sons, 2009), to our more hybrid approach. A book still in development, which promises a thorough-going scholarly approach addressing a narrower field than we do, is *Bitten by* Twilight*: Youth Culture, Media, and the* Twilight *Saga*, to be edited by Melissa Click, Jennifer Stevens Aubrey, and Lissa Behm-Morawitz.

28. Meyer posts playlists for all her novels, including links to play the songs for free, stepheniemeyer.com. Her patronage has boosted the careers of bands like Muse. She also collaborated on a music video for the band Jack's Mannequin.

29. The image of Meyer writing in her kitchen with one child on her lap and the other on her knee very much invokes the image of women writers of the nineteenth century who wrote bestselling popular fiction, including Gothic fiction, and who angered writers like Nathaniel Hawthorne who was not making money off his writing. He described them as that "damned mob of scribbling women." Quoted in Person, Leland S. Person, *The Cambridge Introduction to Nathaniel Hawthorne* (New York: Cambridge University Press, 2007), 24.

30. There is a definite superhero/comic book quality in the image of Bella wielding her "shield" in the final scenes of *Breaking Dawn*.

31. Another image that Meyer seems to borrow from speculative fiction, this time from Mary Shelley's *Frankenstein*, is that of Edward enacting the mad scientist in Carlisle's office as he "creates" the vampire Bella.

Luminous and Liminal: Why Edward Shines

Marijane Osborn

A perfect statue [...] glittering like crystal.[1]

Stephenie Meyer says that she found the characteristics of a vampire on the internet, just as her protagonist Bella does.[2] But Bella soon finds out that the vampires of the Cullen family are not traditional — that is, of the tradition established for Western Europe by Polidori and Stoker and elaborated by later writers. As Edward comments wryly, the Cullens don't exactly "adhere" to the "canon."[3] Re-imagined vampires are not unique to *Twilight*, however, for within the last generation or so, thanks especially to the innovative efforts of Joss Whedon, vampire tradition has been rapidly changing.[4] Once the pale and grotesque vampire prowled by night, emerging hungry from his coffin to seek the human blood that made him immortal, or nearly so, and it took a stake through the heart to slay him,[5] but by the late twentieth century hardly any of the original qualities remain, the most spectacular changes being the vampire's attractiveness and the ability of some to abstain from human blood. Handsome Edward mocks the old tales; when Bella probes him about vampires being burned by sunlight and sleeping in coffins, he responds by laughing, "Myth."[6] Though he does not mock the most central of all vampire attributes (indeed, it torments him), he mocks Bella's casualness about it, and asks her if she isn't concerned about his diet. With uneasy irony, Bella brings up coffins again when she visits the Cullens' luxurious home in the woods. "No coffins," Edward promises.[7] No need; Meyer's vampires don't sleep.

Even with their corpse-like pallor, as early as the nineteenth century vampires were in a transitional mode as they became attractive and charming, and by then there were those of both genders. Male vampires mainly allured young women, the females, young men, and a few vampires were unconcerned with gender difference.[8] By the late twentieth century some vampires began to ache with remorse for what they were forced by their hunger to do, like the thoughtful vampires Louis of *Interview with the Vampire* and Bill Compton of the TV series *True Blood*. In order to avoid killing humans, Bill drinks only artificial human blood ("untrue" blood). Meyer's "vegetarian" Cullens share this reluctance about killing humans; Edward says he doesn't "*want* to be a monster."[9] Though vampires are usually classified among the walking undead, their drinking of blood, by preference human blood, is the single unchanging feature by which a vampire can be distinguished from other monsters today. Some vampires have even lost their fangs. The Cullens have no fangs, but they have sharp teeth and remain hungry for blood. Thus vampires by their very nature are liminal creatures, dwelling on the limen (Latin for "threshold") between the worlds of ordinary people and monsters, human and Other, life and — because they are "undead" — death. But unlike the vampires of old, and many other non-human beings of legend, the Cullens can cross the threshold of a house without invitation; they are not bound by that particular limen.

Though they have no fangs, there is one visual feature that is unusual in the tradition of vampires old and new that marks Edward and his family as non-human (hence liminal beings, despite their attempt to appear human). They sparkle in sunlight, and that unusual feature is the main focus of this essay.[10] When asked in an online chat club, "Why do they sparkle?" Meyer replied, "They sparkle because they have turned to a substance that is somewhat like diamond. Their bodies have hardened, frozen into a kind of living stone. Each little cell in their skin has become a separate facet that reflects the light. These facets have a prism-like quality — they throw rainbows as they glitter."[11] This is an explanation in terms of the physics of the "secondary world" that Meyer has created,[12] and since it is her world, her answer is authoritative; no one can dispute it even should they wish to. This essay seeks an answer different in kind, in terms of our primary world; it explores what might lie behind Meyer's conception of vampires with glittering skin. Here one could argue that Edward glitters simply because Meyer wants to make him as beautiful as possible, but in view of her lively appropriation of fairy tale themes in her story,[13] the explanation is likely to be more complicated than that. It is also likely to be more complicated than any one explanation can offer, a combination of several factors spiced up by Meyer's own rich imagination. Six possible sources of inspiration for Edward's shining are explored in this essay, ranging from a scholarly book Meyer might have read, to modern fantasy novels and medieval stories that she probably has read (including tales of red-eyed monsters), to a childhood experience many of us share, to a book illustration that may have left a lasting impression on Meyer's picture-making mind, and finally to the possible impact of a major icon from her Mormon culture that might also be partly responsible for the vampires' hardness. The possibility of Meyer's debt to C.S. Lewis and J.R.R. Tolkien is especially emphasized.

Bright People, Angels, and the Longaevi: *A Scholarly Source?*

At one point in C.S. Lewis's space novel *Out of the Silent Planet*, the philologist Ransom, that Tolkien the philologist "believed ... was loosely based on himself,"[14] is discussing with a native of Malacandra (the planet Mars) the nature of the eldil, another intelligent species inhabiting that planet. The eldil are barely visible creatures of light that can pass through solid matter. When the Martian says it is strange that these creatures have never visited Ransom's planet, Ransom replies, "Of that I am not certain," and he mentions "the recurrent human tradition of bright, elusive people appearing on the earth."[15] Stephenie Meyer may have derived some of her inspiration for sparkling humanoids from the works of these two Oxford medievalists, Lewis and Tolkien.

In his own persona, Lewis speaks of "bright people" (sometimes capitalized) in *The Great Divorce*,[16] and shining supernatural beings occur also in his other fictions. He devotes an entire chapter in his scholarly book *The Discarded Image* to those beings he calls the *Longaevi* ("long-livers") that are nearly but not quite immortal.[17] Associating them with the High Fairies, a category that includes elves, Lewis describes them with two characteristics shared by today's vampires: the *Longaevi* are typically beings who can die, but their lifespan greatly exceeds that of humans, and because of their extended lifetime they tend to accumulate great wealth. In his Narnia novel *The Silver Chair,* Lewis describes both the great lion Aslan and the Lady of the Green Kirtle (the witch) as "long-livers," the precise translation of *Longaevi*[18]; the word occurs also in *Out of the Silent Planet* and elsewhere. Like vampires (including Meyer's), the lion and witch of Narnia, though long-lived, can be killed. Some of the *Longaevi*'s other attributes listed by Lewis remind us more specifically of Meyer's vampires. In the words of Lewis describing the *Longaevi*, the Cullens are physically "hard" and "bright" and surrounded by "a blaze of wealth and luxury," possessing among other treasures an array of expensive cars. They have a beautiful home into which they welcome their guests with "graciousness and courtesy." Most significantly of all, they are "liberated ... from the beast's perpetual slavery to nutrition."[19] They are liberated from the need for normal food, that is. Throughout the series much is made of Edward not dining with Bella,[20] though of course like all vampires he thirsts for blood, his eyes changing color when he does. In this he is a slave, like us all, to nutrition.

It might seem coincidental that Lewis's description of the *Longaevi* appears to fit Meyer's vampires so neatly at several points, but maybe it is not. Meyer says in an interview that when she was attending Brigham Young University her favorite teacher, "hands down," was Steven Walker. Professor Walker teaches British literature, and his special interest within that area, according to his website, is "the fantasy literature of J.R.R. Tolkien and C.S. Lewis."[21] He has confirmed that Meyer took his course in "Christian Fantasy," in which he encouraged students to "reach out more widely into the genre" by reading other works, and he listed *The Discarded Image* among the works by C.S. Lewis that they might wish to consult,[22] so his syllabus provides grounds for considering the possibility that Lewis's *Longaevi* influenced Meyer's creation of the attractive Cullens.

Several of Lewis's adjectives throughout his description of the *Longaevi* evoke beings that shine, but Meyer vamps up this attribute by having Bella constantly associate Edward with bright angels, both overtly, as in Chapter 23 of *Twilight* that is actually titled "The Angel," and subtly, as when Edward stands in a "halo" made by the light of the Swans' front porch.[23] In Narnia the Christ-figure Aslan also shines: "And one queer thing was that there was no moon last night, but there was moonlight where the lion was."[24] Very much like Edward Cullen, the "Bright People" of Lewis's *The Great Divorce*, spirits clearly akin to angels, are "almost blindingly white" when their skin is revealed.[25] At the end of his discussion of the *Longaevi*, Lewis puts forth among several possibilities the idea that they are semi-fallen angels, who were "almost, but not quite, guilty of sedition," and many of whom "will return to Heaven at Doomsday."[26] The source Lewis gives for this idea is a passage in the medieval *South English Legendary* where the writer mentions that mortals have seen these angels dancing and call them "eluene," elves. This identification of elves with angels, mentioned also in other medieval works, is an unusual and improbable though not unique notion. But all that glitters is not gold, and elves are no more angels than Edward is, though in some respects such "bright, elusive people" (see above) may be *like* angels.

Light-Elves: A Literary and Folklore Source?

In Tolkien's fantasy-world, a world quite different from that of C.S. Lewis, Frodo and his friends encounter elves right near the beginning of their quest in *The Fellowship of the Ring*, and what they first see is the elves' shining: "the starlight glimmering on their hair and in their eyes. They bore no lights, yet as they walked a shimmer, like the light of the moon above the rim of the hills before it rises, seemed to fall about their feet."[27] Later on, when the Lady Galadriel nobly rejects the Ring he has offered her, Frodo watches in astonishment as "there issued a great light that illumined her alone and left all else dark."[28] Long-living but not immortal (in terms of her life in Middle-earth[29]), Galadriel is clearly of the *Longaevi*, though that is not what she would call herself. Her title is "Lady of the Elves," and Boromir, when doubting her purpose, reverses this to "Elvish Lady."[30] Since "Elvish" is a word with ambiguous connotations, Aragorn reprimands him for this. Tolkien the philologist was fascinated with words and often developed his stories from them. Two other ambiguous elf-related words that clearly intrigued and inspired him are the Old Norse *ljós-álfar* ("light-elves") and Old English *ælfscyne* ("elf-beautiful"). The light associated with the elves of Lothlórien and elsewhere is poised against the darkness of Sauron, so clearly they are "light elves." The Icelander Snorri Sturluson (A.D. 1178–1241), the only medieval writer to use this term, describes the light elves as *fegri en sól synum* "fairer than the sun in appearance."[31] Although he does not say that these elves actually shine in the way the sun does, and perhaps did not mean to imply that, for a reader the implication of their shining is present.[32] The other "elf" word, *ælfscyne,* occurs three times in Old English poetry (in various spellings) to describe the beauty of women. *Ælf* means "elf," and the element *scyne,* cognate with German *schön*, means "beautiful," so the compound word *ælfscyne* is normally understood to mean "as beautiful as an elf." In Bosworth's *Old English Dictionary*, however, a volume that Tolkien would have kept close at hand, the adjective *ælf-scínu* at line 14 of the poem *Judith* is glossed "*shining* like an elf or fairy, elfin-bright, of elfin beauty"[33] (my emphasis), and indeed, with the sc pronounced as sh in Old English, the y something like the ee in "sheen," and final-e a soft "eh," the word *scyne* sounds very much like "shiny" to the modern ear. Led by verbal hints like these, the word-loving Tolkien created such figures as the glowing elves that Frodo and his band meet in the Shire, the figure of white light that the elf-lord Glorfindel becomes when he raises a wave to drown the Black Riders, and the glimmering Tinúviel in a song that Aragorn sings. All three of these figures are good elves aligned with "the light," though the tale of Beren and his elf-maid is a sad one in the end. Aragorn calls her "Tinúviel the elven-fair" (elven-fair: *ælf-scyne*), and he begins by singing how the hero Beren first saw her dancing to unseen music, as he came "from mountains cold" into lower woodlands: "And light of stars was in her hair,/ And in her raiment glimmering." She flees, Beren follows and finally wins her love, and they become part of the legendary history of Middle-earth.[34]

Elfwomen dance and elfwomen glimmer,[35] but sometimes that shining is regarded with deep suspicion. In the medieval romance of *Emaré*, which is offered here not as a potential source for Meyer but as an example of people's unease with the uncanny, the entirely human protagonist Emaré wears a gown that glimmers like Tinúviel's. When Emaré in her boat is washed up onto the shore of Wales, her rescuers first see that glow and hesitate because they think it must be something "fey" (fairy, uncanny), but they soon get over their fear and look after her. Later the King of Wales falls in love with the young woman and decides to marry her, and when Emaré comes in her glittering gown into the royal hall where he is waiting with his possessive mother, the old queen, laughing unpleasantly, says, "I never saw a woman half/ So shining and so gay." And then she says what she really thinks (or wants him to think): "My son, that robe ... she is a fiend/ Whom you have thought to wed!" (lines 443–44 and 446–47).[36]

When the *Beowulf*-poet places elves among the uncanny species descended from Cain and then defines them as enemies of God (lines 111–114),[37] he reveals that from early times there was a strong medieval view of such beings as "fiendish," to use the terminology of the Welsh queen in *Emaré.* Although Emaré is a normal human woman, indeed a pious Christian, who happens to be wearing a magical gown (made from Saracen cloth, hence suspect by contagion), the queen perceives her glimmering, or pretends to perceive it, as malignant. Thus the queen links Emaré to "the other side," the dark side inhabited in those times by elves and witches and later by vampires.

Tom Shippey sums up the early English view of elves as follows:

> Texts from totally different times and places come up with roughly similar ideas, indicating two main lines of thought on the origin of the elves: they are humans from some separated branch of humanity; they are spiritual creatures who are neither angels nor devils. They can be hostile, but they are also alluring, especially sexually alluring. The consequences of the allure are not certain, may be disastrous, and may not be distinguishable from the activities of truly diabolical incubi and succubi.[38]

To someone thinking about vampires, Shippey's description of elves is suggestive. Though the earlier blood-sucking undead creature of Eastern Europe is quite different, a terrifying monster of the night rather like Grendel, one has to wonder whether the attractive vampire of the modern West has derived his allure at least in part from this dangerous supernatural and alluring species, the elf.[39]

In his book *Vampires and Their Slayers: A Cultural History of Killing the Dead,*[40] Bruce A. McClelland focuses on a time and place when vampires were thought to be real, and were by no means attractive. In his prefatory essay he offers a perspective on the "curious rash of hysterical vampire epidemics at the fringes of the Habsburg Empire" that helps to explain the impulse behind those historical eighteenth-century "epidemics." It also helps to explain the attitude of the queen portrayed earlier by the "Emaré" poet. In the cultures of Western Europe, uncanny folk were perceived in a negative opposition to Christianity:

> The concept of evil, in the West at least, thus continues to be linked to a fundamental belief in the apostasy of anything that inherently subverts canonical Christian theology. [...] The threat posed by both the witch and the vampire has to do with their special knowledge, acquired through contact with the dead: the witch has the ability to foretell and thus control the future, while the unholy vampire is somehow able to return from the dead without the permission of Jesus or his clergy. This threat, ultimately, goes to the very foundation of Christian eschatology.[41]

From its inception as a popular modern genre, fantasy literature, especially that for children, has always raised anxiety among those deeply concerned with Christian doctrine; even C.S. Lewis, a devout believer who inserted doctrinal messages into his Narnia novels, has been taken to task about the magic he included, and the Harry Potter series with its wizardry has raised a hullabaloo of vast proportions, as have Philip Pullman's novels with more cause. Perhaps one reason that Stephenie Meyer has linked Edmund so strongly with angels is to minimize or even erase the reader's feeling that her beautiful non-humans, especially when perceived as the walking dead and especially when they shine, continue to seem "fiendish" even when they abstain from drinking human blood. This angel connection also helps her to shift the status of the heroine from vampire-slayer like Buffy or vampire-victim like the women in the earlier vampire stories, to enthralled lover unendangered by her vampire (despite Edward's warnings to the contrary).

In *Twilight*, Bella, already dazzled by her love for Edward, finds him more beautiful than ever when she sees his glittering skin, but one can imagine what the ordinary townspeople of Forks, Washington, would make of a sight like that in *Emaré,* of a being "so shining and so gay."[42] The evil old queen in that medieval romance interprets the maiden's shining as the monstrous mark of a fiend, and this endangers the young woman, but even good people in the story find the fact of her shining ambiguous.

Liminality and Fiery Eyes: A Medieval Source?

When it comes to monsters that actually are of the fiendish variety, the otherworldly light that pours out from their eyes is not ambiguous at all, and this gleam is especially threatening when they come suddenly upon us. Such sudden entrances occur in two of the most famous medieval English stories. In *Beowulf*, about which Tolkien wrote so movingly,[43] the hungry monster Grendel, with his red eyes aflame in the darkness, bursts open the door of the royal hall where the confident Danish warriors are fast asleep (lines 118–120). It is a sudden, shocking, interruption of their complacent slumber, and many die. In *Sir Gawain and the Green Knight*, a medieval romance that Tolkien edited and also translated,[44] the giant knight of the title is green with the red eyes of a monster (line 304), but otherwise he is as beautiful as Meyer's vampires, in garments gleaming and glinting (line 172). He comes bursting into King Arthur's hall during a Christmas banquet—"there hales in at the halle dor an aghlich mayster" (line 136)—again a shock to those in the story. Both monsters cross literal thresholds, *limen* in Latin, remember, the entry point of a house that gives us the useful word "liminality."[45] Both monsters remind us that shining associated with the supernatural is not always benevolent, red light in particular marking danger or the demonic.

Monsters entering a human place from a different, wilder space are inherently "liminal" creatures. Vampires are liminal by their very nature (the walking dead in the world of the living), and Meyer introduces her really scary bad vampires with an abruptness that recalls the sudden coming of these two most famous of our medieval English monsters. Part of Meyer's strategy is the way she aligns the "good" monsters in relation to humans. She places three communities of the northwest Washington rainforest in an interesting uneasy relationship: everyday Americans, old-world but "nice" vampires, and Quileute Indians who later become werewolves, each group having its geographically defined territory. The three "races" are focused on three family groups: the "inside" family of Bella and her cop father in the ordinary town of Forks, the Cullen family of vampires across the Calawah River and down an unpaved road in the misty forest,[46] and the Indian boy Jacob and his father on the government-defined Quileute reservation, all three being areas one can trace on the map of the state of Washington. Truly Other are the rogue vampires who enter this carefully maintained détente with the suddenness of the *Beowulf* monster Grendel raging hungry into the hall Heorot or the Green Knight whamming into Camelot. In her essay in this volume, Keri Wolf examines the way *Twilight*'s high-schoolers arrange themselves in the school cafeteria and shows how only Bella is capable of moving between the groups. Bella moves fluidly between the communities outside Forks High School also, as Wolf observes, crossing first from Forks to the Quileute reservation and later being invited to the Cullens' private estate or "castle in the woods"—crossing boundaries from one story-plot to another, and at last, in the final book of the series, crossing even a boundary between species.

My focus here is narrower, upon the theme of the monster-arrival only and the meaning of their gleaming red eyes. The liminal moment in *Twilight*, the moment when the story swings around into a type of narrative more akin to the traditional vampire tale, occurs during a baseball game being played in a huge forest meadow. The Cullens have carefully chosen this wide-open field surrounded by the peaks of the Olympic National Forest as a good and secret place, safe for the vampires' game so long as there is a thunderstorm to disguise the impact of bat on ball.[47] By now Bella has been accepted by the Cullen family of "good" vampires, and the game is progressing smoothly—like the banquet in Camelot, with everyone enjoying themselves and their fellowship together, confident that all is well. At this point, one must remember that Alice Cullen can see the future, though inexactly, and that Edward can read her mind. The scene is full of references to eyes and seeing, seeing in more than one sense. Carlisle comes up to bat and Edward is acting as catcher, when suddenly Alice gasps. As usual, Bella is watching Edward, and she sees his head snap up to look around at Alice. As their eyes meet, something flows between them, and he is at Bella's side before anyone can ask Alice what she sees. Esme asks her tensely, and Alice whispers back that she "didn't see, couldn't tell."[48] As she says this, three vampires, James, Victoria and Laurent, a trio not morally opposed to drinking human blood, are almost upon them, and there is no time to whisk Bella to safety. Simply hiding her is not an option because vampires can smell her delicious blood. Edward, reading the other vampires' minds from afar, knows they are thirsty, and he reacts, angling himself between Bella and those coming. The other Cullens turn in the same direction, hearing sounds that Bella's merely human ears cannot detect. Then the blood-lusting alien vampires emerge one at a time out from the "forest edge."[49]

All that these vampires want at first, as they cross over the rainforest limen, is to join the Cullens in their game, but when a breeze ruffles Bella's hair, the tracker vampire James "whipped his head around," and he looks directly at her, "his nostrils flaring."[50] Carlisle tells them firmly that Bella is with them, and Laurent asks, innocently enough but gruesomely, "You brought a snack?"[51] The leaders of the two groups, Carlisle and Laurent, defuse the situation, but James, a brilliant and obsessive tracker, has caught Bella's scent and is transfixed by it. For the first time, Bella finds herself truly in danger from vampires, and she later sees that James' eyes are different from those of the "vegetarian" vampires she knows. James has the eyes of a demonic limen-crosser, hungry for human blood. Their color is not the gold or black that Bella has come to expect, but, as she reports, "deep burgundy ... disturbing and sinister."[52] Meyer has taken this entrance-of-monsters theme, racked up the tension to an exceptionally high pitch, and balanced the plot of her book upon it.

We are familiar with crossings into a magical otherworld from classical children's literature such as the stories of Alice, Dorothy, and of course the four children going through the wardrobe into Narnia. It is typical of such stories to associate brightness and iridescent color with the otherworld.[53] But an element that modern vampire stories bring to this motif of crossings is the location of the territories of supernatural beings not in a glimmering otherworld like Narnia and Oz, or even in a more shadowy yet faraway Transylvania, but in the everyday landscape, since vampires need the blood of ordinary humans to survive. The American high-school vampire is almost a cliché today, and Meyer locates her vampire family adjacent to a small town of very ordinary humans in an out-of-the-way corner of the state of Washington. While typical of vampire tales, this feature of the extraordinary existing within the realm of the ordinary is unusual for tales of crossings into realms that harbor shining beings.[54]

Meyer's insertion and fusion of a magical realm into the ordinary world is an element of her story-telling that she handles with skill. For example, the Cullens' fairytale castle is a handsome mansion hidden among dark cedars but is itself full of light. Edward and Bella approach it by car through a relentlessly gloomy forest, and, on arrival, human Bella with her hand in Edward's walks toward the house with trepidation through "deep shade."[55] The reader familiar with fairy tales may well be nervous with her. Soon, however, her misgivings are dispelled by the Cullens' warm welcome in their home, where she encounters that "blaze of wealth and luxury" that C.S. Lewis associates with the *Longaevi*. Despite mishaps both major and minor, from then on Bella is essentially at home with them. In *New Moon* Bella hangs out, with ease, in Jacob's workshop-garage on the reservation and later crosses the Atlantic to confront the regal Volturi in their lair. Bella is the single human in Meyer's four novels who crosses a variety of thresholds with impunity, and her initial threshold-crossing into the Cullen home is in high contrast to the confrontation in the forest playing-field that soon follows. That moment in *Twilight*, when the bloodthirsty vampires enter the "safe" meadow, echoes the liminal monster-crossing into the humans' Central Place in two of our greatest medieval narratives, while also thrusting unordinary monsters into the midst of the most ordinary possible scene of Americana, a baseball game.[56]

In my opinion, this bursting in of the thirsty vampires with their sinister dark-red eyes[57] is one of the most striking moments in fantasy literature of any period. But the scariest of all the eyes described in the Twilight novels appear in Bella's dream in *Breaking Dawn* about a monstrous baby, a dream by which Meyer cleverly, deceptively, sets up the reader for the baby that comes later in the book.[58] Here Bella sees a toddler, cherubic, trembling, surrounded by Volturi intent on killing him because he's an immortal child, an out-of-control vampire. Torn by pity, she sprints towards the baby to save him but staggers back as she sees the pyramid of bodies on which he stands, bodies with faces dear to her, and then the "adorable boy" opens his blood-red eyes. That moment itself marks a threshold in the narrative as Bella's own eyes fly open.[59]

Because the thirsty red eyes of the vampires tend to be seen in darkness or gloom (when the sight of them is most frightening) and their uncanny skin only glitters when reflecting light, especially sunlight, Meyer rarely evokes these two features together. But they are mentioned in the same breath in two threshold moments when Bella is transformed, first when Jacob imagines how shocked her father would be to see his daughter "all sparkly white with the bright red eyes,"[60] and later by the newly transformed Bella seeing herself in a mirror, with glistening pale skin and red eyes aflame (like Grendel's).[61]

Angelic People in the Bedroom: A Memory of Childhood's Bright Watchers?

Another kind of threshold crossing in *Twilight*, a literal limen crossing that has elicited negative comment, is the scene where Edward enters Bella's bedroom and watches her while she sleeps. When she first finds out about it, this shocks even Bella,[62] and it appalls some readers who describe Edward as a stalker.[63] But a stalker makes the victim nervous, whereas Bella falls blissfully asleep in Edward's arms as he hums softly into her ear, sounding to her like an "archangel."[64] He does not shine like an angel in the dark, and in another scene Bella makes a point of this. As he walks beside her in the night, she remarks that, while he is, as always, pale and dreamlike in his beauty, he is not the "fantastic sparkling creature" of their sunlit afternoon.[65] Yet if he's anything otherworldly in addition to being a vampire, he is Bella's guardian angel, watching over her even by night.

The benevolent being in the bedroom may be something that many of us have experienced, and here I move into the personal. When I was a child, bright watchers often stood at my bedside or wandered through my room, glowing and white. Apparently this is a common visual phenomenon among children, no doubt caused by the firing of nerves in the optic system and personified by the child. Astronauts are known to see similar figures when in space. According to a NASA–endorsed survey, these figures, scientifically termed phosphenes, "predominantly appear white, have elongated shapes, and most interestingly, often come with a sense of motion."[66] At any rate, to me they seemed friendly—shining like C.S. Lewis's Bright People in *The Great Divorce*, and protective as in the lullaby beginning "fourteen angels guard my bed." Perhaps Meyer's Edward as guardian in the bedroom, angelic-seeming to Bella even though here he does not shine, has more of a kinship with this family of watchers than with stalkers.[67] As we grow up, there is a tendency to forget or suppress the fact that we ever saw such irrational figures, yet they may leave a residual trace upon a receptive imagination.

"It All Began with a Picture" (or a Dream of a Picture): A Fairy-Tale Source?

Although Lewis, Tolkien and Meyer are all creators of worlds vividly engaging our visual imagination, the visual element that Meyer reports as the inception of *Twilight* may align her more with Lewis than with Tolkien. Tolkien's Middle-earth began, as he says in a 1955 letter to W.H. Auden, with words, when he thoughtlessly scribbled a sentence on a blank leaf in an exam he was grading, "I scrawled, 'In a hole in the ground there lived a hobbit.' I did not and do not know why."[68] The story evolved from there. Tolkien is "the Great Philologist," enchanted with words, following them to their source and creative about their implications. About the thinking, moving trees of Middle-earth called ents, he states in another letter, "As usually with me they grew rather out of their name, than the other way about. I always felt that something ought to be done about the peculiar A[nglo-]Saxon word *ent* for a 'giant' or mighty person of long ago."[69] In contrast, C.S. Lewis says of his invention of Narnia, "It all began with images; a faun carrying an umbrella, a queen on a sledge, a magnificent lion."[70] Probably all three of Lewis's images were lodged in his mind from elsewhere, from pictures and things he saw, including statuary like the traditional garden faun and library-guarding lion, from dreams, and even from stories that he visualized as he read them. Lewis was a reader who saw vividly what other authors imagined, and he saw their worlds so clearly that he had a propensity to adopt their visions.[71] Perhaps the most obvious example of an adopted vision, because the source is familiar to many of us, is

Lewis's Narnian "queen on a sledge." This figure, as Colin Manlove has pointed out, "comes straight out of the pages of Hans Andersen"[72]; it is the Snow Queen, "so tall and straight, so shining white."[73] Seating the boy Kay beside her in her sleigh, "she wrapped the fur around him; it felt as if he were sinking into a snowdrift."[74] Likewise in *The Lion, the Witch, and the Wardrobe*, the White Queen, who is the witch of Lewis's title, invites the boy Edmund into her sled, then "put a fold of her fur mantle around him and tucked it well in."[75] These along with various other details confirm Lewis's borrowing as tending toward the visual more than the verbal.

But there is more than an approximation of Andersen's text in Lewis's depiction of his white witch, and here we move into new and scarcely explored territory (nor is there space to explore it sufficiently here). The following example is offered to suggest how not only details of a narrative but an artist's illustration of a narrative, perhaps not remembered at a conscious level, may be contributing to Meyer's imagining of her protagonists in a similar way. When Lewis says that he saw a picture in his mind,[76] he may have seen a literal picture. As he transfers the image of the cruel snow queen who kidnaps little Kay to his own story of the White Witch capturing Edmund, Lewis is apparently influenced both by Andersen's words and by a memory of a particular illustration of the scene.[77]

Despite Tolkien's disapproval,[78] Lewis was comfortable about mixing together different kinds of story, like putting the Danish snow queen into a secondary world along with Father Christmas (Santa Claus) and a Graeco-Roman faun called by what pretends to be a middle-class British name (Mr. Tumnus, probably from Ovid's Vertumnis). Meyer's practice is like that of Lewis in that she draws narrative material from many disparate sources into her world of vampires and werewolves.[79] Probably the story that filters most obviously into the novel *Twilight*, especially with the protagonist being named "Bella," is "Beauty and the Beast" (in the French story the maiden was named Belle). That affinity is as vividly striking as the appearance of Andersen's Snow Queen in the first Narnia novel. But Meyer does not point to a fairy tale (or its illustration) as her initial inspiration for the romance in *Twilight*, any more than Lewis does for his white witch. In a brief account of the origin of her novel on her webpage titled "The Story behind *Twilight*," she claims that she "can say with certainty that it all started on June 2, 2003," when she awoke "from a very vivid dream."[80] Thus her fictional world began, or she would have us believe that it began, in much the same way as Lewis's, with an image, and there is no reason to doubt that she actually had such a dream. Dreams often bring to consciousness what has been bubbling below; Lewis claims that when suddenly the lion "Aslan came bounding into" his story, he'd been having "a good many dreams about lions about that time,"[81] and Meyer's dream could likewise be part of an unconscious impulse to bring her story to the surface. But since our dreams reflect the daylight world, it is legitimate to ask where Meyer's dream of her star-crossed teens might originate.

An interesting juxtaposition is offered to conclude this exploration of graphic art affinities of Edward's shining. A suggestive similarity (proof is not possible, of course) is revealed by placing next to each other Meyer's description of her dream and Alan Barrett's impressionistic gouache painting of Beauty seeing her beloved Beast transform into a handsome prince. In her dream (as reported by Michael R. Walker) Meyer sees[82]

> two star-crossed teens stand in a wood-encircled meadow, talking intensely, obviously in love. While she is average in appearance, he seems without flaw, the sun sparkling on his perfect skin.[83]

In Barrett's painting the two figures of Belle and her Beast-prince are standing in a circle of light, "talking intensely, obviously in love." Even though the light in the picture flashes outward from the prince as if he were aglow, the match of these figures with Meyer's "star-crossed teens" is far from exact. However, Philippa Pearce's account of the transformation that goes with this picture makes it pretty close to the dream, and different from Jeanne-Marie Le Prince de Beaumont's eighteenth-century French version of "Beauty and the Beast" upon which most modern versions are based.[84] In Beaumont's story, Beauty declares her love for the Beast, and she "scarce had pronounced these words, when she saw the palace sparkle with light; and fireworks, music, every thing seemed to give notice of some great event."[85] Pearce in her retelling differs by having the light emanate directly from the Beast himself. When Beauty says "I love you," he at once begins "to shiver and to shimmer and to change."[86] The artist Barrett portrays the liminal moment with the costumed pair standing in a nimbus of light as an explosion of shimmering sparks flies between their hands, flowing, it would seem, from the Prince to Beauty.[87] In Meyer's account of her dream, the two modern teenagers are surrounded by trees and one of them shines, while her words "star-crossed" and "sunlight" and "sparkling" evoke even more light. The sparkling portrayed in Barrett's picture may have nothing to do with Meyer's dream of the couple in love, or it may have lodged forgotten in the depths of her mind ready to blossom (or sky-rocket) forth in her dream — and then into her novel. Or she may consciously remember this romantic picture. In any case, while certainly not a definite source for shining Edward, the radiance issuing forth from Barrett's Beast-prince is highly suggestive.

Naturally enough, upon waking from her dream Stephenie Meyer, like Tolkien with his hobbit, wants to know what happens to these two people, talking so intently and "obviously in love." "I was really invested in what was going to happen next," she says.[88] Because like Lewis she visualizes so vividly in pictures, like him she not only becomes absorbed by her story, as the creator of it who watches from outside, but she also is absorbed into it, rather like Lucy passing through the wardrobe into Narnia, and *Twilight* becomes a secondary world into which, as Tolkien says, "both designer and spectator can enter."[89] Wrapped in her assumed Bella persona and enraptured by fairy tale, dream vision, and perhaps the residual memory of "watchers" and a beloved remembered picture, Stephenie Meyer herself crosses into the strangely ordinary yet magical landscape that she has created, dreamlike, for her shining vampire lover, and for us.

That Diamond Hardness and Vampires Like Statues

But Meyer adds one quality to that shining vampire that this essay has not addressed at all so far: his diamond-like hardness. This takes us back to her explanation (quoted above) of why her vampires sparkle: their skin has become a "substance that is somewhat like diamond. Their bodies have hardened, frozen into a kind of living stone."[90] In another 2006 interview, responding to the question of whether she based Edward on someone in particular, Meyer replies, "Edward is all imagination and wishing. No one is that perfect."[91] Yet there is a possible model for him that might well be considered "that perfect." Central to her Mormon culture is a shining being that appears in a vision having remarkable similarities to the childhood seeing of bright watchers. Here the founder of Mormonism, Joseph Smith, is telling his story:

> I discovered a light appearing in my room, which continued to increase until the room was lighter than at noonday, when immediately a personage appeared at my bedside, standing in the air, for his feet did not touch the floor. He had on a loose robe of most exquisite whiteness. It was a whiteness beyond anything earthly I had ever seen; nor do I believe that any earthly thing could be made to appear so exceedingly white and brilliant. His hands were naked, and his arms also [...]. I could discover that he had no other clothing on but this robe, as it was open, so that I could see into his bosom. Not only was his robe exceedingly white, but his whole person was glorious beyond description.[92]

Compare this description of the angel Moroni with Bella's description of Edward, shortly before the meadow scene in *Twilight*. He is wearing his white sleeveless shirt unbuttoned, and seeing his smooth, white skin she thinks in despair that he is too perfect, that it is impossible that such a "godlike creature" was intended for her.[93] This assessment takes us back to Meyer's before–*Twilight* dream (quoted above): "While she is average in appearance, he seems without flaw, the sun sparkling on his perfect skin."

But besides his perfect skin sparkling, the hardness of Edward's skin is frequently mentioned in the series,[94] and there is nothing hard (like stone or metal) about the angelic being who visits Smith — or about Meyer's handsome dream-man. Yet this quality of "hardness" may provide a link between both Smith's and Meyer's visions and the vampire Edward. In addition to Edward having a hard skin, his perfection is often likened to that of a statue, as when he lies in the meadow with Bella, and throughout the four novels the Cullen vampires are increasingly described as being like statues when immobile. Thus (hard) statues become a theme associated with Meyer's sparkling vampires, and—here is the link this is leading up to—no real-world statues are more shining than those of the Angel Moroni.

Although gleaming metallic statues of Moroni traditionally appear on the steeples of Mormon temples,[95] no statue adorned the Provo temple in the 1990s when Meyer was attending Brigham Young University next door—not until May 12, 2003. On that date a large crowd watched as "Moroni" was raised to complete the spire of that temple, and even a non–Mormon would have to agree that this is a glorious male figure.[96] Was Meyer there for the occasion? Did a good friend or relative convey the excitement of this event?[97] In any case, three weeks later on June 2, 2003, Meyer woke up—in Phoenix, Arizona—from her "very vivid dream" of a girl talking to a shining man in a meadow.

Though Stephenie Meyer is generous in pointing out, both in interviews and by clear allusions in the novels themselves, the sources for many of her images that compel us, others are more obscurely derived and it would be fruitless to invite her to confess where she got them. As a writer working in the frenzy that she claims, it is likely that she herself could not identify the inspiration for many of her bright visions, as they flowed dreamlike, from her life and her reading, through her fingertips into words, weaving a spell to enchant us.

Notes

1. *Twilight* (New York: Little, Brown & Company, 2005), 260.
2. Stephenie Meyer in response to Question 20 in an interview ("Q&A at Fairless Hills") posted 9–12–2007 at http://stepheniesays.livejournal.com/20266.html.
3. *Breaking Dawn* (New York: Little, Brown & Company, 2008), 301.
4. Many of these changes are listed and analyzed by Dowdle in this anthology.
5. This bit of lore is evoked by Sylvia Plath in her poem "Daddy" and hilariously mocked in the film *From Dusk Till Dawn*.
6. *Twilight*, 185–86.
7. Ibid., 329.
8. The vampire Carmilla famously preyed upon young women. Joseph Sheridan le Fanu's novella of the lesbian vampire Carmilla was first published in 1872 in *Through a Glass Darkly*, a collection recently republished as an Oxford Classic (Oxford: Oxford University Press, 2008). Roger Vadim made the story "Carmilla" into a French film released in 1960 and titled *Blood and Roses* in English. Another movie was based on the novel a decade later, *The Vampire Lovers*.
9. *Twilight*, 187.
10. It has been pointed out that Anne Rice's Vampire Lestat describes himself as having "extremely white and highly reflective skin" (*The Vampire Lestat* [New York: Alfred A. Knopf, 1985], 3), but his skin does not appear to sparkle or to be so dominant a feature as it is for Meyer's vampires. The other quality of Meyer's vampires' skin is that it is hard, like stone ("living stone," as Meyer explains; see above in this essay). This hardness that accompanies the sparkling will be addressed below.
11. Meyer's answer was posted in "Personal Correspondence #7" in the "Twilight Lexicon" at http://www.twilightlexicon.com/?p=62 on March 26, 2006.

12. The term "Secondary World" was introduced by J.R.R. Tolkien in his essay "On Fairy-Stories," included in *Tree and Leaf* (London: Unwin, 1964). He says, "When the story-maker's art is good enough [to draw you into believing his story], what really happens is that the story-maker proves a successful 'sub-creator.' He [in Meyer's case, she] makes a Secondary World which your mind can enter. Inside it, what he relates is 'true'; it accords with the laws of that world" (36).

13. This aspect of the *Twilight Series* is discussed in detail by Janice Hawes in her essay in this volume. Other writers also refer to it.

14. Elizabeth A. Whittingham, *The Evolution of Tolkien's Mythology: A Study of the History of Middle-earth* (Jefferson, NC: McFarland, 2008), 29.

15. *Out of the Silent Planet* (New York: Macmillan, 1965), 95.

16. C.S. Lewis, *The Great Divorce.* (New York: Simon & Schuster, 1974 [1946]). Bright People are mentioned, for example, on pages 38 and 60. Reference to some of Lewis's other shining beings will be made later in the essay.

17. *The Discarded Image: An Introduction to Medieval and Renaissance Literature* (Cambridge: Cambridge University Press, 1964), Chapter VI.

18. Lewis, *The Silver Chair* (New York: Collier, 1970 [Macmillan 1953]), 134.

19. *The Discarded Image*, 130–134.

20. Except for when he tries to be accommodating to human custom or expectations: in *Twilight* he takes a bite of pizza, and in *Breaking Dawn* he forces down a slice of wedding cake.

21. See http://humanities.byu.edu/faculty/scw3.

22. Personal letter of 9 February 09.

23. Meyer, *Twilight*, 358.

24. Lewis, *The Voyage of the Dawn Treader* (New York: HarperCollins, 1994 [1952]), 113.

25. Lewis, *The Great Divorce*, 39.

26. *The Discarded Image*, 136.

27. Tolkien, *The Fellowship of the Ring* (London: Allen and Unwin, 1969), 93.

28. Ibid., 381.

29. The "mortality" of elves is a complex issue to which Whittingham devotes an entire chapter in *The Evolution of Tolkien's Mythology* (123–69; see note 14).

30. Tolkien, *The Fellowship of the Ring*, 373.

31. Snorri Sturluson discusses the light and dark elves in chapter 17 of "Gylfaginning" in his *Prose Edda*; an edition by Gudni Jónsson is on the *Fornrít* site at http://www.snerpa.is/net/fornrit.htm. For analysis see Tom Shippey, "Light-elves, Dark-elves, and Others: Tolkien's Elvish Problem," *Tolkien Studies* I (2004), 1–15, and for elves in general see Shippey's more extensive "Alias Oves Habeo: The Elves as a Category Problem," *The Shadow-Walkers: Jacob Grimm's Mythology of the Monstrous*, ed. Tom Shippey (Tempe, Arizona: ACMRS, 2005), 157–87.

32. This is especially the case when one knows that in this description Snorri is adapting a description of angels from an earlier medieval book, an early twelfth-century Latin work called the *Elucidarius*, by which he was "almost certainly influenced" according to Alaric Hall (*Elves in Anglo-Saxon England: Matters of Belief, Health, Gender and Identity* [Woodbridge, Suffolk, UK: Boydell Press, 2007], 25).

33. Joseph Bosworth, *An Anglo-Saxon Dictionary* (London: Oxford University Press, 1898), 15. Early etymology was also responsible for the concept of the shining elf; the online *Wictionary*, citing a source with which Tolkien would have been familiar (J. A. Macculloch, *Mythology of All Races* Series, Volume 2 *Eddic*, Great Britain: Marshall Jones Company, 1930, pp. 220–221), gives this etymology for the word: "Middle English from Old English *ælf* (incubus, elf). Originated from Indo-European root **albho-* (brilliant, shining white) via Teutonic languages." Tolkien was sufficiently intrigued by these words and their definitions to write a poem titled "Ides Ælfsciene," available together with a modern English translation in T.A. Shippey, *The Road to Middle Earth* (London: Grafton, 1992), 306–07.

34. Tolkien, *The Fellowship of the Ring,* 208–9. Tolkien continues to elaborate the tale of Beren and Lúthien throughout several of his works; for details see Whittingham (note 14 above), 135–38. I am grateful to the Tolkien scholars Michael Drout and Yvette Kisor for guiding me to these passages about "shining elves" in *The Fellowship of the Ring.* Professor Kisor points out another similarity to Edward when, in several passages in books II and III of *The Lord of the Rings,* "there are implications that [the elf] Legolas does not sleep, or at least that sleep is optional for him" (e-mail message of 12 June 2009). See also Yvette Kisor's essay in this collection.

35. The beautiful fairy Tryamour (essentially the same creature as an elf) shines similarly in the Middle English romance *Sir Launfal* (ed. A.J. Bliss; London: Thomas Nelson, 1960). Her face *lyght schoone* ("shone brightly," line 936), as does her hair and her crown (lines 937–942).

36. *Emaré* is included in *Romancing the Goddess: Three Middle English Romances about Women,* trans. Marijane Osborn (Urbana: University of Illinois Press, 1998), 69.

37. *Klaeber's Beowulf,* 4th ed. of Fr. Klaeber's *Beowulf and the Fight at Finnsburg,* ed. Robert E. Bjork, R.D. Fulk, and John D. Niles (Toronto: University of Toronto Press, 2008), 6–7.

38. "Alias Oves Habeo," 175.

39. Elves were not initially small; they could be human-sized or even taller, like Tolkien's Galadriel. These beings were active in the English countryside well into the eighteenth century both in song and in the dangerous "elf-fire" of forest and swamp. The alluring elves of British and Scandinavian ballads were usually intent on doing harm to their human lovers, and the gleam of *ignis fatuus,* looking in the night like a distant beacon or lighted window and associated with elves because it seemed intentional, would lure the unwary traveler astray.

40. Bruce A. McClelland, *Vampires and Their Slayers* (Ann Arbor: University of Michigan Press, 2006).

41. Ibid., xii. In this interesting study, concerned to a large degree with the moral issues raised by scapegoating, Bruce A. McClelland goes behind the Transylvanian legend to search out the "deep history" of vampires and their slayers in earlier social and religious conflicts in the Balkans, where the term "vampyr" apparently arose.

42. *Emaré,* line 444, p. 69 (see note 36 above).

43. Primarily in his 1936 British Academy Lecture, *Beowulf: The Monsters and the Critics* (London: Oxford University Press, 1936; from the Proceedings of the British Academy, Vol. XXII).

44. *Sir Gawain and the Green Knight,* ed. J.R.R. Tolkien and E.V. Gordon, revised by Norman Davis (2nd ed., Oxford: Clarendon Press, 1967), and *Sir Gawain and the Green Knight, Pearl, and Sir Orfeo,* trans. J.R.R. Tolkien (Boston: Houghton Mifflin, 1975).

45. Traditionally, unlike Grendel and the Green Knight, many monsters, including vampires, are unable to cross the threshold into a house without being invited. This is another way that Meyer's vampires differ from the norm, as Bella discovers when she finds Edward in her bedroom (discussed in the next section).

46. Meyer, *Twilight,* 320.

47. The folklore theme that Meyer is tapping into here is the traditional "thunder-god ball game," most famously played in the Catskill Mountains of New York in Washington Irving's story of "Rip Van Winkle." Curiously, in Michael Chabon's young-adult novel *Summerland* (New York: Miramax, 2002), the portal to the world "Middling" (this is Chabon's Middle-earth) is Clam Island, Washington, directly across Puget Sound from Seattle and thus adjacent to Meyer's Olympic Peninsula location, and in Middling a Clam Island baseball team plays a game to save the universe, with the God-of-Thunder Thor helping them to walk between the worlds. I am grateful to Julian Meldon D'Arcy for observing and telling me about this coincidental ballgame location.

48. Meyer, *Twilight,* 371–72.

49. Ibid., 374–75. The edge of the forest is a traditional limen in fairy tales. For example, the rapist-knight in Chaucer's "Wife of Bath's Tale" meets the fairy hag "under a forest syde"

("at the edge of the forest," line 990); *The Canterbury Tales Complete*, ed. Larry D. Benson (Boston: Houghton Mifflin, 2000), 100.

50. Meyer, *Twilight*, 378.

51. Ibid,. 379.

52. Ibid., 376.

53. At the beginning of *The Silver Chair*, C. S. Lewis describes the Narnian otherworld as brilliant with splendor against which the child Jill Pole entering it from our world looks dingy, much as Bella sees herself in comparison to Edward. Throughout all four novels until her transformation, Bella continues despairingly to compare his angelic appearance to her own plainness.

54. In the *Wizard of Oz* film, Dorothy and her dog Toto are snatched up by the whirlwind out of black-and-white Kansas into a Technicolor land that is *different* and ruled by *Longaevi*-like witches and a wizard (though he is an imposter).

55. Meyer, *Twilight*, 321.

56. Cp. Edward's definition of baseball as American, *Twilight*, 347.

57. Later, the eyes of thirsty James are black irises ringed with ruby, as he prepares to torture Bella and drink her blood (*Twilight*, 444–45), and most of the vampires coming to aid the Cullens in *Breaking Dawn* also have hungry red eyes. The eyes of the vegetarian Cullens are golden (*Breaking Dawn*, 403).

58. Meyer enjoys offering the reader foreshadowing effects that mislead. In her essay in this volume, Kisor discusses the way Meyer misleads us also with her apparently descriptive epigraphs.

59. Meyer, *Breaking Dawn*, 37 and 38.

60. Ibid., 300.

61. Ibid., 403–4.

62. Meyer, *Twilight*, 293.

63. For example, a student calling herself Rinnybird exclaims, "Does no one realize that if Edward really existed he would be considered a stalker? Everyone tries to excuse that by saying that he's so hot, but that wouldn't change a thing ... if you woke up in the middle of the night and some guy was there, you wouldn't make out with him, you would kick him down and call for your dad to get his gun." Simon and Schuster Teen Forum at http://forums.simonandschuster.com/topic.php?id=140880. Others have commented similarly.

64. Meyer, *Twilight*, 331.

65. Ibid., 292.

66. Astronauts do not personify the figures as children do. See C. Fuglesang and L. Narici, P. Pocozza, and W.G. Sannita, "Phosphenes in low earth orbit: survey responses from 59 astronauts," *Aviation, Space, and Environment Medicine* 77:4 (April 2006), 449–452. "In all, 98 surveys were distributed to current NASA and ESA astronauts. [...] Among the 59 respondents, 47 noticed them sometime during spaceflight. Most often they were noted before sleep." An abstract of this article is available at http://www.ncbi.nlm.nih.gov/pubmed/16676658.

67. Not everyone experiences these phosphenes as benevolent. Eugene Field describes these nighttime forms as frightening in his poem "Seein' Things," *Poems of Childhood* (New York: Scribner's, 1904), 165. Engelbert Humperdinck's version of this old prayer ("Now I lay me down to sleep") comes at the end of Act 2 of his opera *Hansel and Gretel*. It begins: "When at night I go to sleep, / Fourteen angels watch do keep." There are many versions.

68. *The Letters of J.R.R. Tolkien*, ed. Humphrey Carpenter (Boston: Houghton Mifflin, 1981), 215.

69. *Letters*, 208.

70. "Sometimes Fairy Stories May Say Best What's to Be Said," *On Stories and Other Essays on Literature*, ed. Walter Hooper (New York: Harcourt, 1982), 46; Lewis later repeated this idea, mentioning only the lion, in "It All Started with a Picture," *On Stories*, 53.

71. For a preliminary discussion of Lewis's gift of visual appropriation from prose descrip-

tion see Marijane Osborn, "Deeper Realms: C. S. Lewis' Re-Visions of Joseph O'Neill's *Land Under England*," *Journal of Modern Literature* 25 (Fall 2001), 115–120. Details of the two author's descriptions of uncanny lands are so closely parallel that there can be no question about Lewis's borrowing from O'Neill's novel.

72. Colin Manlove, *C. S. Lewis: His Literary Achievement* (Basingstoke, Hampshire: Macmillan, 1987), 127–28.

73. Hans Christian Andersen, *Andersen's Fairy Tales*, trans. Pat Shaw Iversen (New York: Signet/NAL, 1966), 154.

74. *Loc. cit.*

75. C.S. Lewis, *The Lion, the Witch, and the Wardrobe* (New York: HarperTrophy, 1994 [1950]), 36.

76. "It All Started with a Picture," 53.

77. See Milo Winter's illustration of the Snow Queen in her carriage with Little Kay at http://www.surlalunefairytales.com/illustrations/snowqueen/wintersnowqueen.html. This picture is from *Hans Andersen's Fairy Tales*, trans. Valdemar Paulsen (Chicago: Rand McNally & Co, 1916), and Lewis appears to be borrowing details from it that are not specified by Andersen in his story. These appropriations continue in a curious way in the work of the later illustrator Michael Hague. In an illustration published in 1981, Hague gives Andersen's queen a crown of icicles, and just two years later he gives Lewis's queen almost the identical crown, the difference being that he follows Lewis's description by coloring the White Queen's crown golden. No crown of icicles is mentioned in either story, however, and Lewis's original illustrator Pauline Baynes makes the queen's crown spiky but not of ice (*TLWW* 33). Yet by picturing the evil queens' crowns in the two stories as so similar, Hague reveals how he has identified the two icy queens with each other. Compare his illustration of the snow queen in *Michael Hague's Favourite Hans Christian Andersen Fairy Tales* (New York: Henry Holt and Company, 1981; p. 9) to his illustration of the witch in *The Lion, the Witch and the Wardrobe* (New York: Macmillan, 1983); p. 31.

78. Humphrey Carpenter, *The Inklings* (Boston: Houghton Mifflin, 1979), 224.

79. Several authors in this anthology study this phenomenon; see in particular Kisor and Hawes.

80. http://www.stepheniemeyer.com/twilight.html.

81. "It All Started with a Picture," 53. Lewis may also have been half-remembering the picture of the imaginary lion threatening the man in bed in Erich Kastner's novel *The 35th of May*, (trans. Cyrus Brooks (London: Jonathan Cape, 1933), 58, particularly in view of the fact that the protagonists of this story travel in a magical wardrobe (illustrated on p. 177).

82. *Beauty and the Beast*, retold by Philippa Pearce and illustrated by Alan Barrett (New York: Thomas Y. Crowell Co., 1972).

83. "A Teenage Tale With Bite" in *BYU [Brigham Young University] Magazine* (2007). http://magazine.byu.edu/?act=view&a=1972. The flawless young man is a vampire. In "The Story Behind *Twilight*," Meyer describes him as "beautiful, sparkly"—and thirsty for the girl's blood: http://www.stepheniemeyer.com/twilight.html. In this interview she says that Chapter 13 of *Twilight* "is essentially a transcript of my dream."

84. Beaumont tells the story in *Le magasin des enfans* (Londres: J. Haberkorn, 1756), translated into English, apparently by Madame Beaumont herself, as *The Young Misses Magazine* (1783). This most familiar version of the story is reproduced in facsimile by Betsy Hearne as Appendix Two in her *Beauty and the Beast: Visions and Revisions of an Old Tale* (Chicago: University of Chicago Press, 1989), 189–203.

85. Ibid., 202.

86. Pearce, 30.

87. Meyer would certainly have seen the famous 1991 Disney animated movie of the fairy tale at some time. Linda Woolverton's screenplay is based on Beaumont's version, but possibly with some influence from the Pearce version as well. The transformation in the film is similar to Pearce's in that the light is entirely associated with the prince, but it is differently realized.

In the film broad beams of light shoot out from the Beast-prince's hands and feet as he contorts and changes, unlike the shimmering light surrounding the pair in the Pearce/Barrett interpretation of the story.

88. Quoted by Peter Debruge in a report posted on Wednesday, July 30, 2008, at http://www.variety.com/article/VR1117989820.html?categoryid=3193&cs=1. Some commentators have found fault with Meyers' Bella for being passive, constantly being saved by Edward, whereas in the fairy tale it is Beauty who saves the Beast. In terms of the plot their situations are very different, but Belle/Bella transforms him with love in both stories.

89. Tolkien, "On Fairy Stories," 48.

90. http://www.twilightlexicon.com/?p=62 (in Personal Correspondence #7). Sometimes this "hard as stone" quality is manifested in humorous ways in Meyer's story, for example in *New Moon* when Bella, tremendously relieved to see Alice at last, smashes into her as into a cement wall (p. 382).

91. http://www.yabookscentral.com/cfusion/index.cfm?fuseAction=authors.interview&author_id=1564&interview_id=121.

92. "Extracts from the History of Joseph Smith, the Prophet" in *History of the Church*, Vol. I, Chapter 1: paragraphs 30–32. http://scriptures.lds.org/js_h/1.

93. Meyer, *Twilight*, 256.

94. Even the half-vampire baby inside Bella's womb is enclosed in a membrane so hard that ultrasound can't penetrate it; see *Breaking Dawn* (New York: Little Brown and Company, 2008), 192.

95. See the *Wikipedia* article on "The Angel Moroni," under "Sculptors."

96. An excellent photograph of the relatively new Provo statue may be seen here: http://www.flickr.com/photos/19779889@N00/2338267436/.

97. http://www.ldschurchnews.com/articles/43775/Statue-finds-home-atop-Provo-Utah-Temple.html.

Narrative Layering and "High-culture" Romance

YVETTE KISOR

Much of the narrative layering in Stephenie Meyer's *Twilight* series is immediately obvious to the attentive reader. One can observe a variety of narratives used to help shape her tale, varying in genre from fairy tale (Beauty and the Beast, The Ugly Duckling)[1] and Native American legend (spirit travelers) to popular culture (*Buffy the Vampire Slayer*)[2] and vampire lore. These intertwined narratives serve to structure her story and lend it depth. Perhaps the most consciously employed of these narratives are the stories of so-called "high" literature incorporated among them. In each of the novels in the series, Meyer uses a range of canonical literature to guide her storytelling, from Jane Austen to Emily Brontë to Shakespeare. Coupled with her extensive employment of a wide range of narrative types, this use of canonical romantic literature helps give her story a resonance that puts it in dialogue with the archetypal love stories of the western world.

Stephenie Meyer has said as much, identifying specific texts as informing each of her four books in the series: Jane Austen's *Pride and Prejudice* for *Twilight*, Shakespeare's *Romeo and Juliet* for *New Moon*, Emily Brontë's *Wuthering Heights* for *Eclipse*, and Shakespeare's *A Midsummer Night's Dream* and *The Merchant of Venice* for *Breaking Dawn*.[3] The way she does this is relatively simple: the bulk of the four novels is narrated through Bella's first-person experience, and Bella is a reader who, through the first three novels of the series, is in high school. While some of the references are fairly incidental — a reference to something they happen to be reading in English class, for example — often Bella thinks about the books she reads in terms of her own experience, identifies with particular characters or situations, or talks about them with Edward.[4]

Meyer has stated that the novel that informs *Twilight*, the first book of the series, is Jane Austen's *Pride and Prejudice*.[5] This makes sense as Austen's novel largely concerns the fascination of the main character, Elizabeth Bennet, with the mysterious Mr. Darcy. Elizabeth misunderstands and misconstrues elements of his behavior throughout the novel, and both these errors in interpretation and her interest in Darcy are recalled in Bella's attraction to Edward. In particular, much of what Elizabeth construes as actions done in indifference to, or even dislike of, her and her family are eventually revealed to be situations where Mr. Darcy was working to protect either them or someone else. For example, he is instrumental in separating her older sister Jane from Bingley, as Elizabeth accuses him of, but his motives are based on his perception of Jane's indifference and Bingley's tendency to fall in love rather often, not distaste for her family's lower-class status as Elizabeth had assumed, and once he understands his mistake, Darcy encourages Bingley to propose.[6] Further, when her sister Lydia runs off with Wickham, it is Darcy who finds them and provides the dowry so that Wickham will marry Lydia, but he keeps his actions secret; in fact, Elizabeth mistakenly believes he wants no more to do with her because of Lydia's situation.[7] Similarly, Edward's hostility towards Bella turns out to be an effort to protect her. Bella herself comes to realize this, and it is revealed even more tellingly through *Midnight Sun*, the companion novel to *Twilight* that retells the events of that novel from Edward's point of view.[8] Even the initial meetings of the characters, the ball in chapter three of *Pride and Prejudice* and the biology lab scene in the first chapter of *Twilight*, have elements in common; certainly both Bella and Elizabeth are surprised and offended by the way they are treated. Much of Mr. Darcy's arrogance can be seen as parallel to Edward's: in both cases their arrogance is real to a certain extent, and both men send mixed signals as their attraction to the heroine grows.[9]

However, while it may provide an overarching parallel, *Pride and Prejudice* is actually specifically alluded to only once in *Twilight*. Several other literary works are mentioned early in the novel and reflect Bella's growing fascination with Edward Cullen. All references to literature come in the first seven chapters of *Twilight*, as Bella comes to recognize her own attraction to Edward and his dangerous difference from others. The novel's epigraph is biblical, from the book of Genesis: "But of the tree of the knowledge of good and evil, thou shalt not eat of it: for in the day that thou eatest thereof thou shalt surely die."[10] The suggestions here of temptation, knowledge, and mortality are all relevant to the novel, particularly the sense of the attractive danger inherent in temptation. In the novel proper, the first allusion to literature comes in the opening chapter, on Bella's first day of school before she has seen Edward, as she assesses the reading list in her English class. She mentions four authors and describes the list as "basic," asserting that she has already "read everything," a reality she identifies as both "comforting ... and boring."[11] This quick reference establishes Bella as a reader and names two authors, Brontë and Shakespeare, whose work will inform later aspects of *Twilight* and of the series as a whole. It also prepares us to understand Bella's later attraction to Edward and her ability to accept his dangerous desire for her: she is someone who has read widely, who has been immersed in romantic stories like those of Brontë and Shakespeare—and become bored by them. This suggestion of restlessness implies an attraction in Bella to those stories and the emotions they embody, and a readiness to inhabit them more fully.

Bella's predilection for such stories is suggested again in the very next chapter as she pulls out Brontë's novel *Wuthering Heights*, telling us that it is assigned for her English class and that although she has read it many times before, she wants to do so again.[12] This occurs after her initial meeting with Edward in biology when his hostility was so clearly in evidence. It is now her second day of school, when Edward is not there. She has been thinking about him, unable to escape the feeling that his absence is due to her, and it is in this context that she picks up the novel about the mysterious, violent Heathcliff, becoming so lost in it that she loses track of time.[13] That evening she asks her father about the Cullens, a clear indication that her mind is still on Edward and that she is trying to figure out just who he and his mysterious family are, and she is surprised by Charlie's heated defense of them. A third reference to Brontë comes later in the chapter. A week has passed, and Bella has become accustomed to Edward's absence, and her thoughts of him have become sublimated, though not completely. In the context of expressing how comfortable she is beginning to feel in her new environment, Bella relates how easy she found an unannounced quiz on Brontë's novel in English class.[14] With Edward's absence, the novel has gone from something she turns to in the context of her thoughts about Edward back to its "safe" place in her world and original status as an old favorite. And then, just a page later, Bella sees that Edward has returned to school.

Thus Bella's initial encounter with Edward is framed by references to *Wuthering Heights*. Bella's intrigue with Edward and the Cullens, coupled with his hostile treatment of her in biology and later in the high school office (and her misinterpretation of it), may indeed suggest Elizabeth Bennet's relationship to Mr. Darcy, in particular their initial encounter at the ball. However, the references to Brontë's novel also hint at a potentially passionate, destructive love, like that of Cathy and Heathcliff, lingering just below the surface. *Wuthering Heights* will come to the fore again in the third novel of the series, *Eclipse*, and will dominate that novel, but its presence here in the very beginning of the series—three references in the first two chapters—indicates the passion, but also the dangerous obsession, possibly hiding beneath. Specifically, since the novel *Twilight* is told exclusively from Bella's point of view, it hints at Edward's experience, which Bella does not at this point—and arguably, never—fully understand. A look at the first chapter of *Midnight Sun* confirms this, as Edward fights his overwhelming desire for Bella's blood. The violence of his desire suggests Heathcliff's violent obsession, confirming the danger that Bella senses in Edward.

This sense of danger is primary in the second set of literary references found in *Twilight*, congregating in the sixth and seventh chapters. At this point in the novel Edward has saved her from being crushed by a van and helped her recover from fainting when they do blood-typing in biology, and Bella's English class has moved on from *Wuthering Heights* to *Macbeth*. It is in the context of reading Shakespeare's violent and supernatural play that Bella begins to figure out the true danger that Edward poses—that he is a vampire and that she cannot resist him. Chapter six opens with Bella attempting to focus on Act III of *Macbeth*, but really listening for the sound of her truck being returned.[15] The chapter follows the fainting incident, when Edward has driven her home, and concerns the trip to La Push beach where Bella hears Jacob's story of "the Cold Ones." The third act of *Macbeth* focuses on Macbeth's fall into violence and madness as he suborns the murderers to kill Banquo and his son Fleance, and it culminates in the banquet scene where Macbeth is tortured by the spectre of Banquo's ghost, an apparition that is perhaps supernatural, perhaps the guilty prodding of his subconscious. For Bella, the result of Jacob's account of "the Cold Ones" is a dream in which her subconscious reveals that she already knows Edward is a vampire, though it takes her conscious mind a while to catch up.[16] After a frustrated attempt at Internet research, she heads for the woods in what is the culminating moment of the first movement of the novel. Bella wrestles with the realization that Edward is a vampire and recognizes that it does not ultimately matter to her—her need to be with him supersedes any instinct for self-preservation. Once she experiences this realization she returns home: to work on her paper on *Macbeth*.

After the emotional tumult of mind that she has experienced in the woods, Bella finds it fairly easy to focus on her essay on *Macbeth*, realizing that she feels more content and "serene" than she has since the last time she saw Edward, when he drove her home after she almost fainted in biology and she had tried to distract herself by attempting to read the third act of *Macbeth*.[17] Once again Meyer has framed an important stage of Bella's acquaintance with Edward with references to literature: in the first two chapters Bella's initial strange encounter with Edward is framed by references to *Wuthering Heights*, while in chapters six and seven Meyer uses references to *Macbeth* to frame Bella's realization that Edward is a vampire and truly dangerous, yet she cannot stay away from him. Shakespeare's tragedy is untypical, though as we shall see not completely unique, among the canonical works that Meyer uses to inform her story, in that it does not primarily concern love and attraction as most of the others do. It is useful through its suggestion of the possibility of violence and the supernatural important at this stage of the novel, but it has other resonances as well.

In the play we see Macbeth agonize over the killing of Duncan through the first two acts, but once the murder is accomplished he falls rapidly into a downward spiral of violence begetting more violence, with seemingly little remorse and no more effort needed to "screw [his] courage to the sticking place."[18] Once he makes the definitive decision to kill Duncan, the rest follows. There is a parallel here with Bella's own mental processes. She describes her serenity after her turbulent morning in the woods, when she accepts that Edward is likely a vampire and that she loves him, by noting that while the decision was of a different nature from any she had faced before, the process was not. Bella finds it difficult and painful to make decisions, but once the decision is made, she is rarely assailed with doubts and second guesses, feeling instead relief as she "simply follow[s] through."[19] There's a real similarity here to Macbeth's own mode of thought and action as it appears in Shakespeare's play.

Bella's decision is made, but it takes her a while to share it with Edward, since a sunny day intervenes that necessitates his absence from school. In fact, she will not see him again until the rescue in Port Angeles. At this point, Meyer gives us two more references to the essay that Bella has been writing on *Macbeth* throughout her school day. The first comes as she anticipates seeing Edward in school, the calm resulting from her realization in the woods still with her. It comes, however, without a specific mention of Shakespeare's play, as she tells Mike that her essay considers if Shakespeare portrays women negatively.[20] Thus stripped of any mention of the specific play — without the context of the other references there is no way to know what play Bella is writing on — the allusion becomes more innocuous.[21] However, Edward's unexpected absence from school (all the Cullens are absent) sends Bella into a tailspin of "panic" and "desolation."[22] In this mood we get the final reference to *Macbeth* as Bella finds herself "spiraling downward in misery" because of Edward's absence, while she tries to respond to Angela's questions about her *Macbeth* essay.[23]

It is in this state, somewhere between anticipation, desolation, and frustration, that we get the only direct reference in the novel to Jane Austen, whose novel *Pride and Prejudice* Meyer has identified as informing *Twilight*. Returning home on her sunny, Cullen-less day, Bella is looking for something to distract her from her musings about Edward. She turns once again to a beloved book, this time a collection of Jane Austen's works. She names *Pride and Prejudice* and *Sense and Sensibility* as her favorites, opting for the latter, only to abandon it a few chapters in because the protagonist shares Edward's name. She turns next to *Mansfield Park*, only to give up in disgust when that hero turns out to be named Edmund.[24] At this point she closes the book in frustration and falls asleep feeling the warmth of the sun and the light breeze on her skin; the description is quite sensual, and when she wakes she is momentarily confused and struck by the abrupt sensation that someone is there with her.[25] The scene passes without Bella knowing if anyone is responsible for that feeling, but given the sensuality of the description of Bella falling asleep the reader is primed to think of Edward, and chapter eight of *Midnight Sun* confirms that suspicion: Edward is watching Bella from the trees while she is reading and when she falls asleep he approaches her, steals her book, and examines it to determine where she switched stories, and then returning her book he listens as she talks in her sleep, mentioning the two names that were the source of her displeasure, Edward and Edmund, though without the ability to read her thoughts Edward cannot seem to decipher what they mean.[26]

This literary reference is easily the fullest and most complex in *Twilight*. It is the longest and is no mere reference but a full-blown scene. It is also arguably the most sensual scene in the novel, and it is not difficult to see in it the suggestion of Bella's physical desire for Edward, as she feels the light breeze tickle her skin and the sun touch "my eyelids, my cheekbones, my nose, my lips, my forearms, my neck, soak[ing] through my light shirt...."[27] The titillating way she breaks off as she falls into sleep with the heat reaching through her shirt, touching, the continuation of the catalog would suggest, her breasts, coupled with the sense immediately upon waking that someone is there, all create the sensuality of this moment that grows out of her frustrated desire to see Edward. She turns to Jane Austen at the beginning of this scene as to a comfortable old friend (she identifies it as the "shabbiest," i.e., most well-worn, volume in her small library)[28] as she is seeking an escape from her thoughts of Edward. But this time Jane Austen disappoints, as Bella's desire to escape thoughts of Edward is thwarted by Austen's propensity to name her heroes "Edward" and "Edmund."[29] Like the first literary reference in the novel, Bella's reading list in English class, this much fuller one establishes Bella as a reader and a romantic, restless to move beyond the confines of the pages of her books.

There are no more literary references in *Twilight*. Meyer uses them exclusively in the first seven chapters to help anchor Bella's expanding understanding and experience of Edward. Their primary purpose is to emphasize the danger that Edward poses, though there are other resonances as well. References to *Wuthering Heights*, a novel Bella and Edward will discuss in much greater detail in *Eclipse*, function here to frame Bella's initial encounter with Edward and through the character of Heathcliff to suggest both the mystery and the potential for violence present in Edward. References to *Macbeth* occur in the chapters in which Bella finally realizes what Edward is and the danger he poses to her, as well as the fact that she loves him and cannot stay away. The final literary reference in the book, to Austen's novels, provides what Meyer has identified as the key text, and in the sensuality of the episode hits the note that sustains this first novel of the series: the intense desire between Bella and Edward and the danger of that desire. In *New Moon* that danger comes to the fore again, and in that novel Meyer uses only one major text to inform hers: Shakespeare's *Romeo and Juliet*.[30]

Romeo and Juliet is used much more deliberately in this novel than literature was used in *Twilight*. It becomes important to the plot when Edward and Bella's discussion of the play leads Edward to outline his suicide plan. It becomes important thematically when Bella begins to imagine her life in terms of the play and casts Jacob in the role of Paris, ruminating not on suicide, as Edward had, but on the possibility of life continuing without her Romeo. Allusions to the play are clustered in the beginning (the epigraph through chapter three) and end of the novel (chapter sixteen through the epilogue), reflecting this division. The prevalence of references to the play in *New Moon* not only helps to structure the novel's plot, but it also provides some interesting glimpses into both Edward's and Bella's characters through the different ways they use the play to think about their own lives.

Not only does the epigraph to *New Moon* establish the importance of the play to the novel, it also suggests the inevitable nature of the end: "These violent delights have violent ends, / And in their triumph die, like fire and powder, / Which as they kiss consume."[31] This is, of course, a trick, a sleight — the violent end is indeed approached, but ultimately avoided. Both the confrontation with the Volturi and the confrontation between Jacob and Edward, not to mention Edward's attempted suicide, are all begun — but not completed. Even the threat posed by Victoria is never realized in the context of this novel, and all the violence threatened is ultimately dissipated. The novel ends, in fact, in an odd kind of circularity, where all sorts of horrible, violent things have *almost* happened, but in terms of their daily lives Bella and Edward are largely in the same place they were when the novel began. The real changes are internal and future-oriented, as the prospect of Bella becoming a vampire comes to seem more inevitable.[32]

There are three references to *Romeo and Juliet* in the first three chapters of the novel. The first and third are incidental and function to situate Bella's interaction with the Cullens; the middle one is more involved and concerns the discussion of Edward's suicide, a plot point crucial to the novel. In the first chapter of *New Moon*, Bella and Edward's English class is reading the play and Bella uses her desire to watch *Romeo and Juliet* in a failed attempt to put off Alice's plans for a birthday party; Alice responds with derision, suggesting that Bella already knows the play by heart.[33] Here once again Bella's immersion in an archetypal romantic tale is asserted even as Alice and Edward scorn her excuses. Bella's affection for the story of doomed lovers continues to be referenced: when Edward speaks scornfully of Romeo, she is immediately defensive, admitting to herself that Romeo is not just a favorite character, but someone she had "sort of had a thing for,"[34] at least pre–Edward. Upon being questioned by Edward, she admits that she will probably cry as they watch the movie, and in fact she does shed tears in response to Juliet's waking to discover Romeo's lifeless body. Her response to Shakespeare's story confirms Bella's identity as a romantic as well as the depth of her identification with literature. She loves Romeo, and weeps when Juliet finds him dead.

Edward's response to the play couldn't be more different. He finds Romeo irritating, and criticizes his fickleness and his stupidity. He's amused by Bella's tears, and where she becomes immersed in her literary experiences, he is detached, critical. Her identification is emotional, while his is analytical. He does connect with Romeo on some level; even if only in response to Bella's obvious affinity, he analyzes Romeo's actions and even whispers his lines in

Bella's ear — though this is likely due less to a sense of personal connection than an acknowledgement of Bella's. His penchant for analysis leads him to their discussion of suicide, which not only sets up the plot of the novel and prepares us for Edward's dangerous visit to the Volturi, but also reinforces our sense of Edward's detached, analytical nature, as much a part of his character as his passion: perhaps even its inverse. Even in the grips of his desperation to find Bella when James had kidnapped her, when he was filled with desperate fear and desire for vengeance, he asserts that "part of my mind was making contingency plans."[35]

That propensity for detachment is in strong evidence after Bella's disastrous birthday party, and Edward shows himself to be well capable of sublimating his emotions and analyzing the situation coldly. His emotional distance is met with growing panic in Bella, and the final reference to *Romeo and Juliet* in the first part of the novel serves to emphasize the change in circumstances, as Bella is so distracted by Edward's coldness that she has difficulty paying attention in English class and does not hear their teacher question her about the play; the only break in Edward's ignoring her comes when he whispers the answer to her.[36] This reference makes a kind of pair with the first one in the novel, when Bella tried to put off Alice's birthday plans with her desire to watch *Romeo and Juliet*. Both are brief references not integral to the scene and signal Bella's changed relationship with the Cullens: in the first she is trying to put off their attentions while the second indicates her panic at their lack of notice. Both thereby are in contrast to the central discussion of the play by Bella and Edward in the first chapter, where the play becomes integral to the plot and a key to understanding theme and character.

There is only one other direct reference to literature in the first part of the novel before the cluster of *Romeo and Juliet* allusions in the final chapters. This is largely because Bella stops reading. In the deadness of her world after Edward leaves, there is no music, no books—certainly not the kind of reading Bella has hitherto engaged in, where she identifies so strongly with the characters that she comes to inhabit the book. No, the reference to literature that signals her changed relationship with reading is to something quite different from *Romeo and Juliet*: George Orwell's *Animal Farm*, which she calls a "welcome change from the exhausting romances that made up most of the curriculum." One could hardly ask for a clearer indication of Bella's changed attitude and circumstances.[37]

The references to *Romeo and Juliet* return when Bella "wakes up" due in large part to her relationship with Jacob. They come, crucially, after she jumps off the cliff, a decision that sets in motion the series of events that leads to Edward's suicide attempt, though of course she does not realize that. And they come, as is so often the case with Bella, in a dream as her subconscious mind presents what her conscious mind is not quite ready to process.[38] Rather than the dream of endless searching in the forest that has haunted her since Edward left,[39] this is a more ordinary dream, a collection of memories. The final image, though, the one that stays with Bella, is not a recollection. It is a stage set, an image of Juliet on the balcony. Despite asserting twice that the picture is meaningless, when she awakes she cannot shake the image.[40] In spite of herself, Bella begins to think about Juliet, but instead of simply identifying with her and experiencing the play through her, she begins to speculate, wondering what Juliet would have done if Romeo had "left her," having "lost interest."[41] Rather than inhabiting the play, Bella begins to use the play as a way of interrogating her own life. She imagines Juliet's recovery in terms of her own — incomplete, but occurring nonetheless. And she casts Jacob in the role of Paris and creates a relationship between Paris and Juliet that mirrors her own and Jacob's. She ends up discarding this re-imagined play,[42] but a new willingness to consider life with Jacob has crossed her conscious mind through the vehicle of this play, and she has demonstrated a new way of relating to literature.

This new role for Paris and Juliet will come back to Bella in the Epilogue, but in the meantime the chain of events set off by her jump from the cliff moves Romeo swiftly back into the picture. Just as in Shakespeare's play Romeo comes to believe that Juliet has died due to a message that goes awry, Edward's belief in Bella's death is due to a mistaken message, as he misinterprets Jacob's curt reply that Charlie is "at the funeral"[43] to refer to Bella rather than to Charlie's friend Harry Clearwater. This accident coupled with Alice's visions (also misinterpreted)[44] bring Bella to the realization that Edward is going through with his suicide plan, and as might be expected that realization comes in the form of Bella's memory of her earlier conversation with Edward, which is bound up in Romeo and Juliet's tragic end.[45] This memory recurs as she and Alice fly to Italy,[46] and once she finally finds Edward again it becomes clear that she is not the only one who has been thinking about Romeo and Juliet.

"Death, that hath suck'd the honey of thy breath, / Hath had no power yet upon thy beauty."[47] So says Edward when he finds Bella in his arms at the moment he believes to be his death. This is a far cry from Edward whispering Romeo's lines into Bella's ear when they watched a movie of *Romeo and Juliet* back in Forks. There he was teasing her, amused at her emotional response to the play. Now he understands it. Now he understands Romeo and he too connects the play to himself and Bella, seeing the role played by fate and circumstance and determining "never [to] criticize Romeo again."[48] In certain ways he and Bella have moved closer together in terms of their relationship with literature. In the beginning of the novel Bella was inhabiting the world of *Romeo and Juliet* emotionally and identifying with the characters while Edward remained distant, viewing the characters with a critical eye, unable to relate to them. By the end of the novel Edward finds himself understanding Romeo's situation and able, at least partially, to identify with the characters emotionally, greeting his view of Bella's face with Romeo's words at Juliet's tomb.[49] By contrast, Bella's emotional relationship with the play has expanded to include a more thoughtful, speculative aspect, as her re-imaginings of the ending demonstrate.

This speculative exercise comes back sharply to Bella when they return to Forks and Edward and Jacob are brought back into one another's sphere. Once Edward makes clear to her how unlikely it is that he and Jacob can avoid a fight should they meet, and raises inadvertently the possibility that he might kill Jacob, Bella comes back to Paris' role in the play. She suddenly remembers Paris' fate once Romeo returns, tersely expressed in the descriptions: "*They fight*" and Paris "*falls.*"[50] Just a few pages later, the inevitable confrontation at hand, the same stage directions come back to her.[51] This is the Epilogue to the book and it sets up the conflict to follow in the third novel of the series. Further, the way literature is used in *New Moon* sets up its use in *Eclipse*.[52] By focusing on one main literary work and allowing characters to use the work to think about their own lives, Meyer gives readers a tool for understanding how her characters think and how they grow and change. Her use of *Romeo and Juliet* shows Bella progressing from an emotional, romantic soul to one capable of considering other more realistic possibilities—contingency plans, if you will—yet doing so with an imagination born out of her ability to inhabit the literary texts she encounters. Conversely, his use of Shakespeare's play shows Edward's growth from detached criticism to a deeper understanding of what motivates characters—people. Meyer also gives us patterns we can use to understand where her story is heading, not simply as templates but as possibilities, sometimes realized and sometimes subverted. She will use a similar technique in *Eclipse*, though here the work she uses is not Shakespeare but Emily Brontë's *Wuthering Heights*.

Wuthering Heights is the main text referenced in *Eclipse*, but it is not the only one. The epigraph, Robert Frost's poem "Fire and Ice," signals the main conflict in the novel, because in spite of the threat posed by Victoria and the newborns in Seattle, the real conflict is between Edward and Jacob.[53] The difference in their body temperatures is the most obvious significance of the fire and ice allusion, but the title of Frost's poem speaks to differences in temperament as well. Jacob not only gives off more heat physically, he is more hot-tempered and apt to lose control; similarly Edward's body is not only cool to the touch, but he is icy in his self-control. The temperature differences also lead to the explosive situation in the tent as Bella requires Jacob's body heat to survive the winter storm, yet that awkward physical situation leads to the emotional confrontation between them ... which leads in turn to the physical confrontation with Victoria. And, oddly enough, that results in the strange alliance between werewolf and vampire, fire and ice, figured in Seth's loyalty to Edward and Edward's affection for him, culminating ultimately in the alliances of *Breaking Dawn*. All this may be too much weight for one epigraph, but it must be noted that, just as the epigraph of *New Moon* implied an explosive, fatal ending that did not occur, so too Frost's poem is loaded with intimations of the end of the world, of desire and hate, yet there is no such ending either in this novel or the final one of the series.[54]

The main literary point of reference for *Eclipse*, though, is not Robert Frost's poem but *Wuthering Heights*. Three references in the first chapter alone establish its importance, and the discussion Bella and Edward engage in about it suggests both how it will function in *Eclipse* and the growth of Bella and Edward's relationship. The first reference establishes the novel's place in Bella's imaginative life. Like Austen's novels, this is one that Bella has read many times before; she refers to her "much-abused copy" as well as her desire to "lose" herself in the novel.[55] Once again we are reminded of Bella's devotion to such romantic fare, a devotion that predates her involvement with Edward but is in some sense realized through it. Upon his arrival Edward spies the novel and responds skeptically,[56] expressing, once they are alone, both amusement and bewilderment at her affection for such novels. It's not just the fact that Bella returns to it over and over again; Edward questions the appeal of the two protagonists, whom he declares "ghastly people" who destroy one another. He professes incomprehension at the status Cathy and Heathcliff have attained as legendary lovers, mentioning the texts that inform the first two novels of Meyer's series, *Romeo and Juliet* and *Pride and Prejudice*, as featuring much worthier romantic pairs, and finally asserting that *Wuthering Heights* "isn't a love story, it's a hate story."[57]

There is a parallel here with Edward and Bella's different responses to *Romeo and Juliet*, as there too Edward initially found Bella's immersion in the text somewhat amusing and the hero to be wanting. However, their ensuing conversation demonstrates how their relationship has grown. Edward does not simply tease her about her literary tastes, he enquires about them with what appears to be a genuine interest that Bella finds disarming.[58] Their differing responses to *Romeo and Juliet*, and in particular the way in which Edward came to understand Bella's position in *New Moon*, inform this desire to understand. Bella responds in somewhat uncertain terms, but she attempts to elucidate her position, focusing on the "inevitability" of Cathy and Heathcliff's love and the impossibility of anything separating them for long, "not her selfishness, or his evil, or even death, in the end...." This reference to Cathy's selfishness marks the course of Bella's identification with the heroine, which will be more fully realized as the novel progresses and Bella finds herself unwilling to give up Jacob. To Edward's objection that neither Cathy nor Heathcliff has any redeeming quality, Bella can only maintain that "[t]heir love *is* their only redeeming quality."[59] Their mutual identification with the main characters of Brontë's novel is asserted as Bella counters Edward's warning against falling for someone "so ... malignant" with her hope that he has the sense to avoid someone "so selfish," contending that Cathy, not Heathcliff, is the one primarily responsible for their misfortunes.[60] Yet as the events of the novel unfold, Edward too will find elements in the novel with which he can identify.

Edward's guilt over the pain he caused her when he left her in *New Moon* has left its mark. That guilt, in the face of Bella's unwillingness to give up Jacob, leads Edward, by chapter eleven, to a new willingness to allow Bella to spend time with Jacob, in spite of his fears for her safety, and to a new understanding of Cathy and Heathcliff. Rather than allowing his protectiveness of Bella and potential jealousy of Jacob to rule him, he gives way, placing that decision in the context of *Wuthering Heights* and a new understanding of Heathcliff and his situation. He has been reading Brontë's novel as Bella sleeps after her day with Jacob, during which she had heard the old legends of the Quileute around the bonfire. Upon waking, Bella looks with curiosity at the passage he had been reading, wondering about his earlier remark that he could "sympathize" with Heathcliff.[61] It is the passage, which Meyer quotes at length, in which Heathcliff asserts both the enormity of his hatred for Linton and the utter impossibility of his hurting him as long as Cathy cares for him. The words that catch Bella's eye, though, and provoke her refusal to believe that this could have been the passage Edward was reading, are "drank his blood": Heathcliff's contention that "[t]he moment her regard ceased, I would have torn his heart out, and drank his blood! But, till then ... I would have died by inches before I touched a single hair of his head!"[62] The violence of Heathcliff's hatred of Linton, not his refusal to act on it, is clearly what Bella shies away from acknowledging here.

In the face of the enormity of her need for both men, Bella continues to push away any deep recognition of either Edward's suffering or Jacob's. She goes so far as to use Edward's guilt about leaving her in *New Moon* to manipulate him into sitting out the confrontation with Victoria and the newborns. She feels her own guilt over this, but continues in the course she has begun. This leads to the confrontations in the tent, and the increasing of both men's pain, culminating as she sends Edward after Jacob, who has fled in response to the intense anguish that the knowledge of her acceptance of Edward's proposal causes him. As she waits for both men to return, Bella is overcome with remorse at the suffering her selfishness has caused, and she turns in her thoughts to Cathy, reproaching herself for being as cruel and selfish as she.[63] It is in the throes of this identification that she turns to the other story that she has been identifying with out of her sense of helplessness in the face of forces more powerful than herself: the Quileute tale of the Third Wife.

Her attempt to act out the role of the Third Wife and sacrifice herself, however, turns out to be a useless gesture due to her misunderstanding of Edward's, and especially Seth's, tactics as they battle Victoria. By the conclusion of the novel, once Bella has cried herself out in Edward's arms as she lets go of Jacob, Edward and Bella's identification with Cathy and Heathcliff is so strong that they turn to Brontë's novel to explain how they feel, literally reading passages to one another. When Bella tries to make clear to Edward that no matter how great the pain of letting go of Jacob is to her, it is nothing compared to her need for Edward, she demands that he hand her copy of *Wuthering Heights* to her. She turns to the most well-worn passage, and though she calls Cathy a "monster," she acknowledges the rightness of her love for Heathcliff.[64] Bella's self-loathing for her selfishness is still in evidence here, but what is primary is the strength of her love for, and need for, Edward; the passage she reads is Cathy's declaration of what Heathcliff means to her: "If all else perished, and he remained, I should still continue to be; and if all else remained, and he were annihilated, the universe would turn to a mighty stranger."[65] We are back to Bella's original attempt in chapter one to explain the appeal of Cathy and Heathcliff's story. While Cathy's selfishness has been in strong evidence through Bella's own, she has come back to what drew her to the novel to begin with—the inevitability of the love between Cathy and Heathcliff that perseveres in spite of their faults. This time Edward understands and concurs, quoting Heathcliff: "I *cannot* live without my life! I *cannot* live without my soul!"[66] Once again a literary work has brought Edward and Bella from a place of not understanding one another to a place of mutual insight and appreciation. In the absence of any ability to read her thoughts, Edward needs to understand Bella's relationship to the literature she loves, and he is able to understand her when he can grasp that relationship.[67] Like their discussions of *Romeo and Juliet* in *New Moon*, in *Eclipse* Edward and Bella use *Wuthering Heights* to explain their own relationship, and there is a similar movement towards comprehension when they can do so. In each case, the books become a meeting ground for Edward and Bella, in terms both of understanding their own minds and desires and of understanding each other's.

Whereas Meyer's use of canonical literature in the middle two novels of her four-part series, *New Moon* and *Eclipse*, is relatively straightforward, allowing one novel to set the tone for each, in the fourth and final novel, *Breaking Dawn*, the literary references work in a more complex and subtle way.[68] Once again, she turns to Shakespeare, this time to *A Midsummer Night's Dream* for Book Two and to *The Merchant of Venice* for Book Three. In each book, she signals the resolution of the main conflicts to the discerning reader, as well as suggesting deeper resonances concerning the larger themes of her work as a whole. Edward and Bella have grown in their relationship to the point where there is less to work out between them, and the fundamental conflicts concern Jacob's role in their lives and the larger problem of the place of the Cullens, now including Bella, in the wider vampire world—i.e., the showdown with the Volturi.

Breaking Dawn is divided into three books, each titled by its narrator. Book One is the shortest of the three and, in terms of literary resonances, the least complex. It recounts the wedding and honeymoon and ends with the realization of Bella's pregnancy and her turning to Rosalie for protection. Given its content, moving Bella from fiancée to wife to expectant mother, the epigraph seems appropriate: the opening lines of Edna St. Vincent Millay's poem "Childhood Is the Kingdom Where Nobody Dies." The poem as a whole, however, resonates somewhat differently from the opening three lines given in the epigraph. The poem concerns the speaker's grief for her mother's death and the reality that it is that, a mother's death, which signals the end of childhood. But the three lines quoted here do not suggest anything about a mother's death; they suggest instead the movement from childhood to adulthood and raise the spectre of immortality: "Childhood is not from birth to a certain age and at a certain age / The child is grown, and puts away childish things. / Childhood is the kingdom where nobody dies."[69] In isolation, the three lines quoted here are germane to the content of Book One, but through their difference from the meaning of the entire poem they signal the kind of "trick" Meyer has played on the reader in previous books. Like many of her epigraphs throughout the series, this one suggests, for readers who know the work it comes from, a direction the plot will go that is ultimately unrealized—though toyed with. Just as the epigraphs to *New Moon* and *Eclipse* suggest an explosive, fatal ending that is approached but never reached, the poem excerpted at the beginning of Book One of *Breaking Dawn* implies not simply Bella's entrance into adulthood, but that the approach will come through the loss of her parents. The loss of her family is indeed anticipated as one of the costs of her choice to become a vampire, but it is not realized in the course of the novel. She expects to lose Charlie once she becomes a vampire, but thanks to Jacob's intervention, she gets to keep him in her life. Rather than loss, Bella gains both Jacob and Charlie as she enters her vampire life, as well as, and arguably through, the unexpected arrival of Renesmee, the magical child who unites all the disparate elements of Bella's life. Ultimately she *has* lost her parents to mortality as she chooses the immortal life of the vampire, but in the context of the novel, that loss does not occur. It is postponed beyond the confines of Meyer's story.

Other than the epigraph, there are almost no specific literary resonances in Book One of *Breaking Dawn*, though given the primacy of the wedding in this section, *Anne of Green Gables* can be seen as a kind of touchstone. The specific references to Lucy Maud Montgomery's novel come not in *Breaking Dawn* itself but in the previous novel in the series, *Eclipse*. Yet both allusions to *Anne of Green Gables* relate to the vision that comes to fruition in Book One of *Breaking Dawn*, Bella's wedding to Edward. Bella's acquiescence to Edward's demand for marriage—a long process, granted—is signaled through her ability to picture herself in the time of his human life, on his arm. During his drawn-out attempt to convince her to marry him, her true assent is signaled by her vision of herself in the garb of his time period, the early twentieth century. She sees Edward in a complementary guise and, in spite of her attempt to brush away the vision, referring scornfully to Montgomery's novels, she *has* seen it, she has seen his side, as he requested.[70] This is not the moment in which she accepts his proposal, but it is the moment in which she begins to concede to his desire for marriage, and that vision is realized in the final chapter of *Eclipse* when Alice shows her the wedding dress she has created for her.[71] *Anne of Green Gables* is not specifically mentioned in *Breaking Dawn*; the only literary reference is again to Jane Austen, as Renee tells Bella that she looks like she belongs in an "Austen movie" when she appears in her turn-of-the-century bridal gown.[72] The *Anne of Green Gables* vision she saw in *Eclipse* is made real when she marries Edward in the first part of *Breaking Dawn*, and in the traditional, even old-fashioned implications of Montgomery's novels, Bella's pregnancy during their honeymoon — the first time they make love, in fact — makes an odd kind of sense.[73]

Where literary references are sparser in Book One of *Breaking Dawn*, Book Two contains perhaps the clearest references to literature. It uses only one major text, and that is Shakespeare's *A Midsummer Night's Dream*. The play provides the epigraph for the book, a quote from Act III, Scene i: "And yet, to say the truth, reason and love keep little company together now-a-days." The line is Bottom's,[74] and signifies his bemusement at finding Titania in love with him: but in its suggestion that reason can play no real role in resolving the problems of love, it looks forward to the solution to the love triangle of Jacob, Bella, and Edward, as well as to the conflict between Sam's werewolf pack and the Cullens, that the conclusion of Book Two offers. The hint has already been provided in the third book of the series, *Eclipse*, when Edward uses Shakespeare's play to describe the imprinting that werewolves undergo as "magic."[75] And indeed imprinting is the piece of fairy magic that will resolve the conflict between Edward, Jacob, and Bella. Much as Puck's flower-juice resolves the problem of that play by redirecting Demetrius' affections from Hermia to Helena, the moment of Jacob's imprinting on Renesmee resolves the seemingly insoluble problem of the love triangle of Bella, Jacob, and Edward: now Bella gets to keep Jacob in her family, Jacob is happy, and Edward, though rather bemused, is content and can even, within this new configuration, grow to love Jacob as a brother — or a son.[76]

Other than the epigraph, though, there is only one specific reference to Shakespeare's play in Book Two. The dearth of literary references is due in large part to the change of narrator. Book Two of *Breaking Dawn* is the only part of Meyer's series not narrated by Bella, and whereas Bella is a reader actively engaged in the stories she reads, Jacob is not.[77] Books are not important to him, and thus the only specific reference to Shakespeare's play comes from Bella, a reference back to Edward's characterization of the werewolves' imprinting as similar to the magic of *A Midsummer Night's Dream*.[78] Here Bella is explaining her "magical" belief that her pregnancy will work out somehow, even though she herself cannot quite see how it will happen. The analogy she chooses is more accurate than she realizes, of course, because Jacob's imprinting on the child she carries will indeed make everything work out. She affirms her belief in magic based on everything she's been through,[79] and goes on to describe her conviction — that her pregnancy will have a positive result — as "*faith*."[80]

Jacob, however, is not buying it. He ignores the specific Shakespeare reference, which has no reality for him, and focuses instead on Bella's use of the word "magic." He hears it next from Carlisle who, like Bella, has his own share of faith and has come, during the abbreviated course of her pregnancy, to a belief that things will work out, though his is based, at least in part, on his medical confidence. He is not specifically talking about Bella's pregnancy, though, but rather musing on the genetic divergences of vampires and werewolves from the human species, describing the werewolves' variance as "[m]agical."[81] Once again, Jacob responds dismissively, muttering "Bibbidi-Bobbidi-Boo" under his breath and likening the doctor to Bella with his "magic garbage."[82] Jacob's attitude is a far cry from the faith that Bella and Carlisle, and eventually Edward, can espouse, and when Jacob runs off to Seattle and considers the unlikelihood of his ever being okay again, he muses to himself that "[m]agic wasn't going to save me."[83] But he is wrong. Magic will save him. It comes in the form of Renesmee, and she saves them all: Bella, from the moment she nudges her *in utero*; Edward, once he can hear her thoughts; and Jacob — when he imprints on her. Like the fairies in *A Midsummer Night's Dream*, she fixes all the problems that seemed insoluble.[84]

The final book of *Breaking Dawn* is by far the most complex in its resonances. As she does in the previous book, Meyer uses a Shakespeare play to signal to the attentive reader the resolution of the book's main conflict, here the confrontation with the Volturi. However, *The Merchant of Venice* does not come into play until deep in the novel, chapter twenty-nine, when Alice uses a page from Bella's copy of the play to leave her secret message to Bella. The epigraph utilizes a quite different text. It comes from Orson Scott Card's *Empire* and speaks directly to the situation that Bella and the Cullens face as they confront the Volturi in the final book: "Personal affection is a luxury you can have only after all your enemies are eliminated. Until then, everyone you love is a hostage, sapping your courage and corrupting your judgment."[85] Like other epigraphs, it is a trick. It suggests war; it suggests the sacrifice of loved ones. Both are anticipated, even come to seem inevitable, as the final book moves towards its conclusion, but neither occurs. There is no vampire war, and no loved ones are sacrificed.[86] The aspect of the epigraph that *is* realized, though, is the sense of expansion outward. *Empire* is a speculative fiction that imagines the left/right political divide in the United States leading to a second Civil War. The last book of Meyer's final novel in the series has a similarly wide view. The previous books of the series have been fairly insular, focused on Forks and the Cullens with superficial forays to Arizona, Italy, and Isle Esmee, and brief incursions inward as the nomads James, Victoria, and Laurent, and the Denali coven, not to mention a group of the Volturi, make short visits. Now the canvas expands to include the whole vampire world, as so many covens and nomads converge on Forks that Meyer includes a "Vampire Index" to help the reader keep track of them all.[87] Like so many of the epigraphs in the series, this one provides both a clue for reading the following book, and a red herring.

The corrective to the red herring and the predominant text for the third book of *Breaking Dawn* is Shakespeare's *The Merchant of Venice*.[88] Meyer has affirmed this, and confirmed that it is her hint to the reader that the ending is not going to be a battle, but a courtroom scene: "I put a clue into the manuscript as well. Alice tore a page from *The Merchant of Venice* because the end of *Breaking Dawn* was going to be somewhat similar: bloodshed appears inevitable, doom approaches, and then the power is reversed and the game is won by some clever verbal strategies; no blood is shed, and the romantic pairings all have a happily ever after."[89] As Meyer notes, Shakespeare's play enters the novel because the page on which Alice writes her note telling the Cullens that she and Jasper are leaving is from Bella's copy of the play.[90] Acting on that hint, Bella goes back to retrieve the book and finds that on the title page opposite the page she had torn out, Alice had written her a message.[91] That's as much as Meyer gives us, but by this point in the series, given how she has used literary references throughout, it is more than enough. It does indeed suggest the resolution of the novel, for just as Shylock will get no pound of flesh from Antonio and exact no vengeance, Aro will acquire no gifted vampires nor eliminate any competing ones. The key parallel comes when Edward, with his gift of hearing the thoughts of others, senses Alice's approach and the evidence she brings before anyone else can, and as a consequence he is able to ensnare Aro in his own words, forcing him to declare that the only point of contention between them is their inability to know how Renesmee will develop. Once he has Aro's statement of that fact and his assurance that with that knowledge there will be no conflict,[92] then he has Aro and the Volturi trapped, just as Shylock is trapped by his insistence on a single pound of flesh — no more, no less.

That is the main function of the reference to Shakespeare's play, as Meyer has affirmed.[93] It is not, however, the only way the allusion to that play operates. It opens up other resonances that reach deeper into the themes of Meyer's work, and allows other points to be interrogated. In a traditional reading of Shakespeare's play, Shylock is the villain. He traps Antonio into his bond for a pound of flesh due to his hatred for Antonio as a Christian, as someone who lends money at no interest and rails against the Jews as usurers,[94] and Shylock receives his comeuppance through his refusal to heed Portia's call to practice mercy.[95] Shylock is a usurer whose greed drives him to place the loss of his money on the same plane as the loss of his daughter, as is suggested by his well-known lines "My daughter! O my ducats! O my daughter! / Fled with a Christian! O my Christian ducats! / Justice! the law! my ducats, and my daughter!"[96] Similarly, Aro's greed is in clear evidence. He is acquisitive not for money but for uncommon gifts — he desires to acquire vampires with special talents, and his desire for Alice, with her unique ability to see the future, is pre-eminent.[97] Aro is a collector, and even in the final climactic scene he expresses his desire for those aligned with the Cullens who possess special talents: Edward, Bella, Kate, Zafrina, Benjamin.[98] Given Aro's acquisitiveness, established repeatedly throughout Meyer's series,[99] and the Volturi's insistence on the strict letter of the law, they can be associated with the Jews of Shakespeare's play. In this reading the Volturi can be seen as representing the old way and the old law, and the Cullens as representing a new way and a new law. It is this that the Volturi find so threatening in the Cullens—they have found a new way to live that trades the natural craving of vampires for human blood, for a deepening of the bonds of love and family. Since the most obvious difference between the Volturi and the Cullens is the latter's choice to abstain from human blood, there is a certain fitness in the analogy with Shylock's "pound of flesh," for the verbal technicality that gets Antonio off is that the bond does not allow Shylock to shed any blood: "This bond doth give thee here no jot of blood; / The words expressly are 'a pound of flesh.'"[100] Much of this is expressed in Garrett's speech to the Volturi witnesses, as he affirms that the Volturi call for justice is a sham and their true desire is to eliminate a new group that threatens their power.[101] In this can be seen a reference to the conflict between the Jews and the early Christians (to push the parallel as far as it can go).

But the association of Aro and the Volturi with Shylock and the Jews as villains of the piece is not the only possible reading. The Volturi are the power figures in the vampire world who represent the law. As such they correspond better with the Christians of Shakespeare's play than with Shylock. In their upholding of the law they protect the vampire world from discovery; as Edward tells Bella, her negative view of the Volturi fails to acknowledge the role they play in maintaining the relative peace of vampire society.[102] It is possible to see many of their actions as serving the greater good, and even their utilization of special talents as weapons, such as Chelsea's ability to loosen bonds of alliance or Alec's to incapacitate, can be seen as merciful, allowing "justice" to be served without needless cruelty.[103] The problem, of course, is hypocrisy, for Aro and the Volturi do not always seek to enforce justice as their primary goal. Sometimes acquisition or power is also an objective, and sometimes those ends supersede justice to the extent that justice becomes just an empty show. Such is the case with the "trial" at the end of *Breaking Dawn*, and many of Aro's speeches have the ring of the lawyer espousing justice when in reality seeking a more self-interested goal. But in this he resembles not Shylock but Portia. It can be argued that in her legal representation of Antonio, Portia seeks not justice but the maintenance of power for the controlling authority, even revenge: that her famous speech urging mercy is as empty as Aro's speeches. After all, the traditional reading of Shakespeare's play that sees Shylock as the villain and the Christians as innocent has been energetically interrogated in the last half-century, to the degree that Shylock becomes a tragic, even heroic figure in many modern productions.[104] Even those who hold with a more traditional reading must acknowledge that Shakespeare gave Shylock the famous "Hath not a Jew eyes?" speech that suggests that Shylock's desire for vengeance is not without cause,[105] and while he gave Portia the famed speech on mercy,[106] it is a mercy that she herself refuses to practice, denying Shylock even his principle, confiscating his goods, and forcing him to convert.

But that's the point, of course. Aro and the Volturi can be seen as *either* Shylock *or* the Christians because both Shylock and the Christians can be understood to twist justice for their own ends. Shylock uses the legal contract between himself and Antonio, his bond for a pound of flesh, in order to exact his revenge on Antonio. Portia uses the laws of Venice not simply in order to free Antonio, her new husband's friend, from what amounts to a death sentence, but also to exact revenge on Shylock — that's why she insists on ruining him financially, and she and Antonio between them require that he turn both his goods and his soul over to the Christians. Thus Lorenzo, the Christian who stole Shylock's daughter, becomes heir of his goods and Shylock must become a Christian; nothing less than Shylock's total defeat is called for. An interrogation of the Volturi in terms of *The Merchant of Venice* reveals the problem with systems of justice: they can be twisted to serve selfish ends. That is the resonance of the conclusion of *Breaking Dawn*, as Siobhan gives voice to a vision of a future "free of the Volturi altogether."[107] It is a utopian vision, but it has been prepared for by the events of Meyer's series. As the vampire world discovers a new way of functioning, one modeled on the Cullens' choice and implied through the expansion of the Denali clan, a world becomes possible that does not require the authoritarian structures of the Volturi to enforce peace and civility.

This sense of a changing world order is implied several times in the closing chapters of *Breaking Dawn*. Eleazar has already modeled it, leaving the Volturi, though he believed in their mission, to join the Denali clan and embrace the new way of life. Garrett chooses it at the end of the confrontation with the Volturi after delivering the rousing speech that encapsulates what is wrong with the Volturi system and notably directing his words to the Volturi witnesses. And Bella observes the change several times, noting that "everyone could feel it."[108] It is not simply the reality of such vampire-human hybrids as Renesmee and Nahuel that is referenced here — it is the sense of family that becomes possible when bonds of love are forged through the choice to live differently, i.e., without preying on the humans around them. With this, then, Meyer's use of *The Merchant of Venice* as a touchstone for the final book of her final novel in the series becomes much more than simply a clue to the reader that the conclusion will be a courtroom scene rather than a battle. It becomes a tool with which to interrogate systems of justice and consider the ramifications of a choice such as the Cullens'. After all, Carlisle too lived with the Volturi and experienced their way of life, but like Eleazar he ultimately found it wanting and found his own way — a new way.

This essay has sought to explore some of the methods by which more canonical narratives serve to structure Meyer's story, and also to elucidate some of the resonances they suggest in terms of theme and character identity. Meyer's use of references to canonical literature throughout her series serves multiple purposes, deepening the story she tells. In *Twilight* she establishes Bella as a reader and uses several texts, primarily Jane Austen's *Pride and Prejudice*,

Emily Brontë's *Wuthering Heights*, and Shakespeare's *Macbeth*, to ground Bella's growing realization that Edward is a vampire who thirsts for her blood, yet she loves him and cannot stay away. In *New Moon* and *Eclipse* Meyer uses one main text for each novel, Shakespeare's *Romeo and Juliet* for *New Moon* and Brontë's *Wuthering Heights* for *Eclipse*, to suggest the movement of each novel, and then to play with that expectation, and also to show Bella and Edward's growth towards understanding one another as each is able to use literature in different ways and to find through that literature a common meeting ground. In her final novel of the series, *Breaking Dawn*, she uses Shakespeare's *A Midsummer Night's Dream* and *The Merchant of Venice* to suggest the resolutions of the main conflicts, and to give the reader tools through which to understand the ramifications of the vampire world she has created. By placing her tale in dialogue with some of the canonical texts of western literature, Meyer has given it a depth that allows her to move beyond simply telling a story of star-crossed young lovers to speak to the larger issues that literature addresses: the nature of love, the reality of justice, and what it means to be human.

Notes

1. These are the two fairy tales suggested in the first and last name Isabella (Bella) Swan. For perhaps the clearest indication of the fruition of the Ugly Duckling tale, see *Breaking Dawn* (New York: Little, Brown and Company, 2008), 523–4. In addition, see Janice Hawes' "Sleeping Beauty and the Idealized Undead" in this volume for a different examination of Meyer's use of fairy tale.

2. Meyer has affirmed that she has "never seen an entire episode of *Buffy* or *Angel*," though she identifies her sister, who read drafts of *Twilight*, as a "huge Buffy fan" who urged her to watch; "10 Second Interview: A Few Words with Stephenie Meyer," Amazon.com, http://www.amazon.com/Twilight-Book-1-Stephenie-Meyer/dp/0316160172. She has also stated that, once she is finished writing, "I'm going to get 'Buffy' and watch the whole thing back-to-back, because I love Joss Whedon—I can't believe I've never seen it." Stephenie Meyer, interviewed in Larry Carroll, "'Twilight' Tuesday: Stephenie Meyer Says She May Revisit 'Twilight' Universe Someday," MTV.com, August 5 2008, http://www.mtv.com/movies/news/articles/1592141/story.jhtml. There are potent parallels: Joss Whedon's creations feature a high school setting in the first three seasons of *Buffy the Vampire Slayer*, and the star-crossed love of the human teenager Buffy and the vampire–with-a-soul Angel is an important through line for both series. Like Edward and his family, the character Angel is a "vegetarian," abstaining from human blood and drinking animal blood. He seeks to "do good," and the series *Angel* even features a "miraculous" pregnancy (here two vampires) and a pregnant mother willing to sacrifice herself to bring the baby to birth. *Buffy the Vampire Slayer* ran from 1997 to 2003 on the WB network (1997–2002) and UPN (2002–3); *Angel* ran from 1999 to 2004 on the WB network.

3. This has been widely reported; for just two examples see Maurine Proctor, "Stephenie Meyer's Vampire Series Makes Readers' Blood Rush," *Meridian*, August 8, 2008, http://www.meridianmagazine.com/books/080806vampire.html and John Timpane, "High Blood Pleasure; Arts & Entertainment," *PhillyNews.com*, August 2, 2009, http://www.philly.com/philly/entertainment/20090802_High_blood_pleasure.html.

4. In fact, looking back at her human life and assessing her former mediocrity, Bella identifies reading as the one thing she was good at, though she notes that few prizes are given out for "reading books" (*Breaking Dawn* 523). Meyer has talked about the importance of Bella's

reading: "Bella is a reader. ... she ... sees her life through the filter of the stories that she's read." See "Video & Transcript: Q+A at Vroman's, Pasadena, CA" August 25, 2007, http://stepheniesays.livejournal.com/3221.html.

5. See note 3. Meyer describes the first book as "sort of my *Pride & Prejudice*" less because of specific parallels but because Austen's novel is "kind of the epitome of a people meet & fall in love story for me" ("Video & Transcript: Q+A at Vroman's, Pasadena, CA."). While the movies made of the series are not the subject of this essay, it should perhaps be noted that the *Twilight* movie does not include any literary references, either visually or through dialogue. In fact, the only shot of Bella "reading" per se is of Bella holding up a book on her second day of school as a signal to her high school admirers that she is too busy to join them. The paperback cover is folded back, and the book cannot be identified, but it appears from the lineation of the text to be poetry rather than a novel or a play. For the second movie, *New Moon*, however, it is a different story. See note 30.

6. Jane Austen, *Pride and Prejudice* (New York: Signet, 1980), 167–72, 311–2. First published 1813.

7. Ibid., 269–73.

8. As of this writing, *Midnight Sun* has not been published, but the author has posted a rough draft of the first twelve chapters to her website: StephenieMeyer.com, 2008, http://www.stepheniemeyer.com/pdf/midnightsun_partial_draft4.pdf.

9. In addition, like Elizabeth, Bella has a somewhat scatter-brained mother and a more sensible father with whom she has a deeper relationship; there are also similar class differences between the Cullens and Bella's family as exist between Darcy and the Bennets. See Shirley Kinney and Wallis Kinney, "The Jane Austen—*Twilight* Zone," Jane Austen Society of North America, http://www.jasna.org/film/twilight.html.

10. Gen 2:17 (King James translation).

11. Stephenie Meyer, *Twilight* (New York: Little, Brown and Company, 2005), 15.

12. Ibid., 34–5.

13. In the final chapter of that novel, Nelly Dean even wonders if Heathcliff is "a ghoul, or a vampire" (301). Emily Brontë, *Wuthering Heights* (New York: Bantam Books, 1981). Originally published 1847.

14. Meyer, *Twilight*, 38.

15. Ibid., 110.

16. Ibid., 130–1.

17. Ibid., 140.

18. William Shakespeare, *Macbeth*, I.vii.60. *The Riverside Shakespeare*, 2nd ed., ed. G. Blakemore Evans (Boston and New York: Houghton Mifflin, 1997).

19. Meyer, *Twilight*, 140.

20. Ibid., 143. The subject of Bella's essay seems somewhat ironic, given some of the negative criticism Meyer has received that finds her *Twilight* series to be "anti-feminist." The clearest response Meyer has given to the criticism can be found at "Frequently Asked Questions: *Breaking Dawn*," StephenieMeyer.com, http://www.stepheniemeyer.com/bd_faq.html.

21. In this way it is similar to Bella's earlier characterization of a quiz on *Wuthering Heights* as simple, for in both cases her sense of calm is reflected in a literary reference that indicates her control over the material. See note 14.

22. Meyer, *Twilight*, 145.

23. Ibid., 146.

24. Ibid., 147–8. This is the only time *Pride and Prejudice* is named in *Twilight*.

25. Ibid., 148.

26. Meyer, *Midnight Sun*, 160–2.

27. Meyer, *Twilight*, 148.

28. Ibid., 147.

29. Others have moved beyond the confines of Austen's books in "interesting" ways. Dare one reference here the new *Pride and Prejudice and Zombies* by Jane Austen and Seth Gra-

hame-Smith (Philadelphia, PA: Quirk Books, 2009) or *Sense and Sensibility and Sea Monsters* by Jane Austen and Ben H. Winters (Philadelphia, PA: Quirk Books, 2009)? Or even *Vampire Darcy's Desire: A Pride and Prejudice Adaptation* by Regina Jeffers (Berkeley, CA: Ulysses Press, 2009)?

30. Unlike the movie made of *Twilight* (see note 5), the film of *New Moon* makes strong use of the book's literary references. The first few minutes of *New Moon* are replete with references to *Romeo and Juliet*, some based on those of the book and others new: the lines from *Romeo and Juliet* that form the epigraph of *New Moon* are read as a voiceover by Bella; Bella wakes from her dream of Edward and herself as an old woman with a copy of *Romeo and Juliet* on her pillow; as she arrives at school her high school friends greet her with reference to the R & J essay being due and Mike Newton hails her with "Wherefore art thou, Bella?"; Bella and Edward's discussion of his suicide plan takes place in their English classroom as the class watches a movie of Shakespeare's play while the camera pans over the teacher mouthing the words and Bella's friends emotionally entranced by the movie (except Mike, who is bored); the teacher pauses the movie to ask Edward to repeat the last lines heard and he recites part of Romeo's final speech (V.iii.109–15); Bella and Edward continue their conversation about suicide now focused on the Volturi while in Edward's house, looking at a picture of Carlisle with the Volturi. While the discussion of Edward's suicide plan is necessary to the plot, it does not need to be linked with *Romeo and Juliet*, and certainly the number of references in the early moments of the movie suggest the importance of the parallel. Its importance is emphasized by the innovation of having Edward recite Romeo's final words before drinking the fatal poison.

31. Shakespeare, *Romeo and Juliet*, II.vi.9–11; quoted in Meyer, *New Moon*.

32. Meyer originally chose a different passage from *Romeo and Juliet* for the epigraph, part of Juliet's soliloquy to night as she waits impatiently for Romeo (III.ii.20–4); Juliet's Nurse comes instead with the news that Romeo has slain Tybalt. In discussing her change, Meyer has stated that she "wanted the epigraph to be more representative of danger and potential heartbreak. Though this quote also has some nice foreshadowing, I had to choose — the romance or the warning? I went with the warning." "*New Moon* Outtakes," StephenieMeyer.com, http://www.stepheniemeyer.com/nm_outtakes.html.

33. Stephenie Meyer, *New Moon* (New York: Little, Brown and Company, 2006), 11.

34. Ibid., 17.

35. Ibid., 18.

36. Ibid., 63–4.

37. Ibid., 99. In an earlier draft Meyer included a fuller version of this idea, shifted later in the book, as Bella, the day after going to see a movie with Jessica, finds herself "...suddenly wishing I had a book. I hadn't read anything for a while, outside of school. And even then, when some ridiculous love story was part of the curriculum, I would cheat with cliff notes. It was a relief to be working on *Animal Farm* now. But there had to be other safe books. Political thrillers. Murder mysteries. Grisly murders were no problem; just as long as there was no starry-eyed, romantic subplot to deal with" (3). "Scholarship," StephenieMeyer.com, 2006, http://www.stepheniemeyer.com/pdf/nm_outtakes_scholarship.pdf.

38. An example of Bella's subconscious at work is her dream in *Twilight* that presages her understanding of Jacob's tale of "the Cold Ones": her dream-understanding that Edward is a vampire (130–1). The dream also suggests that, even though she does not process it consciously for some time (not until the second book of the series, in fact), she knows on some level that Jacob is a werewolf (*New Moon*, 291–2).

39. See pages 122–3 for the fullest account of this nightmare. It corresponds in some fairly obvious ways to other dreams Bella has, such as the forest dream in *Twilight* (130–1).

40. Meyer, *New Moon*, 369.

41. Ibid., 370.

42. Ibid., 371.

43. Ibid., 412.

44. Jacob's role in these misinterpretations cannot be ignored, for though he does not intend them to, his actions lead to both Alice's and Edward's mistakes. The reason Alice does not see Bella being pulled from the water is because she cannot see past Jacob, and though Jacob thinks he's speaking to Carlisle, his curtness creates Edward's misunderstanding. What Jacob *would* do if he understood the consequences of his actions is, of course, another question.

45. Meyer, *New Moon*, 418.

46. Ibid., 426–7.

47. Shakespeare, *Romeo and Juliet*, V.iii.92–3; quoted in Meyer, *New Moon*, 452.

48. Meyer, *New Moon*, 508.

49. See note 47. Meyer has alluded to the importance of Edward's ability to relate to characters like Romeo in *New Moon*: "And the second one [*New Moon*] was more about how Edward saw himself in relation to fictional characters" ("Video & Transcript: Q+A at Vroman's, Pasadena, CA").

50. Shakespeare, *Romeo and Juliet*, V.iii.70, 72; quoted in Meyer, *New Moon*, 552.

51. Meyer, *New Moon*, 555.

52. In this accounting I have left out one literary reference in *New Moon*, and that is Bella's determination, as she flies back to the U.S. with Edward, still under the impression that he will leave her shortly, to stretch out her time with him "Scheherazade-style" (495).

53. The phrase "Fire and Ice" is also a chapter title in *Eclipse*, chapter twenty-two, which features the lengthy conversation between Jacob and Edward in the tent overheard by Bella as she drifts in and out of sleep. While the epigraph does indicate most clearly the conflict between Jacob and Edward, it can also be seen to reference the secondary threat posed by Victoria, as Victoria's strongest identifying characteristic is her fiery red hair (a feature in addition to her icy white skin common to vampires). This association may be encouraged in the novel; the only other reference to Frost comes in chapter three as Edward recounts to Bella, through passing notes in English class, the vampire/werewolf chase of Victoria while their teacher reads aloud an unspecified poem by Frost (86). Robert Frost's poem "Fire and Ice" was first published in 1920 in *Harper's Magazine* and reprinted in his collection *New Hampshire* (New York: Holt, 1923), 80.

54. In an odd throwback, Bella uses the same phrase, "fire and ice," to refer to the successful consummation of her marriage on her wedding night with Edward (*Breaking Dawn* 87).

55. Stephenie Meyer, *Eclipse* (New York: Little, Brown and Company, 2007), 9.

56. Ibid., 19.

57. Ibid., 28.

58. Ibid., 29.

59. Ibid. (italics Meyer's).

60. Ibid.

61. Ibid., 265.

62. From chapter fourteen of Brontë's novel, as Heathcliff demands Nelly Dean's aid in securing a private meeting with Cathy (136); quoted in Meyer, *Eclipse*, 266.

63. Meyer, *Eclipse*, 517. In response to a question about the parallels between *Wuthering Heights* and *Eclipse*, Meyer describes Bella's identification (perhaps even over-identification) with Cathy this way: "So it's not that the story is actually that related to *Wuthering Heights*; it's psychosomatic, it's in her head. It's how she sees herself. She has always read the story and seen the characters in a certain way, but as time goes on in *Eclipse* she more and more starts to see the bad aspects of this one character in herself and starts to realize how she's doing things wrong and how she's behaving badly. And so it's just more about *her* idea of how she sees herself and how she relates to fictional characters" ("Video & Transcript: Q+A at Vroman's, Pasadena, CA"; italics Meyer's).

64. Meyer, *Eclipse*, 610.

65. The quotation comes from chapter nine as Cathy attempts to explain what Heathcliff means to her, even as she prepares to marry Edgar Linton (74); quoted in Meyer, *Eclipse*, 611.

66. Heathcliff speaks these words in chapter sixteen, upon hearing the news of Cathy's death (153, emphasis Brontë's); quoted in Meyer, *Eclipse*, 611.

67. Edward has demonstrated this intuition before, though to a lesser degree; during his 'day of endless questions,' Bella reports that her reading habits were a frequent focus (*Twilight* 229), and upon his first surreptitious visit to her room at night while she sleeps, Edward immediately wishes to examine the titles of her books, a desire he repeats on his second trip, though in neither case does he do so (*Midnight Sun* 107, 153).

68. Meyer has compared *Breaking Dawn* to *Twilight* in its more subtle use of other literature: "Book Four is going to be like *Twilight* in that the novel that I'm kind of running with won't be linked as much, there won't be quotes, there won't be references so much" ("Video & Transcript: Q+A at Vroman's, Pasadena, CA").

69. The phrase "puts away childish things" also suggests the well-known passage from St. Paul about the nature of love (1 Cor. 13:11). The poem "Childhood Is the Kingdom Where Nobody Dies" was published in Edna St. Vincent Millay's collection *Wine from these Grapes* (New York and London: Harper, 1934), 21.

70. Meyer, *Eclipse*, 277.

71. Ibid., 614.

72. Meyer, *Breaking Dawn*, 44–5. Renee is off by about a hundred years, of course, as Austen wrote at the beginning of the nineteenth century, not the twentieth.

73. It also makes Montgomery's series an appropriate touchstone, as her books about Anne Shirley follow her heroine, like Bella, from adolescent to wife to mother. The eight books of the Canadian series were published from 1908–1921. Meyer has acknowledged this connection; see "10 Questions for Stephenie Meyer," Time.com, August 21, 2008, http://www.time.com/time/magazine/article/0,9171,1834663-2,00.html.

74. Shakespeare, *A Midsummer Night's Dream*, III.i.143–4; quoted in Meyer, *Breaking Dawn*, 141. Bottom, as the human with a donkey's head, is perhaps an appropriate referent for the only section of Meyer's series to be narrated by a werewolf.

75. Meyer, *Eclipse*, 418.

76. Edward refers to him as such when he lifts Renesmee onto Jacob's back before what they expect to be the final battle with the Volturi, thereby expressing the fulfillment of this progression (723); it is anticipated in Book Two when Jacob returns from his trip to Seattle and Edward asks for his permission to violate the truce, telling him he sees him as both a "brother" and a "comrade in arms" (341).

77. The only references to "literature" that Jacob makes in the section he narrates are to the children's story *The Little Engine That Could* (190) and *The Wizard of Oz* (329). In an early draft of *New Moon*, Meyer included another *The Little Engine That Could* reference, this time by Bella; in this rejected version of the Epilogue, as she tries to maintain her equilibrium during Edward's first absence to hunt after their return from Italy, Bella tells herself that "I felt like the little engine who could — over and over again I had to tell myself, you can do this, you can do this, you can do this" (7–8). "Jacob," StephenieMeyer.com, 2006, http://www.stepheniemeyer.com/pdf/nm_outtakes_jacob.pdf.

78. Meyer, *Breaking Dawn*, 189.

79. Ibid., 189.

80. Ibid., 190 (emphasis Meyer's).

81. The genetic properties of vampire, human, and werewolf DNA are not irrelevant to the "magical" solution of Jacob imprinting on Renesmee. As a half-human, half-vampire, Renesmee is actually closer genetically to a werewolf (Meyer, *Breaking Dawn*, 236–7).

82. Meyer, *Breaking Dawn*, 237.

83. Ibid., 335.

84. There are other brief references to magic in the third book of *Breaking Dawn*: Bella's description of the cottage as magic (479 and 490) and observations of Renesmee's magical effect on those around her, human, werewolf, and vampire (515, 525, and 595). These confirm the promise of the second book and demonstrate that the magic Renesmee brings extends to

all those within her sphere. Further, the idea of magic is anticipated in Book One when Bella looks at Billy Black at her wedding and sees in him the power and magic that stretches back through his ancestors and forward to his son (52).

85. Orson Scott Card, *Empire* (New York: Tor Books, 2006), 64; quoted in Meyer, *Breaking Dawn*, 365.

86. The only death is Irina's, and while as a member of the Denali clan, she is close to the Cullens, and her death grieves them, it does not approach the level of losing a Cullen. Certainly she could not be described as a "loved one" of Bella's.

87. Meyer, *Breaking Dawn*, 756.

88. I am passing over the mention of Tennyson in the discovery that Renesmee can read (529). The lines she reads are the opening ones of the choric song from "The Lotos-Eaters"; Alfred Lord Tennyson, *Poems* (London: Bradbury and Evans, 1833), 111.

89. Stephenie Meyer, "Frequently Asked Questions: *Breaking Dawn*."

90. Meyer, *Breaking Dawn*, 558.

91. Ibid., 563.

92. Ibid., 731.

93. See note 89.

94. Shakespeare, *The Merchant of Venice*, I.iii.41–52.

95. Ibid., IV.i.184–205.

96. Ibid., II.viii.15–7. It must be pointed out, however, that these are not Shylock's lines directly, but his speech reported by the Christian Salanio, who refers to Shylock as "the dog Jew" (14) as he relates his speech; almost certainly it is a mocking, exaggerated version.

97. According to Meyer, for Aro too familial love does not outweigh greed. Aro killed his own sister Didyme, whom he loved, in order to keep her husband Marcus in the fold, because he valued his gift. Stephenie Meyer, "Frequently Asked Questions: *Breaking Dawn*."

98. Meyer, *Breaking Dawn*, 729.

99. This is perhaps most fully expressed in Bella's assessment of Aro (532) as well as her reference to Jane and Alec as the prize items in "Aro's collection" (684); Aro himself refers euphemistically to collecting "histories" (698) and exclaims over Renesmee's uniqueness (693, 698). In relating his desire to acquire the werewolves, Bella refers to Aro's "longing," describing him as "appraising Jacob openly," as well as the other werewolves (699). Here his unadulterated desire for acquisition is in clear evidence.

100. Shakespeare, *The Merchant of Venice*, IV.i.306–7.

101. Meyer, *Breaking Dawn*, 717–9.

102. Ibid., 580.

103. Ibid., 603. Once the trial begins and Edward can hear their thoughts, of course, this interpretation is countermanded; as Edward tersely notes that their motive is to "incapacitate" in order to prevent "escape" (726). But even Edward's knowledge is incomplete and cannot encompass every instance; in particular he cannot know what the Volturi's goals have been in the past.

104. The 2004 movie from Sony Pictures starring Al Pacino as Shylock is an example of this trend. *William Shakespeare's "The Merchant of Venice*," DVD, directed by Michael Radford (Culver City, CA: Sony Pictures Classics, 2004).

105. Shakespeare, *The Merchant of Venice*, III.i.58–73.

106. Ibid., IV.i.184–202.

107. Meyer, *Breaking Dawn*, 743.

108. Ibid., 734.

I would like to thank my daughter Kate, for introducing me to the *Twilight* universe, and my mentor Marijane Osborn, for convincing me that if I could write about hobbits, I could write about vampires.

Carlisle's Cross: Locating the Post-Secular Gothic

LORI BRANCH

On the screen or on the page, fangless "vegetarian vampires" fly in the face of creatures we have learned to expect from Gothic literature and film. Particularly in the sunlit Cullen mansion or the Forks High School cafeteria of director Catherine Hardwicke's *Twilight* (2008), the *Twilight* series' connection to the Gothic tradition seemed tenuous at best. But with the November 2009 film release of *New Moon*, the Gothic undertones of the *Twilight* saga swept into big-screen surround-sound. Chris Weitz's cinematic adaptation of *New Moon* chills moviegoers with more traditional Gothic spectacles, particularly in the unreformed Volturi, the vampire aristocracy, who rule their netherworld from medieval thrones and feast on unsuspecting tourists in the bowels of their castle. Even with Stephenie Meyer's departures from traditional vampire lore, in the paper-white faces of Aro, Caius and Marcus, in their blood-hungry gazes and impulsive cruelty made wily and brazen by immortality, we see on screen what Meyer presents to us in her novels, a world of vampires both distinct from and yet clearly connected to recognizably Gothic conventions.

The *Twilight* saga, then, both in its print and film versions, raises fascinating generic questions: what exactly is the series' connection to the longstanding Gothic literary tradition, or more simply, is *Twilight* Gothic? What does its connection to the Gothic tradition mean for our understanding of the series? And how does its quasi–Gothic, postmodern–Gothic, or pseudo–Gothic status contribute to its popularity? Using classic Gothic texts and contemporary critical understandings of Gothic fiction to set the *Twilight* saga in relief, this essay positions Meyer's blockbuster novels within the history of Gothic fiction, of which, I contend, it is squarely a part. Examining the saga's continuities with and innovations within the Gothic literary tradition enables us to use the tools of contemporary Gothic criticism to help us understand the deeper cultural meaning of the series and its immense popular appeal. Gothic fiction scholar Kelly Hurley has followed Annette Kuhn in encouraging us to think of literary genres in terms of their "'cultural instrumentality': how a genre functions within the culture that produces and consumes it, how it expresses something significant, or negotiates some salient problem, for its readership." For Hurley, "The Gothic is rightly, if partially, understood as a cyclical genre that reemerges in times of cultural stress in order to negotiate anxieties for its readership by working through them in displaced (sometimes supernaturalized) form."[1]

Keeping one eye on *Twilight*'s recognizably Gothic characteristics and another on its unique elements in its contemporary context, I suggest that we can fruitfully locate the *Twilight* series as a uniquely American, late-capitalist, post-feminist, and post-secular Gothic phenomenon, and that we can understand its immense appeal in terms of the culturally satisfying ways it negotiates a particular set of concerns that hearken back to the Enlightenment origins of Gothic literature — guilt and forgiveness, desires and fears related to the family, and the tensions of belief and hope in an increasingly rationalized world — yet in a way peculiar to our own postmodern moment. Families (dysfunctional or ideal), forgiveness, and faith are as interwoven in classic Gothic literature as they are in the *Twilight* series, and we can usefully take Meyer's image of Carlisle's cross as an image of their interconnection. The cross that hangs outside Carlisle's study, we learn in *New Moon*, was made by his fundamentalist father, whose vampire-hunts were ironically, unintentionally, the occasion of Carlisle's transformation into a vampire. It is from his father's faith that Carlisle has retained, paradoxically and at once, his sense of damnation, his ideals of nonviolence and love for others, and even his hope, against all hope, for his and his family's redemption. Carlisle's cross evokes both the image of a horribly dysfunctional family and the religious hope that would heal that dysfunction. The popularity of the *Twilight* series, I would argue, helps us locate what we might call the post-secular, Gothic consciousness of its readers, caught as they are between the specific forms of guilt over consumerism and the versions of redemption that Meyer's fiction so compellingly portrays.

The Cullens: American Family Gothic

In his immensely interesting and helpful guide to the circuitous 250-year history of Gothic fiction, Jerrold Hogle defines "the Gothic" in a laudably balanced way. Acknowledging that the Gothic has proven to be a particularly pliable and malleable form of fiction and that this flexibility accounts in part for its success, he nevertheless specifies "some general parameters by which fictions can be identified as primarily or substantially Gothic."[2] These include four traits that Gothic fiction fans can spot as easily in eighteenth- as in twenty-first-century works — an antiquated space, secrets from the past, haunting ghosts and monsters, and elements of the supernatural[3]:

> A Gothic tale usually takes place (at least some of the time) in an antiquated or seemingly antiquated space—be it a castle, a foreign palace, an abbey, a vast prison, a subterranean crypt, a graveyard, a primeval frontier or island, a large old house or theatre ... or some new recreation of an older venue.... Within this space, or a combination of such spaces, are hidden some secrets from the past (sometimes the recent past) that haunt the characters, psychologically, physically, or otherwise at the main time of the story. These hauntings can take many forms, but they frequently assume the features of ghosts, specters, or monsters (mixing features from different realms of being, often life and death) that rise from within the antiquated space, or sometimes invade it from alien realms, to manifest unresolved crimes or conflicts that can no longer be successfully buried from view. It is at this level that Gothic fictions generally play with and oscillate between the earthly laws of conventional reality and the possibilities of the supernatural ... often siding with one of these over the other in the end, but usually raising the possibility that the boundaries between these may have been crossed, at least psychologically but also physically or both.[4]

For Hogle, the power and persistence of Gothic fiction stem from the way it helps us simultaneously address and avoid "some of the most important desires, quandaries, and sources of anxiety, from the most internal and mental to the widely social and cultural, throughout the history of western culture since the eighteenth century."[5]

At the center of these swirling and often "contradictory fears and desires," Hogle (with a host of critics) claims, is the family: most especially the middle class family and the new, modern, bourgeois individuals that make up and, not infrequently, trouble that family.[6] Those new selves, like the emerging middle-class readers that made the original Gothic novels popular, find themselves caught between throwing off oppressive, often aristocratic father figures and creating new forms of family, all the while negotiating the guilt of destroying the older order of things and the potentially destructive force of their own individualism. The first Gothic novel in English, Horace Walpole's *The Castle of Otranto* (1764), is the quintessential tale of a dysfunctional family, tyrannized and torn apart by the merciless political ambitions and threatened incest of its patriarch, Manfred. As a result of Manfred's guilt, his son is crushed by an enormous, supernatural helmet and killed; in the aftermath Manfred attempts to divorce his wife and rape his daughter-in-law, finally murdering his daughter, while his wife submits pathetically to degradation after degradation.

Walpole's self-destructive family, as much as his haunted castles and spine-tingling chases through dimly lit subterranean passages, became a fixture of the Gothic genre he inaugurated. Matthew Lewis's *The Monk* (1794), an exemplar of the early Gothic novel so salacious that its author was threatened with charges of blasphemy, also revolves around a family—every member of which is dead by the end—torn apart over two decades by an autocratic father's refusal to accept the daughter of a humble shoemaker as his daughter-in-law. Like the Gothic heroines of his rival Ann Radcliffe, Lewis's Agnes and Virginia are left at the end of *The Monk* in ostensibly loving marriages with men who, in comparison to the novel's villains, appear sensitive and enlightened, evoking the eighteenth-century English dream of the companionate marriage. In Jane Austen's novel about reading Gothic novels, the metafictional *Northanger Abbey* (composed 1798–99, published posthumously in 1818), the real horror of the eponymous abbey is nothing so sensationalistic as General Tilney's having murdered or imprisoned his wife, as the Gothic-reading Catherine imagines, but rather the completely un-supernatural prospect of years trapped in a loveless marriage brokered for wealth, a horror which Catherine and Henry respectively escape, at the novel's end, in their union of true love. And in Bram Stoker's *Dracula* (1897), the marriage of the well-heeled Lucy Westenra and Sir Arthur Holmwood is subverted by Count Dracula, a monstrous, aristocratic, child-eating vampire-father, whose bloodlust also threatens the union of Jonathan and Mina Harker. The Count is finally destroyed, the Harker family is preserved, and in the process a second sort of family is created — the band of Van Helsing's quasi-religious, scientific disciples, bonded through their quest to destroy the Count.

In the primordial rainforest and glaciated mountains of the U.S. Pacific Northwest, haunted by supernatural monsters and ancient treaties and secrets, *Twilight* comes into focus in a unique place in this Gothic heritage, brilliantly expressing the contradictory desires and fears of our own cultural, historical moment circling around the family. Bella Swan expresses a longing for a loving, close-knit family that clearly connects her and her fans to the readers of the original Gothic novels. That is, she shares the ideals of Austen's famously endearing reader of Gothic novels, Catherine Morland, that made her fear the tyrannical father and dysfunctional family: the desire for love, romance, and (later for Bella, in *Breaking Dawn*) children. For all that has been made about Bella's love for Edward, the series itself makes abundantly clear that almost as much as she desires Edward, Bella desires to be a part of the Cullen family: a family that — with their quotidian loves for baseball, home improvement, birthday parties, and shopping, their pairings unbroken through struggles and reconciliations, and their deeply shared moral code, vampirism notwithstanding — represents an uncanny image of American family perfection, both in its stereotypical trappings and in its deeper ideals. An only child from the "broken home" of her low-emoting father, police chief Charlie Swan, and Renée, her hopelessly flighty, narcissistic mother, who floats from one self-help fad to the next, Bella craves the bonded connection and fierce loyalty represented by the Cullen couples and their family as a whole. And the saga reaches its climax and excessive, fantastic, fairy-tale ending in Bella's fulfilled desire to be in a loving, sexual union with Edward and in a full-time mothering relationship with their daughter Renesmee, living near and helped by his extended family, forever.

One of the most fascinating aspects of *Twilight* and the key to understanding its significance in the Gothic tradition, then, is the way it turns the Gothic tradition on its head, or more precisely, brings it full circle: the saga shares the dream of a loving, harmonious family, but now, what is "Gothic" is not the dysfunctional family but *the functional family itself.* One of the most compelling concepts in Gothic criticism today, and one that can help us understand this shift, is an understanding of the monsters of Gothic fiction in terms of what Julia Kristeva calls the "abject." In *Powers of Horror*, Kristeva argues that ghosts and grotesques are created explicitly to embody contradictions in the form of the abject and products of abjection; from the literal meaning of the word, the abject is what we "throw off" or "throw under," according to Kristeva, all that is "in-between ... ambiguous ... [and] composite" in our beings, the internal inconsistencies that prevent us from declaring a coherent identity to ourselves and others.[7] Kristeva's ideas owe a great deal to Sigmund Freud's earlier, related concept of the uncanny, that which we find foreign and frightening, precisely because it speaks to us both of what we have repressed and of the very fact and means of our repression, in the unconscious.[8] The looming, all-important question posed by the *Twilight* phenomenon, when seen as part of this Gothic tradition, concerns what it means for the most popular fictional series of the last decade to make our central cultural ideal — the functional, loving family — into a family of *vampires*, the vampire being arguably the hallmark of contemporary Gothic literature and the definition of the abject, the monstrous contradiction of the undead. What does it mean to locate the functional, loving family in the very place and figure of the abject? Dismissing the amiable, enviable Cullens as simply the gentrification of the vampire or its very ceasing to be abject is too easy and fails to interpret the signature innovation of Meyer's series, that is, the way it not only tolerates its vampires but venerates them as ideal, and to the approval of an unprecedented mainstream American readership. Why make the ideal family into, of all things, the Gothic, abject figure of the *vampire*?

This is the surprise at the heart of the *Twilight* saga and is how the Cullens are the uncanny products of a large scale cultural abjection that we hide from ourselves. That is, the saga reveals how the U.S. cultural ideal of family life — as Bella, Edward and Renesmee with the larger Cullen clan represent that ideal — *is* outside the realm of possibility and experience. The novels reveal that it is in fact an ideal that is impossible for the vast majority of Americans to achieve, and that we, as an economy and a culture, have made it that way. The saga reveals and shrouds at the same moment, in quintessentially Gothic fashion, the strange and painful truth that, as members of late-capitalist, consumer culture in this century, a vast readership craves the very sort of family life that it has made a thing of the past — a form of family life that we as a culture and as individuals abject, quite literally, because it would deny us the sort of coherent selves we have come to imagine under late capitalism. Meyer's novels themselves make abundantly clear the extent to which the family life that the Cullens represent is at odds with the "normal" world around them and its ideals. This fact accounts in great measure for Edward's reluctance to transform Bella. In order to join his vampire family, to marry him, to be eternally young with him, to have children with him, Bella would have to give up precisely the definitive markers of identity, economic life and independence in our society—a college education and a career—and the decade or more of dating around that generally accompanies that process. Shockingly, gothically, Bella refuses that romantic "shopping around" and an economic route to self-definition, instead declaring again and again over the course of 2,000 pages that she would readily forego all that for the love of Edward and for family.

In an essay titled "The Contemporary Gothic: Why We Need It," Steven Bruhm has perceptively claimed that Gothic literature offers us "purchase on the person in society looking for acceptance while at the same time remaining abject and individualized," and that the contemporary Gothic often registers the felt "impossibility of familial harmony, an impossibility built into the domestic psyche as much as it is into domestic materiality."[9] In Bella, we are invited to identify with the odd-girl, only child of divorced parents who seeks acceptance and fulfillment with Edward and his extended family. But in accepting this invitation to see her longed-for family life *as* impossible—as supernatural, Gothic, vampiric and conventionally abject—we ratify a deeper truth and recognition about our desires and our culture, the truth of an impossibility built not simply on domestic but on cultural materiality: Bella literally must die to "life"—a life conceived of as college, career, and 20-something independence—in order to have the sort of union, love, and family she desires. What makes *Twilight* Gothic and the Cullens uncanny is that creepiest of secrets which this mesmerizing tale half conceals, half reveals, that *we* as a culture have made this dream impossible; by putting our desire for family love and togetherness into the usually abject realm of the vampire, we confess that we have made unnatural and impossible the very thing we most desire or profess to desire, despite a seemingly ubiquitous U.S. cultural allegiance to "family values."

This is why critics who rail against Bella's antifeminism miss the larger, more important truth, that the novel's conundrums about whether Bella should become a vampire point to the widespread *acceptance* of feminism as narrowly and economically defined in the U.S. cultural context, that is, in what our demographics show is the widespread assumption that women should postpone marriage and childbearing (and along the way, almost necessarily separate love from marriage and childbearing) in the interests of a college education, career and economic self-sufficiency. After remaining relatively steady for four decades, the median age of first marriage for women in the U.S., according to the U.S. Census Bureau, has increased steadily from 20.3 in 1970 to 26 years in 2007.[10] As a result, more women than ever before have entered the workforce and hold college degrees, and the sort of traditional or ideal family the Cullens represent, in which Esme and Bella stay home with their families full-time, makes up a small and declining portion of U.S. households, according to tabulations from the Census Bureau's 2002 Current Population Survey, only 7 percent.[11] And for those who postpone marriage and childbearing and maintain two jobs, it is not just that family life is postponed but that it is indelibly altered. Robert Putnam's 2000 best-seller *Bowling Alone* amassed a wealth of statistics to demonstrate the plummeting of all forms of social togetherness (what he dubs "social capital"), including that among families, famously citing a 43 percent drop in the number of family dinners eaten together in the last quarter of the twentieth century.[12] According to the Bureau of Labor Statistics report on the care of household children for the years 2004–2008, adults living in households with children under 6 spent an average of only 2 hours per day providing primary childcare to their children.[13] It is fair to say that demographics paint a portrait of the American family headed in the opposite direction of the Cullens' eternal togetherness.

Writing outside her novels, Meyer herself seems to reference the lack of choice this economic reality represents for women. Asked whether Bella is an anti-feminist heroine, Meyer replies on her website:

> In my own *opinion* (key word), the foundation of feminism is this: being able to choose. The core of anti-feminism is, conversely, telling a woman she can't do something solely because she's a woman — taking any choice away from her specifically because of her gender.... One of the weird things about modern feminism is that some feminists seem to be putting their own limits on women's choices. That feels backward to me. It's as if you can't choose a family on your own terms and still be considered a strong woman. How is that empowering? Are there rules about if, when, and how we love or marry and if, when, and how we have kids? Are there jobs we can and can't have in order to be a "real" feminist? To me, those limitations seem anti-feminist in basic principle.[14]

It is in this sense that we should understand what I am calling Bella's post-feminism: not an over-and-done-with feminism, but feminism as thoroughly inhabited by our culture, at least in its economic and educational dimension. The remarkable phenomenon here is the recognition in Meyer's fiction, in its Gothicization and abjection of Bella and her choices, of the abjected "Gothic" desires of our culture.[15] Bella's popularity as superstar Gothic heroine reveals precisely that we as a culture have already travelled a feminist road, and that it has left apparently not a few readers with very particular unfulfilled longings and misgivings.

But qualms about the temporal sacrifices Bella must make for love account, as mentioned earlier, for only a portion of Edward's reluctance to transform her. The other reason Edward does not want to transform Bella is the religious one: the fear that she will lose her soul, that she will be unforgivably damned. This, too, is a concern that stretches back to the very origins of Gothic literature in the heart of the ostensibly secular Enlightenment, and one that is profoundly connected to the guilty recognition of our consumer, capitalist complicity in making impossible the form of family life and love to which we profess a profound cultural allegiance.

The Lion and the Lamb: Gothic Guilt, Gothic Forgiveness

Gothic fiction has, since its origins, been famously haunted by guilt. Monsters are often haunting figures of our sins and crimes which prevent us, in Kristeva's terms, from portraying ourselves, to ourselves or others, as morally upright or coherent. Walpole's Manfred, for instance, for all his villainy, is widely recognized as a cipher for rising middle class guilt over usurping the power of the old regime. Manfred may be a monster and we may be the rightful heirs to the castle, so to speak, but Manfred is overcome, as the novel's creepy and ambiguous prophecy foretells, only when the castle's rightful heir grows too large to inhabit it: thus the creepy specter of the massive helmet (of the usurped rightful heir) that crushes Manfred's son and, later, the colossal knight-in-armor that stalks his castle grounds. It is the new Enlightenment self, caught like Theodore (the descendent of the rightful heir to Otranto) between peasant and aristocratic identities, that has grown too large to inhabit the very castle it seeks to purge of tyranny. Having routed the feudal tyrants from our society, the Gothic reveals, we are too full of ourselves and, implicitly, of our own potential for tyranny to sustain that society. Likewise in *Dracula*, Mina's sympathy for the Count expresses a similar ambivalence and even guilt about progress. In pitying the hounded vampire, Mina voices anxieties about the pitiless scientific spirit in which the men seek to exterminate the Count and "sanitize" the earth in which he rests, such that this supernatural being, and perhaps any supernatural being, cannot inhabit it.

But to say that Gothic fiction is haunted by guilt is also to say that it yearns for forgiveness, and its pages are often palimpsests for deep explorations of the very possibility of salvation in particularly modern contexts. No less sensational a villain than Matthew Lewis's Ambrosio offers a prime example. Lewis's *The Monk* is the story of a pious priest and captivating orator, renowned for his virtue, brought low by his egocentric pride and concomitant moral rigidity. Unwilling to show mercy on the fallen nun Agnes for fear of appearing lax, Ambrosio is susceptible to Matilda's seductive idolatry of him and is consequently unable to imagine his own forgiveness once he has fallen. In the final hair-raising pages of the novel, he signs his soul over to the devil in order to escape torture in the Inquisition, precisely because he is sure that his sins are so black that he would never find forgiveness from God in any case. Ambrosio completes the deal only to discover that he had been moments from pardon; he has damned himself not as much by his horrific crimes as by failing to sustain his hope in God's infinite mercy, the cornerstone of Christian belief which he, as an aspiring doctor of the church, should most certainly have understood but has entirely failed to grasp. The novel leaves readers two harrowing images of hell: Ambrosio's torturous death because he could not hope for forgiveness, and Agnes's hideously being kept alive in the dungeons of her convent, with (as her captors continuously emphasize) no hope of mercy. In a novel that is sometimes considered the pinnacle of the eighteenth-century Gothic, the ultimate misery and Hell itself is to bear the consequences of guilt with no hope for mitigating tenderness or chance for repentance. The case of the brilliant, casuistic Ambrosio serves to highlight a particularly Enlightenment anxiety over the irrationality of forgiveness and how reason is at a loss either to account for or generate it.

In the guilt-ridden Gothic tradition, *Twilight* stands out for its striking hope for precisely the impossible forgiveness that Ambrosio cannot imagine: forgiveness for having forfeited one's soul to the powers of darkness. Where Carlisle holds out hope that he and his family might escape damnation by virtue of their valiant resistance to their thirst for human blood, his "son" Edward is less optimistic and thus loathe to risk Bella's soul by making her a vampire. However cavalier she may seem about her own eternal destiny, when Bella looks at Edward, his family, their virtue and sacrifice, she is absolutely sure of their salvation. As she puts it in *New Moon*, "I couldn't imagine anyone, deity included, who wouldn't be impressed by Carlisle. Besides, the only kind of heaven *I* could appreciate would have to include Edward."[16]

The four novels, from their first volume, are in fact quite explicit in their imagination of a supernatural, cosmic redemption worked, not surprisingly, through Bella and Edward's love. What is surprising about their love, though, is the theological specificity and scope of the cosmic redemption it posits. The announcement of this hope for redemption comes in the thirteenth chapter of *Twilight* ("Confessions"), the chapter that Meyer claims is "essentially a transcript" of a "very vivid dream" she had on the night of June 2, 2003, and which is arguably the heart of the series:

> In my dream, two people were having an intense conversation in a meadow in the woods. One of these people was just your average girl. The other person was fantastically beautiful, sparkly, and a vampire. They were discussing the difficulties inherent in the facts that A) they were falling in love with each other while B) the vampire was particularly attracted to the scent of her blood, and was having a difficult time restraining himself from killing her immediately.[17]

In a chapter that itself could account for the romantic runaway-success of the series, we see both Edward's ennobling moral complexity and the form of love that makes him what we might rightly call an anti-vampire. Edward confesses his love for Bella in explicitly anti-consuming terms, wedged in between his desire to be with her and his great fear of harming her by that desire. Love in this chapter means precisely not pursuing the experience of consuming the one he loves, either literally or sexually. Edward explains to Bella that "every person smells different, has a different essence," and it is this Bella-ness that he savors: he craves her company and her essence, her very life, and this is what makes him more dangerous to his beloved than to anyone else.[18] Bella, in turn, confesses to the reader that she "was filled with compassion for his suffering, even ... as he confessed his craving to take my life," and to Edward she declares that she wants to be with him even if that means her death, however idiotic that may seem.[19] In the climactic passage of the chapter, Edward agrees that she is an idiot, the two laugh together "at the idiocy and sheer impossibility of such a moment," and Edward murmurs one of the most significant lines in the novel: "And so the lion fell in love with the lamb...." "What a stupid lamb," Bella responds, to which Edward half-jokingly retorts, "What a sick, masochistic lion."[20]

The idea of the lion falling in love with the lamb lends a decidedly romantic cast to the Biblical icon of peace in which the "lion lies down with the lamb." Drawn from the book of Isaiah, this image has historically expressed the deepest Christian hopes for the redemption of the world and was repeatedly rendered, for instance, by the American Quaker and folk artist Edward Hicks (1780–1849) as the "Peaceable Kingdom." Under the rule of the Messiah, as the eleventh chapter of Isaiah prophesies, righteousness, equity and faithfulness will be established in all the earth:

> The wolf also shall dwell with the lamb, and the leopard shall lie down with the kid; and the calf and the young lion and the fatling [lamb] together; and a little child shall lead them.... Their young ones shall lie down together: and the lion shall eat straw like the ox.... They shall not hurt nor destroy in all my holy mountain: for the earth shall be full of the knowledge of the LORD, as the waters cover the sea.[21]

Across two millennia of the Christian tradition, this image of peace has inspired the radical hope for the *apokatastasis panton*, the restoration of all things to their primordial condition and to Edenic peace.[22] At the end of time, violence — and particularly here, we should note, deathly consumption of another — shall be no more, for the lion shall be drastically transformed; as Isaiah later foretells, "No lion shall be there, nor any ravenous beast shall go up thereon ... but the redeemed shall walk there."[23]

In the pivotal chapter containing Edward and Bella's mutual confessions of love, their love is thus connected not just to themselves and to the family in general but to a more radical vision of the cosmic restoration of all things from their fallen to their paradisiacal state. Though, as the novel so often points out, it is Bella's fearlessness that in some sense makes her relationship with Edward possible, the metaphor of the lion falling in love with the lamb stresses Edward's transformation. Redeeming love — love as passionate, non-consuming care for the other and as life-giving, eternal communion — is made possible by the conversion that Edward's falling in love with Bella embodies. His love for her represents nothing less than the dramatic turn of a creature prone to draw its deathly existence from destroying and consuming the lives of others, irrespective of their personal qualities (effectively homogenizing them all as raw material for itself), toward all that Bella represents in the novels, namely her distinctive, personal essence and, as Edward declares explicitly in the unfinished *Midnight*

Sun, her unique selflessness.[24] Edward, and with him perhaps Carlisle and the rest of his family, is redeemable and redeemed, we might say, because he comes to love, in the particularly non-consuming and life-giving way in which Meyer's novels define the word.

The romance of Bella and Edward, then, both redeems the Gothic family and shows the family itself to hold the promise of redemption, an equally American and simultaneously Christian and Mormon theme: die to your old self and to a devouring way of viewing and desiring others, and be born again into a new existence of love, of shared life and of communion with others.[25] When Bella professes "I love you," in *Twilight*, Edward answers simply and totally, "You are my life now."[26] Whereas literary critic Brian Frost characterizes the vampire as fundamentally a parasitic force or being, malevolent and self-seeking by nature," and Michael Dennison views the vampire as inherently disordering and entropic, "tak[ing] life energy and turn[ing] it into something irrevocably negative," Elizabeth Sanders rightly identifies the Cullens as the antithesis of "creatures of consumption or disorder."[27] As Sanders argues in her perceptive essay, "Virtuous Vampires: Self-Denial and Relationship in Stephenie Meyer's *Twilight*," Meyer's vampires are "reversal[s] of the concept of the vampire as essentially a creature of consumption."[28] However "natural" their desire to consume may be, the Cullens resist those urges in order precisely not to be monsters, and this resistance makes possible something unique for both the humans and the vampires in Meyer's imaginative world: the ability to band together and to form close relationships.[29] Their asceticism makes possible the deep bonds of love made real in daily family life and, in turn, grounds the novel's hope for ultimate, cosmic redemption and a mode of life that is not consuming and deathly but truly loving and life-giving.

To return to a Kristevan understanding of the Gothic appeal of *Twilight*, we might say that the series is concerned with guilt, forgiveness, and the hope of escaping a deathly life of consumption through love, because we are ourselves concerned with these things; it reveals the horror of guilt over consumption. In the Volturi, Meyer shows us the familiar specter of the vampire as a figure of deathly consumption. But what appears even more vividly in *Twilight* is the way that we have equally abjected or Gothicized the hope for forgiveness for and escape from that egocentric consumption as impossible to us, from the vantage point of selfhood and identity as lived in our late-capitalist society. In other words, our late-capitalist culture, both in its economic organization and its mindset of endlessly shopping for and changing partners, has made the real living-out of love seem either impossible or supernatural. It is not surprising, then, that it should be haunted by guilt, hoping longingly for the redemption and forgiveness that the union of Bella and Edward gestures towards.

What makes the *Twilight* saga Gothic, then, and remarkably so, is that, in our technologized, postmodern age, it consigns this very homely vision of salvation to the realm of the supernatural, to the realm of sparkling, transfigured, immortal beings who once were human. That is, it recognizes this hope for faithful, human love as truly "idiotic," extra-rational and supernatural, as properly religious as it is deeply and abidingly human. To my mind, this recognition of the basic religiousness of the series is as important as plumbing the extent to which Meyer's vision is distinctively Mormon. Given the series' popularity, perhaps rather than invoking its Mormonism we should account for its resonance with contemporary American religious sensibilities asking: what sort of religiousness does the *Twilight* series present?

Situating the Post-Secular in Twilight

From its origins in eighteenth-century England, the Gothic novel has fostered a religious idiom, set as it so often is in monasteries, churchyards, cemeteries, ruined abbeys, and peopled by fallen religious figures and victimized saints, usually in the Catholic countries of Italy, France, and Spain. In part these images express English anti–Catholicism and a Protestant derision of the "superstitious" faith of which it violently purged itself in the sixteenth-century but which it continued alternately to fear and be fascinated with in the seventeenth and eighteenth centuries. But they also reflect the larger intellectual and cultural trend of self-conscious secularization that England underwent, intellectually if not in practice, in the period of roughly 1650–1750. To put it tersely, in Enlightenment, the supernatural is expunged as darkness and superstition, and thus returns in and as the repressed; in terms of the Enlightenment, religion, like the supernatural, is Gothic. Children's literature scholar John Granger has recently accounted for the popularity of *Twilight*'s supernaturalism in terms of a secular cultural context not wholly removed from that of the original Gothic novels:

> [Meyer's books] meet a spiritual need. Mircea Eliade, in his book *The Sacred and the Profane,* suggests that popular entertainment, especially imaginative literature and film, serves a religious or mythic function in a secular culture. When God is driven to the periphery of the public square, the human spiritual capacity longs for exercise, and it often finds it in the "suspension of disbelief" and activity of the imagination that are available in novels and movies.[30]

In his groundbreaking volume *True Religion*, Graham Ward has given an eloquent, nuanced account of secularization in the West that is particularly powerful in the way that it accounts not for the decline of religion after the seventeenth century, but rather for the persistence and transformation of religion after the seventeenth century, along with its causes. The seventeenth-century European Wars of Religion were fought largely between Catholic and Protestant countries, though in the case of England, that war was among Protestants and internal to a Protestant country itself. According to Ward, it is after the seventeenth-century Wars of Religion that faith in doctrinal Christianity declines in the West and that religiousness becomes more and more embroiled in colonization, in individualism, and eventually, in a commodity culture which religion as "special effect" serves only to baptize with the allure of a false transcendence.[31]

It seems no coincidence, then, that *Twilight* situates its origins and its own horizon of possibility in the world following the seventeenth-century Wars of Religion. Despite the fact that Bella tells us that her life "was fairly devoid of belief," in the pages of the *Twilight* series we find a single, stark religious symbol, a Christian cross hanging prominently in the hallway of the Cullen home, outside Carlisle's office, which becomes the occasion for Edward relating Carlisle's history to Bella.[32] Carlisle was born in the 1640s during the English Civil Wars, to an intolerant Anglican (and, we can infer from the description, Puritan) minister who violently persecuted Catholics and led hunts for witches, werewolves, and vampires. It was during one of these raids that Carlisle was bitten and transformed by a wraith from the London sewers. Loathing what he had become but, as a vampire, unable to end his life, Carlisle discovered that he could sustain himself on the blood of animals; he found he could live "without being a demon," Edward tells Bella, and so "found himself again."[33] Through decades of effort, Carlisle perfected his self-control to the point that he could live among human beings and study medicine. By the dawn of the new millennium, as we learn in *New Moon*, he is able to draw great pleasure from healing people and even performing surgery, putting his enhanced vampiric senses to philanthropic uses.[34] As he tells Bella:

> I'm hoping that there is still a point to this life, even for us. By all accounts, we're damned regardless. But I hope, maybe foolishly, that we'll get some measure of credit for trying.... I look at my ... *son*. His strength, his goodness, the brightness that shines out of him — and it only fuels that hope, that faith, more than ever. How could there not be more for one such as Edward?[35]

While we may usefully situate *Twilight* at the historical moment of secularization and capitalization that Ward describes, its religiousness may not be as flat as the special effect or false seal of transcendence that he teaches us to expect. Rather, it seems truer to the theological texture of Meyer's story to situate precisely the kind of religious belief her tale embodies, or in Danièle Hervieu-Léger's terms, to understand the particular transformation of religion in postmodernity that the *Twilight* saga represents.[36] Following scholarship in what has been hailed as the "return of religion" in the humanities, I would suggest that we can fruitfully understand Meyer's novels as post-secular Gothic.[37] We can ground this understanding at the cultural place where Bella's previous lack of belief and her hopeful desires intersect with Carlisle's cross and his hope-against-hope for redemption. That is, we can locate the appealing post-secular religiousness of the *Twilight* series fairly specifically between the residue of the dysfunctional family and faith of Carlisle's youth and Bella's diffuse hope and yet lack of formalized belief.

With his characteristic wit, philosopher John Caputo claims that one of the most important things "post-modern" might have meant, "had it not been ground senseless by overuse," is post-secular.[38] "The 'post-' in 'post-secular,'" Caputo writes, "should not be understood to mean 'over and done with' but rather *after having passed through modernity.*"[39] What is most distinctive about postmodernity, Caputo claims, is not its unreason but its embrace of a humbler epistemology and chastened reason, a post-secular reason that recognizes that no thinking is devoid of belief and that deconstructs the idea of "rigid borders between faith and reason, public and private, subject and object, politics and science or religion" as "an artifice."[40] Postmodernity represents thus not a rejection of Enlightenment reason but, according to Caputo, a "more enlightened Enlightenment":

> A more enlightened Enlightenment is no longer taken in by the dream of Pure Objectivity[;] ... it deploys a new idea of reason that is no longer taken in by the illusion of Pure Reason. It has a post-critical sense of critique that is critical of the idea that we can establish air-tight borders around neatly discriminated spheres or regions like knowledge, ethics, art, and religion.... In the wake of Nietzsche and many others— Wittgenstein and Heidegger foremost among them — philosophers today have largely rejected the idea that there is some proud over-arching thing called "Reason" and have settled instead for the humbler idea of "good reasons," in the plural and lower case. Their idea is not to reject reason but to redefine and historicize it as a historically contingent "take" we have on things— which makes it look a lot more like "faith"— the best one available at the time and the one we go along with until we are forced to revise it by some unexpected turn of events.[41]

Caputo defines a post-secular religious sensibility as "that movement of living on the limit of the possible, in hope for and expectation of the impossible, a reality beyond the real, which I take to be the mark of a religious sensibility, [which] has survived the secularizing and reductionistic critiques that have been directed against religion for the better part of the last two centuries."[42] In our post-modern, post-secular moment, "the religious sense of life turns on what I am calling the *hyper-real*, by which I mean a reality beyond the real, the *impossible* that eludes modernity's narrow-minded idea of what is possible"— chief among them, we might add, forgiveness and love.[43] Caputo is particularly suggestive when he insists that the post-secular does not return us to a pre-modern past but rather opens up connections between the pre- and post-modern: "I have been arguing," he writes, "for opening up the lines of communication between the life of faith before modernity and the post-secular moment we are presently experiencing."[44]

As post-secular Gothic, *Twilight* imagines just such a re-opening of lines of communication between pre-modern and postmodern faith, and joins Ward in locating the rupture between the two at that seventeenth-century moment of the Wars of Religion and the secularizing century that followed.[45] In Meyer's fictional universe, at precisely the mid-seventeenth-century moment in which an increasingly rationalized Western Christianity begins to find it difficult to believe in forgiveness, in God, and in the existence of the supernatural, Carlisle Cullen undergoes his Gothic birth as a vampire who, it would seem, paradoxically preserves the radical hope for forgiveness, salvation, divine love and the restoration of all things in the only place they can be preserved, beyond the bounds of the Enlightenment, where his sparkling skin is too bright for the light of reason. Carlisle breaks out of the hopeless moment in which rationalized religion excuses violence against its enemies by refusing such violence even as he becomes its living embodiment, and by hoping for redemption against all hope. Carlisle's religion is uncannily the postmodern, post-secular sort that Caputo approves: religion as hope for the impossible in a world of uncertainties and belief, a religion that is "for lovers."[46] It is a religion that in going through Enlightenment secularism has come out recognizing the faith of faith. It neither disavows reason nor imagines itself as confined by reason, but swears off the violence of certainty with all the quiet fervor with which Carlisle lives out his convictions as convictions. Carlisle's is a hopeful, religious vision for a salvation that joins this world to the next, and the appeal of this vision to a massive readership — including fans who have coined the term "Cullenism" — is evidence of what we might think of as a wide-spread cultural post-secularity.[47]

But there is another clue that the religion we see in *Twilight* is post-secular in the sense of coming after the Enlightenment, and that is its having been stripped down to a particular list of essentials: it is a religiousness that is identifiably Christian in an undeniable but understated, almost shy or embarrassed way. In this sense, the religiousness of Meyer's series is not unlike what we find in Caputo's own writings, which, for all their talk of impossibility and love and Christian faith from Augustine to Abelard, have exactly nothing to say about the Cross or the Resurrection. Caputo's philosophy, like Meyer's novels, gives a powerful voice to religious sensibilities and a properly post-secular recognition of the supernatural religiousness of the sort of love, life, and forgiveness that readers are not shy about craving, at the same time that they testify to the ways the market and modern rationality strip faith of its teeth, so to speak. In these post-secular novels, a connection has been created between our historical moment and pre-modern faith — almost. Almost, because although *Twilight* can gesture towards premodern faith, it cannot reach back behind the rationalized fundamentalism of the Puritans and the Wars of Religion. Carlisle is in a very real way stuck in the seventeenth-century Protestant moment of his vampiric birth; he hopes for a forgiveness that his father's religion, decreeing that heretics were beyond salvation and thus to be violently exterminated, denied, but he cannot reach beyond that historical moment to any church or congregation that believes in the radical possibility of the *apokatastasis*. Carlisle's family is a non-denominational, apolitical, de-centralized congregation, with no hope for the change of the larger social order (the Volturi are to be avoided, not overthrown) but hope only for the select few who, through whatever extraordinary circumstances, join their family. With the Cullens we are not far from the form of religion that Max Weber so famously describes in *The Protestant Ethic and the Spirit of Capitalism*: a faith that would regard Carlisle's good deeds in the world as indirect evidence of an otherworldly election, grace or forgiveness that is never surely communicated in the material world.

In trying to situate the post-secular in *Twilight* and to understand the precise nature of the religiousness that it represents, we must keep in mind both the aspects of religion that it retains and the ones it has left behind. As in Stoker's *Dracula*, we see in the *Twilight* series the Gothicized or abjected belief that the spiritual is real and will triumph over the powers of darkness, even in a culture (like Stoker's) haunted by the evils contracted through and enacted by empire, capitalism, and global trade, represented by Harker's firm literally bringing the Count to England and giving him purchase on English soil, in pursuit of profit and advancement. But in *Twilight* as in *Dracula*, there is no real communion with God; Dr. Van Helsing and his band of men use the physical wafer of the Eucharist as a defense against evil, not as the means for communion with God or the transfiguration of the human person. In a similar way, Carlisle's cross, made by his father, bars connection with God more than it offers it, only symbolically testifying to the hope he has salvaged from the shipwrecked religion he inherited. Both novels share a belief in God's goodness, and perhaps even in God's somehow working in the world. But for all the breaking up and spreading around of the Eucharistic wafer, no one in *Dracula* receives Holy Communion, and in a post–Puritan world haunted by the specters of the Wars of Religion and the cyclic returns of all sorts of fundamentalisms in modernity, belief in the radical redemption of the person through direct communion with God, through God's presence in the world, is the faith that dare not speak its name. For all Meyer's profoundly religious, moral vision, God is even hazily less visible in *Twilight* than in *Dracula*. And so between these landmark vampire tales, a century and the Atlantic apart, we see a telling shift. The last traces of a sacramental faith identified with the church in Stoker's novel give way to a religion of hope and of love: a hope directed towards a mysterious, absent God, and of a love strange and beautiful like Bella's mysterious protective force field in *Breaking Dawn*, but nonetheless confined to the particular members of one's own family — a family whose very existence the novel points to as supernatural.

Twilight's Transformation of the Gothic

> Perhaps the best way of encapsulating the gist of an epoch is to focus not on the explicit features that define its social and ideological edifices but on the disavowed ghosts that haunt it, dwelling in a mysterious region of nonexistent entities which none the less *persist*, continue to exert their efficacy.
>
> — Slavoj Zizek, *The Fragile Absolute*[48]

This essay has argued that the appeal of the *Twilight* series lies at least partly in terms of the Gothic way it articulates the vexed desires for family, forgiveness, and faith that circulate in its storyline. In so doing it poses the question of what it means that these fears and desires have themselves become Gothic, taking the quintessentially Gothic form of a vampire tale. If the Cullens, and the form of family and hope for eternal salvation they represent, are in any sense unsettling or haunting, it is because they testify to the extent to which it is readers themselves who have participated in abjecting these desires. By living an allegiance to a particular lifestyle of economic productivity and consumption, a significant swath of readers has created its own guilt, made its desired salvation seem impossible, and moreover, has repressed those hopes and desires in the service of a capitalism and consumer culture that not even Meyer's hopeful fiction can fully disavow. Perhaps the most problematic aspect of the series is the way that, for all its monogamous, vegetarian asceticism and its hope for supernatural, redemptive, non-consuming love, it cannot imagine that love without an expressly capitalistic form of wealth. The mansions, the beautiful clothing, the luxury cars, the limitless recourse to travel and every imaginable gift, are the result, we learn, of a particularly twentieth- and twenty-first century form of capitalism: long-term investments of money, accruing interest and strategically managed with the benefit of Alice's foresight into market trends. The fact that even such a compelling fantasy of reprieve from consuming, consumer-oriented, versions of romantic desire cannot shake off that very capitalistic ideal of commodity-luxury is perhaps the most telling point of all.

The resonance of the *Twilight* series in contemporary culture seems to suggest two things: that we as readers know that self-denial is somehow in the recipe for love and redemption, and that, despite this knowledge, we have trouble imagining that redemption outside the unfettered consumer indulgence that is at the root of the problem. Even in our fantasies of salvation, we may all be consumers, all vampires in beautiful cars and clothes, but still this novel imagines hope: hope in the form of family, forgiveness, and a post-secular, pared-down religion of love, of doing no harm through limiting oneself to good consumption, and of carefully specified forms of self-control. Where some might argue that this is just romantic fantasy (and it certainly may function that way for many readers), it is also potentially more than that. The imagination at work in the series, steeped (as Professor Osborn has shown in her essay) as it is in the religious-imaginative works of C.S. Lewis and J.R.R. Tolkien, recognizes the particular religiousness necessary to face up to the vulnerable uncertainties of hope and forgiveness that are abjected in the Enlightenment. In ascribing eternal consequences to the evils of consumption, it in some sense calls sin "sin," and its compelling vision is of redemptive love shown through bravery and vigilant self-control. The even braver insight of *Twilight* is to show us how we have abjected all this, and how profoundly our culture and our economy is opposed to the values and practices that would give it what it professes to value or, better, what it might love. The tempting apple of the cover and the epigraph of *Twilight* (from Gen. 2:17) themselves suggest such a reading of the novels. In our postmodern, post-secular moment, a belief that would choose monogamy, childbearing, and the hope for eternal love over our culture's fairly rigidly enforced paths to economic identity and self-sufficiency, seems like a forbidden temptation, the consequences of which we can only fantastically imagine, hope for, and desire, in a newly Gothic way.

Notes

1. Kelly Hurley, "British Gothic Fiction, 1885–1930," in *The Cambridge Companion to Gothic Fiction*, ed. Jerrold E. Hogle (Cambridge: Cambridge University Press, 2002), 189–207 (quotation on 194).

2. Jerrold E. Hogle, "Introduction: The Gothic in Western Culture," in *The Cambridge Companion to Gothic Fiction*, 1–20 (quotation on 2).

3. Gothic fiction is connected to but not to be confused with the goth subculture, which originated in the UK punk music scene of the late 1970s and early 1980s and combines images from nineteenth-century Gothic fiction with a range of identifiable musical, aesthetic, and fashion tropes.

4. Hogle, "Introduction," 2–3.

5. Ibid., 4.

6. See for instance, Hogle, 4–5 and Leslie Fiedler, "Charles Brockden Brown and the Invention of the American Gothic," in *Love and Death in the American Novel*, Rev. ed. (New York: Dell, 1966), 126–61, esp. 129. Quotation in this sentence is from Hogle, "Introduction," 5.

7. Julia Kristeva, *Powers of Horror: an Essay on Abjection* (1980), translated by Leon S. Roudiez (New York: Columbia University Press, 1982), 4.

8. Sigmund Freud, "The 'Uncanny,'" *Penguin Freud Library*, Vol. 14 (Harmondsworth: Penguin, 1991), 339–376.

9. Steven Bruhm, "The Contemporary Gothic: Why We Need It," in *The Cambridge Companion to Gothic Fiction*, 259–76 (quotations on 261, 264).

10. Figures from the U.S. Census Bureau tabulated at http://www.infoplease.com/ipa/A0005061.html.

11. Figures from the Census Bureau's 2002 Current Population Survey (March supplement) tabulated by the Population Reference Bureau (PRB): http://www.prb.org/Articles/2003/TraditionalFamiliesAccountforOnly7PercentofUSHouseholds.aspx.

12. Robert D. Putnam, *Bowling Alone: The Collapse and Revival of American Community* (New York: Simon & Schuster, 2000).

13. Bureau of Labor Statistics Report on the Care of Household Children (by Adults in Households with Children) for the period 2004–08: http://www.bls.gov/news.release/atus.nr0.htm. The same report indicates that these parents spent an average of 5.6 hours per day providing secondary childcare (i.e., while doing leisure or household activities, which may include time when children sleep).

14. From Meyer's FAQ page on *Breaking Dawn*: http://www.stepheniemeyer.com/bd_faq.html.

15. We can thus think of *Twilight* as representing a Gothic truth not only for readers who see the reality it presents as impossible, but also for women like Meyer herself, who may feel their own stay-at-home existence as Gothic or abject in the face of the prevailing cultural and economic norms.

16. Stephenie Meyer, *New Moon* (New York: Little Brown, 2006), 37.

17. See http://www.stepheniemeyer.com/twilight.html.

18. Stephenie Meyer, *Twilight* (New York: Little Brown, 2005), 267.
19. Ibid., 272.
20. Ibid., 274.
21. Isaiah 11: 6, 7, 9. All Scripture references to the King James Version.
22. For two historical and theological treatments of the *apokatastasis*, see Kallistos Ware, "Dare We Hope for the Salvation of All? Origen, St. Gregory of Nyssa, and St. Isaac the Syrian," in *The Inner Kingdom* (New York: St. Vladimir's Seminary Press, 2000) and Andreas Andreopoulos, "Eschatology and Final Restoration (Apokatastasis) in Origen, Gregory of Nyssa and Maximos the Confessor," *Theandros: An Online Journal of Orthodox Theology and Philosophy* 1.3 (2004), http://www.theandros.com/restoration.html.
23. Isaiah 35:9.
24. Stephenie Meyer, *Midnight Sun*, 43 (http://www.stepheniemeyer.com/midnightsun.html).
25. Meyer strongly self-identifies as a member of the Church of Jesus Christ of Latter-day Saints or a Mormon, and the relationship between Mormonism and the *Twilight* series is explored by chapters in this volume by Jeffers and Schwartzman. Latter-day Saints (LDS) theology declares unequivocally that "the family is central to the Creator's plan for the eternal destiny of His children"; see the important Mormon document, *The Family: A Proclamation to the World*, presented by LDS President Gordon B. Hinckley at the General Relief Society Meeting held September 23, 1995, in Salt Lake City, Utah: http://www.lds.org/library/display/0,4945,161–1–11–1,00.html. Significantly for the purposes of this essay, the *Proclamation* states that "By divine design, fathers are to preside over their families in love and righteousness and are responsible to provide the necessities of life and protection for their families. Mothers are primarily responsible for the nurture of their children. In these sacred responsibilities, fathers and mothers are obligated to help one another as equal partners."
26. Meyer, *Twilight*, 314.
27. Brian J. Frost, *The Monster with a Thousand Faces: Guises of the Vampire in Myth and Literature* (Bowling Green, OH: Bowling Green State University Popular Press, 1989), 27, and Michael J. Dennison, *Vampirism: Literary Tropes of Decadence and Entropy* (New York: Peter Lang Publishing, 2001), 89, both quoted in Elizabeth Sanders, "Virtuous Vampires: Self-Denial and Relationship in Stephenie Meyer's *Twilight*" (unpublished manuscript), 4. Many thanks to Elizabeth Sanders for permission to cite her wonderful paper and for many passionate and enjoyable conversations about all matters *Twilight* and many that are not.
28. Sanders, "Virtuous Vampires," 6.
29. Ibid., 7–8.
30. John Granger, "Mormon Vampires in the Garden of Eden: What the Bestselling *Twilight* Series has in Store for Young Readers," *Touchstone* 22.8 (2009): 24–29 (quotation here from 24).
31. Graham Ward, *True Religion* (London: Blackwell, 2003).
32. Meyer, *New Moon*, 36.
33. Meyer, *Twilight*, 337. For Carlisle's history, see *Twilight*, 330–43.
34. Meyer, *New Moon*, 34.
35. Ibid., 36–37.
36. Danièle Hervieu-Léger, *Religion as a Chain of Memory* (New Brunswick, NJ : Rutgers University Press, 2000).
37. References to the return of or to religion in humanities study abound, particularly within literary theory and with reference to the current work of Slavoj Zizek and the later work of Jacques Derrida. In 2005, Stanley Fish prophesied in *The Chronicle of Higher Education* that religion will "succeed high theory and the triumvirate of race, gender, and class as the center of intellectual energy in the academy"; Stanley Fish, "One University Under God?" *The Chronicle of Higher Education*, 51 (18) Friday, January 7, 2005, page C1.
38. John Caputo, *On Religion* (London and New York: Routledge, 2001), 37.
39. Ibid., 60

40. Ibid., 65.
41. Ibid., 61,
42. Ibid., 67.
43. Ibid., 91.
44. Ibid., 132.
45. Caputo and Ward agree with other contemporary scholars of religion including Talal Asad in pointing out that religious fundamentalism is not so much a product of a premodern past as of modernity itself; it is when religion (or secularism) rationalizes itself as knowledge and not faith that it authorizes violence in its name. On this point, see Caputo, chapter 4, "Impossible People," pp. 91–108.
46. Caputo, 1–7.
47. Cullenism is a discussion group on the Twifans website, currently at 245 members, complete with buttons that read "Cullenism: my new religion" (though the group definition denies its religious status); see http://www.twifans.com/group/cullenism. I am grateful to Marijane Osborn for this reference.
48. Slavoj Zizek, *The Fragile Absolute: Or, Why is the Christian Legacy Worth Fighting For?* (London and New York: Verso, 2000), 3.

I am grateful to the friends and students whose generous readings and responses improved earlier versions of this essay: Sondra Gates, Elizabeth Sanders, James Lambert, Cory Hutchinson-Reuss, Lindsey Row-Heyveld, Andrew Williams, and Johanna Tomlinson, in addition to the editors of this volume.

Eco-Gothics for the Twenty-First Century

James Mc Elroy and
Emma Catherine Mc Elroy

Stephenie Meyer's first loves include an admixture of gothic and romance fiction with Charlotte Brontë's *Jane Eyre*, Jane Austen's *Pride and Prejudice*, and Emily Brontë's *Wuthering Heights* heading up the list, while a host of assorted Shakespeare plays—*Romeo and Juliet*, *The Merchant of Venice*, *A Midsummer Night's Dream*—take up the rear. Quite apart from the obvious links between such texts and Meyer's commercially successful novels (she confesses that she has reread *Jane Eyre* "literally hundreds of times" and "can't go through a year without re-reading" Jane Austen),[1] it is often forgotten that these same texts and, yes, this applies to the intricate eco-tapestries that come with reading Shakespeare as an Elizabethan Green, instantiate specific nature-based narratives which leave, in their wake, a certain brand of eco-gothics that Meyer has rebranded for a twenty-first century reading audience.

The most obvious Gothic tropes that emerge in the pages of *Twilight*, and here we might mention Ann Radcliffe's *The Mysteries of Udolpho* and Mary Shelley's *Frankenstein* as further influences, find their conscious and unconscious ecological antecedents in a diverse tradition where the name of the game is to situate writing in a range of ecological habitats with the most popular being dark primeval forests, uninhabited mountain ranges, isolated moorlands, remote (rugged) beaches, and turbulent, tempestuous seascapes. It is amidst such alluring topographies, whether wilderness or other, that the Gothic and like-minded fictions prepare their ecological narratives so that nature and culture, as suppositional binaries, can come into play. No surprise then that such suggestive semiotic spaces make way for the kind of formative eco-cultural values which enjoin Ann Radcliffe's Emily St. Aubert to protect a noble stand of trees that adorn her father's estate, entice Mary Shelley's Frankenstein, as scientific "*conquistador*," to wander adrift in a desolate alpine landscape,[2] and inveigle Bram Stoker's *Dracula* (Meyer claims she has never read *Dracula*) to find solace, if that is the word, in the wilds of the Borgo Pass and Carpathian Mountains.[3]

In all such cases, writes Roderick McGillis, these texts locate their Gothic "chronotype in sublime settings."[4] Margaret Homans says much the same thing about *Wuthering Heights,* which she believes could not survive without the imposing "presence of nature."[5] She adds, quite rightly, that the narrative weight Brontë brings to her novel means that, even though few scenes are actually set outdoors, "the reader leaves the book with the sensation of having experienced a realistic portrayal of the Yorkshire landscape."[6] Another expression of the same link between natural landscapes and designated protagonists in Brontë is something Joseph Carroll points to in his article, "The Ecology of Victorian Fiction," where he reminds us that *Wuthering Heights* provides an "intense but by no means anomalous example of the way person and place interpenetrate in Victorian novels."[7] As example, Carroll cites the symbiotic link between Thrushcross Grange, which is situated in an oh-so-pleasant setting with the Lintons in residence, and Wuthering Heights, with its bleak and beckoning topography inhabited by the otherwise brutish Earnshaws.[8] Carroll goes on to argue that the ties which bind environment and person together in *Wuthering Heights* are so complete that even when it comes to questions of life and death, or even life after death, the Yorkshire moors figure as nothing less than a transsubstantive topographical semiotic: "This interpenetration of person and place is so complete that after their death the spirits of Heathcliff and Catherine Earnshaw continue to walk the moors, like spectral emanations of the ground."[9]

Meyer's *Twilight* features some if not all of the same eco-expansive elements in more contemporary guise. While it is true that she does not fetishize wilderness as something in its own right, there are decidedly eco–Gothic elements at work in her sylvan location of Forks, Washington, with its attendant meteorological conditions (wet rains), botanical lushness (damp/dank greeneries), apposite forest clearings (Edward and Bella's Edenic-inclined meadow), and remote beach sites as select border habitats with the liminal First Beach at La Push serving as an effective buffer zone throughout the series. To better understand these ingredient ecologies it is essential to see just how much and how often, even in a text that is viewed as an integer of pop culture rather than being in any sense ecological, nature and the environment is featured as an irreducible trace within Meyer's select romance-goth discourse. In this, of course, she is not that much different from many of her Gothic forebears, since *Twilight* is set in a crepuscular world where light is made present through "absence," or, if we turn the same point on its side, where such seemingly absent light acquires untold narrative significance "through the threat of its loss."[10] Much more to the point, it is somewhere inside such "absence" that Meyer constructs a kind of textual diorama where her creature subjects slowly come to light (as it were) in a determinate ecological locale suited out as a kind of prelapsarian/postlapsarian Eden.

Clearly, then, Meyer's immediate sense of eco-construction brings with it an imbricative narrative that hosts a transformative intersection between external environment and cultural meaning. Such a Meyerean landscape accommodates both the standard sense of endarkened woodland as a prime location of wilderness as evil and/or wilderness as mystery while, in the same arboreal trope, setting down mixed rural habitats as safe havens situated apart from the interposing threats and anxieties of the world's encroaching urban sprawl. Meyer's denominational sense of the environment, circa 2010, thus carries with it all or most of the deficits and pluses of Gothic nature narratives, including elements of a particularly American tradition (Cooper, Hawthorne, Poe, Melville) and its appetite for the newest and, as simultaneous moment of the same phenomenon, oldest "frontier" sites.[11] It comes as no great surprise, then, that Meyer's own line in frontiers serves as an important ecological semiotic, providing a ready means of negotiating territorial/textual borders as well as (and at the same time as) passing betwixt and between the conscious and the unconscious, the urban and the rural, the civilized and uncivilized; between, that is, those centrifugal terms that run to "nature" and "culture."

Just take Meyer's chosen beach which, and this is true of many such coastal habitats and harbor locations, embodies certain traces of unspoken violence and historical loss. This is, after all, the kind of interstitial coastline where, to employ Rose Lovell-Smith's terms of reference, a given people have met "the other."[12] As such, La Push with its astute ecological properties furnishes *Twilight* with a rich econic resource whose pluridimensional meanings suggest that "acknowledgement of its ambiguous, sinister, haunted, and conflicted sides is well overdue."[13] (Let us not forget that La Push also serves as the place where Bella finds out for the first time about Edward and the "cold ones."[14]) Meanwhile, the same textual intersections that take place between Meyer's fictive topographies also mark her attempts at bringing together, under one cover, variant creature species. To wit, she uses her Gothicized topographies to fashion a textual world filled with assorted species types who/which co-exist in a veritable "Twiscape." In so doing, Meyer gets to number her pages with creatures— Emmett as bear, Edward as sleek cat, Jacob as wolf— that mirror a close species interchange between vegetarian vampires, indigenous human lupines, large (but largely unseen) feeder mammals, and omnivorous humans.

While Tony Norman has every right to protest the narcissism of Meyer's key protagonists as creatures who have moved us to that point where vampires as designer ghouls (fine bone structure, hair gel, and so on) no longer represent "the dark, unconscious corners of mankind's psyche," this is not the whole story by a long shot.[15] Likewise, Norman's open concern about the generational difference between the altogether hot vampires of now as compared to the fire and brimstone guys of old—"Their undead personas were so gangsta they would have put stakes through their own hearts rather than wait for the phone to ring on weekends, like the creatures dominating popular culture today"—does not, in final analysis, get us any closer to looking at Meyer's revisionist taxonomic species as part of a culturally complex ecological interchange wherein she defines animals, humans, and others outside the usual positivist Linnaean taxonomies. Hence, as much as Norman might rail against the Gothic urgencies of now, the fact remains that *Twilight* posits an interesting shift in species relations with "composite creatures" inhabiting its extant eco-gothic discourse.[16]

In *Limits of Horror: Technology, Bodies, Gothic* Fred Botting suggests that such a generational difference in ghoulish vampires reflects a paradigmatic (with small "p") shift in our understanding of normative patterns as per Monsters Inc: "No longer exceptions, the monsters off and on technical screens are no different from the norms they once negatively defined."[17] In this brave new world of smooth and angular composites, Edward Cullen personifies a chic species of familiar otherness as Gothic hero turned hybrid (whether that be bi-racial, bi-cultural, bi-somatic) and so fosters mixed identification protocols that ensure he can be intensely attractive, in a Johnny Depp kind of way, while remaining true to his own unique species: a pedigreed human/vamp mix. These variegated inter-species are what Botting likes to call, à la Derrida, "normal monstrosities."[18] Botting continues his critical remarks with a few comments on the theoretical premise that the intrepid vampires under discussion seem "strangely human, if not more than human."[19] He adds that this—all this—betokens a "flight towards a disembodied and decontextualized posthumanity" and that the recent appearance of cross-species intimacies symptomatizes an ongoing struggle with the "swiftly changing meanings of what it is to be human, or, for that matter, inhuman."[20]

Of course this "flight" towards the disembodied involves more than just some easy exchange of elderly Transylvanian types, Frankenstein, Dracula, Wolf Man, for the more metrosexual likes, and looks, of Edward Cullen as invasive vampire species. Rather, Meyer's vampires, no matter how buff or bodacious—perhaps because they are so buff and bodacious—help us to better understand how whenever we foreground "transitional states" we inscribe a positive potential for "posthuman transformation."[21] The same work of posthuman definition goes on inside *Twilight* as and when Meyer works with a neat assortment of reference lines. These include her predator-prey reference to the lion that is Edward and the lamb that is Bella. Even more crucial for the purposes of eco-critical analysis are those especially special moments when Bella threatens to change species allegiance as a morphological crossover in kind. Perhaps the most obvious or telling instance of this near-species intercourse comes towards the end of the novel, when Bella is prepared, in the name of love, to engage in an act of total surrender and become a postmodern vampire in her own right.

As it turns out, of course, Meyer does not allow her young charges to exchange sexual/sanguinarian favors in *Twilight*. Rather, she underwrites their various feats of abstinence and so bypasses that venerable tradition of recent interspecies mating patterns on the Hollywood scene as evidenced by *The Little Mermaid* (Ariel becomes human to wed Eric), *The Lord of the Rings* (Arwen switches from immortality and elfdom to get with the human Aragorn), and *Beauty and the Beast* (the Beast becomes human in order to woo, and wed, the ever eligible Belle). At one level, at least, Meyer — in bringing Edward and Bella so close together while never allowing consummation to take place — uses the potentiality of "unnatural" union to talk about what is natural while, at one and the same time, skirting around some important social issues that have to do with "racial and social mixing."[22] In fact, Meyer's introduction to the whole concept of cross-species mating, as both threat and promise, seems to provide an involuntary means of working through racial taxonomic practice insofar as such vampish taxonomies register an anxiety-free means of articulating what remains unsaid about the nature of race/species relations in contemporary society.[23]

Read in this way, Meyer's creation of a particular ecological worldview cast with select inhabitants interacting on cue, hides, as "repressed," what is said amidst the inter-textualities of the unsaid: such determinate species-constructs, as part of *Twilight*'s taken line on nature, serve as a pretext for sorting through interracial and/or interspecies union.[24] Miscegenation in such a confined ecological space means that the trope of reproductive union becomes a normative feature of Meyer's portentous discourse, while nature and what is deemed natural are defined in accordance with, and set within the limits of, otherwise aberrant or unnatural cross-species practices. In this way Meyer's readers encounter, from inside her world of mixed race speciesisation, "figures of the new humanity."[25] What adds to this ongoing sense of new humanities in *Twilight* is the fact that Meyer's modish vegetarian vampires find their live blood source, both off screen and off page, in an unexpected realm: in and among an assortment of four-legged rather than two-legged mammals.

Jean Kazez, in "Dying to Eat: The Vegetarian Ethics of *Twilight*," puts this anomalous circumstance in context right away when she writes (tongue in cheek) that "Animal blood is like tofu, for the Cullen family,"[26] In the same vein — as it were — George Beahm in *Bedazzled: Stephenie Meyer and the Twilight Phenomenon* makes the related point, obvious to real *Twilight* aficionados, that in Meyer's books "there are no lingering scenes of bloodletting, no blow-by-blow descriptions of wholesale slaughter, no pages covered in blood."[27] And yet the killing and consumption of edible mammal species is present in the vamp-turned exchanges common to Edward's kith and kin. So much so, in fact, that even though the standard apotropaics of cross, garlic, or some such, are pretty much off the table in *Twilight*, Meyer's urbane vampires remain confirmed sanguinarians without all the horrible mess of blood and guts that is so often associated with truly vampiric, as in savage, types.

It is clear that Meyer goes to great pains to humanize her chosen others and make them attractive properties on the teen scene in and around Forks. What she also does in the process is to situate her shimmering counter-species inside a definite environmental schema with established modes of interaction between them and her other dramatis personae. Every bit as important as how or where Meyer situates her competing species is the fact that her Gothic lovelies are an intrinsic part of an involved and intricate ecological system. One means of assessing the impact of having a hip crowd of "vegetarian" vampires living inside a functioning ecological system is to look at their treatment of the environment in which they dwell. Isla Myers-Smith, in "The Ecological Consequences of Vampirism," is someone who does just that. In fact, Myers-Smith is eager to make it clear, 100 percent clear, that the Cullens and their ilk are anything but green-friendly inhabitant types. Beginning with the statement that "Vampires are not green; they're wan," she proceeds to accuse the Cullens of indulging in a wasteful round of suspect environmental practices.[28] She hammers them for their mindless and excessive auto acquisition and use by identifying the following inventory as damning evidence of their needless indulgence: Edward's Volvo, the silver S60R, Rosalie's BMW M3, Carlisle's Mercedes S55 AMG, Emmett's Jeep Wrangler, and Alice's Porsche 911 Turbo.

To drive her point home Myers-Smith then waxes eloquent about how the Cullen clan sashays around at "fuel-inefficient speeds" and so guarantees that the "ecological cost of vampirism becomes very substantial."[29] The irony in all this, as far as Myers-Smith is concerned, has a lot to do with the intervening truth that the Cullens—carbon neutral since there is no breathing or CO2 emissions to be had—"squander their carbon neutrality" by spewing out gross car emissions and living in a modern architectural dream house with attendant resource expenditures. (As James Wolcott puts it with reference to the Cullen homestead, they have an "elevated taste in architecture — no gewgawed McMansion for them."[30]) None of this is made any easier by the fact that the same Cullens who consume so much are also on the go (once again that carbon footprint thing) with a breathtaking 24/7 schedule — quite literal, since they do not sleep — wherein more and more lights are used and more and more stuff is required on an *ad infinitum* basis.

All told, the Cullens, compliments of Stephenie Meyer, feature as speciate vamps with insouciant, middle-class values and tastes. The fact that they purchase but never eat generous servings of cafeteria food is just one more no-no when it comes to looking at their carbon footprints. So the Cullens are, it appears, guilty as charged. Meanwhile, their highly suspect vegetarian practices, in light of the fact that they draw exclusively on a single mammalian demographic in Washington State, means that their favorite local prey species will be culled, devoured, and wiped out without so much as a word or a whimper. What this also means, of course, is that such a dwindling population of large resident mammals cannot and will not be replenished over time. To make this point, Myers-Smith cites basic population principles to reinforce the thesis that a concentrated population of predatory vampires (given their capacity as serial killers) can wreak havoc on a finite mammal population in a given habitat range and so accelerate species extinction whereby one species after another is wiped out and the balance of nature is undermined in the course of unwarranted acts of eco-genocide.[31]

Here is how Myers-Smith looks at the question of predation under the stewardship of the Cullens as they go about their annual "harvest" of local prey species: "Immortal predators will exact a continuous predation pressure on populations of large mammals along the West Coast. If each Cullen vampire is feeding on 4—12 cougars or grizzly bears per year (a conservative estimate based on the novels, I might add), this is a substantial annual harvest."[32] Myers-Smith rounds out her critique of *Twilight* by noting that if Meyer really wanted to have her metrosexual vampires live out their interminable lives in harmony with bona fide vegetarian principles, all she had to do, though admittedly this might have taken the edge off her finished text, was to have them take a page from HBO's vampire series, *True Blood*, and head down to the local blood bank for a quick, intravenous fix. (Myers-Smith's alternate suggestion that the Cullens could ingest large quantities of "invasive European Starlings"—one assumes as aviate appetizers?—is almost as anomalous as an eco-narrative where vegetarians are defined as vegetarians because they consume non-human meats.)[33]

Given all this, it is now clear that Meyer's particular brand of Gothic discourse relies on established species configurations to ensure that her Bohemian predators are able to gorge themselves in order to, as Matthew Offenbacher puts it in "Green Gothic," initiate "a semblance of life, an anti-ecology, a reversal of the nitrogen cycle."[34] Indeed, at the same time that "Team Edward" establishes "a semblance of life, an anti-ecology," Meyer's wolfeans, as in "Team Jacob," also establish distinctive species characteristics in their departure from older lupine conventions: the Quileute shape-shifter echoes the environmental practices and longstanding values of native American tribes along the Northwest Coast, while affording a semblant counter-species to the Cullens. The mere presence of such human/lupine inhabitants signals a further paradigmatic shift (with another small "p") in how species and environment are treated in Meyer's published text. Certainly, Meyer's wolf-like species, as compared to the traditional wolves and werewolves of Gothic lore, suggest a far more eco-friendly set of wolves—whatever about their massive size and fierce appearance—as endearing literary figure and cultural trope. Chantel Bourgault du Coudray in *The Curse of the Werewolf: Fantasy, Horror, and the Beast Within* makes the further point that the characterization of wolves in modern culture has become altogether positive (her term, "benevolent") and that this positive tag affirms an ongoing rehabilitation of the wolf within the cultural environment at large.[35]

Of course, such a new appreciation of things lupine goes hand in hand with recent trends in ecological thinking, whereby the natural world has been moved center stage as part of an enlarged and enlarging sense of our own public ecological discourse. At the same time that the environment has become a hallowed if not sacred cultural centerpiece or icon, the "human" has also assumed a quite different and much revised role in the scheme of things. This is certainly the case with Meyer's Quileute who, by adhering to many of the same ecological values common to Native American tribes, promote, at the level of rhizome, a sense that the human creature is but one small part of an intricate ecological system and that people should therefore recognize, no matter how belatedly, that far from being part of a superior species called *homo sapiens*, they are only one finite speciate element in a planetary eco-system which humans depend on for their survival.[36]

All of which brings us to a quick question about *Twilight* as an occasion of eco–Gothics in a "new" age: Do the ecological principles that Meyer draws on in her novel — the eco-system that she draws in her novel — provide sufficient grounds to conclude that her work deserves some real critical attention at the level of ecocritical practice? While the answer to this question might result in a mixed review of Meyer's twilight ecologies — always being mindful not to confuse her crepuscular sense of nature with nature as "alien" presence — it is clear that *Twilight* does situate the meadows, forests and oceans of the natural world in a positive if subdued environmental light. Meyer also appears, for the most part, to locate her shape-shifting wolf people in an almost convivial natural environment which does not force them to behave, as was so often the case in the Gothics of old, like savage beasts. (It should be noted that the Cullens also live in relative harmony with their immediate surroundings even though, as discussed, their hunting sprees and carefree or careless environmental practices leave much to be desired.[37]) In fact, Meyer's text allows for a largely harmonious relationship to hold between person and/or wolf inside what is very much a shared environment. Meanwhile, her preferred wolf creatures develop, within their species, kind, positive and accepting notions of their own "inner wolf."[38] The same Coudray mentioned above makes the additional point, though not about *Twilight*, that a lot of recent goth material has even gone so far as "to cast werewolves as defenders of the environment."[39]

Here, much as before, Meyer's creature types appear to be in sync with today's cadre of celebrity horror figures who are no longer constrained by dark and fearsome animal urges, but are actively given over to protecting and preserving their territories, their homes, and their people — their "species." Another expression of this newfound sense of ecological harmony is part of a growing interdependence between the spiritual and the natural worlds, with spiritual riches being "attained," proposes Coudray, "through an immersion in or connection with nature."[40] In fact, as Coudray points out, one recent theme in modern interspecies conflict as depicted in literature is that in which "good native American werewolves with an intimate connection to the land" fight it out with "bad werewolves from Europe who have forgotten their origins in nature."[41] Sound familiar? Well, it should. This — and no great stretch here — is altogether reminiscent of the competing species values and ecological tenets that define the difference between the adversarial "species" Meyer places at the top of a food chain where "the cold ones are the natural enemies of the wolf."[42]

When James Wolcott writes in *Vanity Fair* that *Twilight's* Edward is "ecologically correct" because, or so Wolcott assumes, he flosses after each woodland kill,[43] Wolcott's seeming eco-speak carries within its terms of reference a brand of criticism that is limited. His concentration on the anthropomorphic with some stuff about Edward's "immaculate physique" and how he is "irradiated with moonlight, putting nature itself in the shade" passes over what is actually ecological, rather than interrogating the ecological possibilities that define Team Cullen on their hunting trips and their variable acts of waste management (or lack thereof).[44] The need to thematize the unsaid and the unrecognized means that we must now begin to problematize, as cultural *a priori*, the idea that gothic-romance is nothing more than a surface phenomenon based on human subjects alone. Also demanding scrutiny is the premise that it is somehow acceptable to eschew the purpose and presence of a grammatological universe of environmental alterities fitted out with an ecological lexicon (a grammar of trees, meadows, shores, species) just because such things are made subordinate to human characters amidst the need to talk about character profile, plot development or vamped-up Goths.

In contrast, the ecocritical disposition outlined here takes the following thesis as a constant: traditional Gothic texts with their engraved ecological narratives have started to give way to more reflexive ecological potentialities based on "differing valuations of the forces of nature and biology."[45] To get to that point where reading nature in eco-gothic texts becomes an essential critical consideration thus requires us to see, as in a new and more radical optique, that even though the Gothic might be the "opposite of the pastoral" it is necessary to re-imagine books like *Twilight* as ecological resource materials which incorporate nature/wilderness as conscious and unconscious facets of an appealing narrative written in commercial mode.[46] It is also necessary to think beyond the premise, not uncommon among critics like Eric W. Jepson, that Meyer's brand of fictionalized creature is not based on any environmental consideration but, instead, is somehow the direct outcome of Meyer's unique Mormon cosmology.[47] Jepson's main point, that Meyer's imagined world of vampires and werewolves "connects most clearly not to the supernatural literature of horror, but to the supernatural literature of the Latter-day Saints," immediately leaves out of account the fact that Meyer's species and attendant eco-systems are based on specific ecological precepts rather than being part of a supernaturalist literature founded on Mormon catechetics.[48] The same can be said about Christine Smallwood's criticism of *Twilight* in her recently posted article, "Vampire Studies," where even though she makes a compelling case with reference to Meyer's creation of "unrebellious" vampires, her entire discussion ends up being centered on Meyer's Mormon family values without any—any—discussion of vampires, wolves, and others in terms of the environment they inhabit:

> I'm a little concerned about *Twilight*, because these are the most unrebellious vampires we've ever seen. They are essentially Mormon vampires; the author is Mormon, and the Cullen family has Mormon values. And *Twilight* is not a cult phenomenon. It's mainstream. The vampire has gone from being a horrible monster to the kid next door. So we'll see what happens. Perhaps Edward Cullen will be the last vampire.[49]

So, yes, it is not enough to criticize Meyer on the grounds that her texts are Mormon-based offerings while ignoring or repressing the ecological abundance that stirs inside the narrative nooks and crannies that make *Twilight* what it is—a rich environment of rivers, beaches, pelicans, gulls, eagles, anemones, eels. In the same way, while critics like Terry Eagelton have a legitimate point about Gothic discourse sometimes being "allergic to depths," it must be said that such criticism stops short whenever it comes to talking about nature and the environment. Much the same thing can be said about Eagleton's argument that the Gothic form serves conservative ends—"The political unconscious of a middle-class society which has thrust its anxieties and persecutory fantasies into the safe keeping of its fiction"[50]—because, just as before, his refined political critique never once takes into account how the "unconscious" relates to ecological issues. And this, give or take, is what also happens in the criticism of Linda Bayer-Berenbaum who insists that Gothicism includes all that is "generally excluded" while she herself, in *The Gothic Imagination: Expansion in Gothic Literature and Art*, never stops to ask if what is "excluded" might include something ecological in nature.[51] Ironically, then, critics like Bayer-Berenbaum and Eagleton help to make an open and shut case for ecocriticism precisely because they try to deny its presence; try to stifle what could be a rewarding critical debate about the intimate relationship between the natural environment and literature. Thus, the same critics who tend to silence the possibilities that come with a new mode of ecocriticism end up challenging us to move beyond the constraints of what is called standard critical discourse and pose a new generation of questions about how to read and write ecological narratives as part of Gothic literature—as part of a *Twilight* craze that has caused such a stir at the beginning of the twenty-first century.

Notes

1. Karen Valby, "Stephenie Meyer: 12 of My 'Twilight' Inspirations," September 29, 2009, http://www.ew.com/ew/gallery/0,,20308569 20308554,00. html. Stephenie Meyer, Interview, http://www.hachettebookgroup.com/9FA6868D6CC441738975A4C8D11EA37A.aspx.

2. Kevin Hutchings, "Ecocriticism in British Romantic Studies," *Literature Compass* 4, no. 1 (2007): 184, 185.

3. Roderick McGillis, "The Night Side of Nature: Gothic Spaces, Fearful Times," in *The Gothic in Children's Literature: Haunting the Borders*, edited by Anna Jackson, Karen Coats, and Roderick McGillis (New York: Routledge, 2008), 230.

4. McGillis, "The Night Side of Nature: Gothic Spaces, Fearful Times," 230.

5. Margaret Homans, "Repression and Sublimation of Nature in *Wuthering Heights*," *PMLA* 93 no. 1 (1978): 9.

6. Ibid., 9.

7. Joseph Carroll, "The Ecology of Victorian Fiction," *Philosophy and Literature* 25 no. 2 (2001): 308.

8. Ibid.

9. Ibid.

10. Rebecca F. Stern. "Gothic Light: Vision and Visibility in the Victorian Novel," *South Central Review* 11 no. 4 (1994): 27.

11. David Mogen, Scott P. Sanders, and Joanne B. Karpinski, eds., *Frontier Gothic: Terror and Wonder at the Frontier in American Literature* (Rutherford, NJ: Fairleigh Dickinson University Press; London: Associated University Presses, 1993), 15.

12. Rose Lovell-Smith, "On the Gothic Beach: A New Zealand Reading of House and Landscape in Margaret Mahy's *The Tricksters*," in *The Gothic in Children's Literature*, edited by Anna Jackson, Karen Coats and Roderick McGillis (London; New York: Routledge, 2007), 94, 93.

13. Ibid., 98.

14. Stephenie Meyer, *Twilight* (New York: Little, Brown and Company, 2005), 124.

15. Tony Norman, "The Twilight of the Monsters Has Arrived," *Pittsburgh Post-Gazette*, November 27, 2009, http://www.post-gazette.com/pg/09331/1016613-153.stm.

16. Anne Rice provides a similar venture in un/human narrative species in *The Vampire Chronicles*; see McGillis, "The Night Side of Nature: Gothic Spaces, Fearful Times," 228.

17. Fred Botting, *Limits of Horror: Technology, Bodies, Gothic* (Manchester: Manchester University Press, 2008), 9.

18. Ibid., 10.

19. Ibid.

20. Ibid., 41, 42.

21. Ibid.,14.

22. Donna J. Haraway, "Universal Donors in a Vampire Culture: It's All in the Family: Biological Kinship Categories in the Twentieth-Century United States," in *Uncommon Ground: Rethinking the Human Place in Nature*, edited by William Cronin (New York: W.W. Norton, 1996), 322.

23. Ibid., 340.

24. Ibid., 345.

25. Ibid., 364.

26. Jean Kazez, "Dying to Eat: The Vegetarian Ethics of *Twilight*," in *Twilight and Philosophy: Vampires, Vegetarians, and the Pursuit of Immortality*, edited by Rebecca Housel and J. Jeremy Wisnewski (Hoboken, NJ: John Wiley, 2009), 25.

27. George Beahm, *Bedazzled: Stephenie Meyer and the Twilight Phenomenon* (Nevada City, CA: Underwood Books, 2009), 63.

28. Isla Myers-Smith, "The Ecological Consequences of Vampirism: AKA, Wherein an Ecologist Takes Down *New Moon*," 30 November 2009, http://www.inklingmagazine.com/articles/the-ecological-consequences-of-vampirism/.

29. Ibid.

30. James Wolcott, "The *Twilight* Zone," *Vanity Fair*, December 2008, http://www.vanityfair.com/culture/features/2008/12/twilight200812.

31. Myers-Smith, "The Ecological Consequences of Vampirism: AKA, Wherein an Ecologist Takes Down *New Moon*," http://www.inklingmagazine.com/articles/the-ecological-consequences-of-vampirism/.

32. Ibid.

33. Ibid.

34. Matthew Offenbacher, "Green Gothic," http://www.artsjournal.com/anotherbb/2009/08/green-gothic-by-matthew-offenb.html.

35. Chantel Bourgault du Coudray, *The Curse of the Werewolf: Fantasy, Horror, and the Beast Within* (London: I.B. Tauris, 2006), 139.

36. Ibid.

37. Ibid., 140.

38. Ibid.

39. Ibid.

40. Ibid., 143.

41. Ibid., 140.

42. Stephenie Meyer, *Twilight* (New York: Little, Brown and Company, 2005), 124.

43. Wolcott, "The *Twilight* Zone," http://www.vanity fair.com/culture/features/2008/12/twilight2008.

44. Ibid.

45. Coudray, *The Curse of the Werewolf: Fantasy, Horror, and the Beast Within*, 140.

46. McGillis, "The Night Side of Nature: Gothic Spaces, Fearful Times," 228.

47. Eric W. Jepson, "Saturday's Werewolf: Vestiges of the Premortal Romance in Stephenie Meyer's *Twilight* Novels," *Reading Until Dawn* 1, no. 2 (2009) 1.

48. Ibid.

49. Christine Smallwood, "Vampire Studies," November 29, 2009, http://www.nplusonemag.com/vampire-studies.

50. Terry Eagleton, "Allergic to Depths," review of *Gothic: Four Hundred Years of Excess, Horror, Evil and Ruin*, by Richard Davenport-Hines, *The London Review of Books* 21 no. 6 (18 March 1999): 7.

51. Linda Bayer-Berenbaum, *The Gothic Imagination: Expansion in Gothic Literature and Art*, (East Brunswick, NJ: Associated University Presses, 1982), 145.

Noble Werewolves or Native Shape-Shifters?

KRISTIAN JENSEN

> It is against everything we stand for to take a human life. Making an exception to that code is a bleak thing. We will all mourn for what we do tonight.[1]

So laments Sam Uley, Alpha leader of the Quileute guardian wolves, as he orders his pack to destroy Bella and the dangerous being she carries inside her. The wolf-men of La Push live by a simple code: protect the tribe at all costs. Though Bella, the Cullens, and even some Quileute refer to these wolf guardians as "werewolves," as represented in the narrative they are technically shape-shifters. In *Breaking Dawn* Aro, the supreme leader of the Volturi, explains to his gathered vampire legion (and to the reader) that the Quileute ability to shape-shift into wolves was purely by chance; they pass on their shape-shifting ability to each new Quileute generation; and there exists no kinship between them and actual werewolves—the "Children of the Moon."[2] While the Quileute exhibit some traits characteristic of typical werewolf legends harkening back to medieval Eastern Europe, Meyer's shape-shifters are distinct from werewolves in several ways. These can mainly be attributed to her incorporation of Indian material; an examination of Quileute and other Northwest Coast American Indian legends reveals that Meyer conducted some limited research to authenticate her Quileute characters. These characters and myths are, however, more a product of her imagination and of the romantic and patronizing Western stereotype of the "Noble Savage," than of a faithful attempt to represent the Quileute culture.

Nevertheless, as she blends some attributes of the Western werewolf with aspects of the Quileute shape-shifter, Stephenie Meyer forms beings uniquely her own. Unlike the "Children of the Moon"[3] or European and Eurasian werewolves, Meyer's Quileute shape-shifters change without regard to the lunar cycle, control their transformations over time, and function to protect, rather than harm, humans. But like traditional werewolves, anger can trigger their transformation; they have the wolf's voracious appetite for raw flesh, but not that of humans; and they are virile, passionate beings.

Meyer not only fuses shape-shifter and werewolf lore, she also mingles two kinds of werewolf tales. Sarah Higley distinguishes between two main types of traditional werewolf legends: those based on the positive traits of the pack including craftiness and comradery, and those influenced by the Omega wolf, the outcast and anti-social loner who breaks from the pack.[4] These two types serve different literary or folklore functions: pack werewolves represent a respect for the wolf's ferocity and martial ability, while depiction of the lone-wolf Omega, more typical of werewolf legends since the Renaissance, expresses loathing toward the violent outsider or outlaw. The Quileute pack, as headed by Sam Uley, matches more closely the first type of werewolf. When Jacob Black breaks from the pack, however, he becomes the Omega wolf; later, when Seth and Leah Clearwater join him, he earns the status of Alpha leader of his new pack.

According to Higley, werewolves themselves can also be divided into two distinct types: the "constitutional," a man who completely transforms into a beast, and the "sympathetic," a shape-shifter who maintains human perceptions and thinking when transformed. Meyer's shape-shifters certainly belong to the "sympathetic" category, as we observe when Bella first sees Jacob transformed and peers into his perceptive, human-like eyes. Though they are not cursed like a "sympathetic" werewolf, Jacob and some of the other Quileute boys initially perceive their new state as an unwanted affliction. They cannot control their transformations at first, and even though he acquires these powers from several generations before him, Jacob views his new condition more as a curse—a view common in werewolf lore—than as an inherited gift.

Not only are Meyer's wolf-men—or Noble Werewolves as I view them—"sympathetic," but they also embody the condescending image of the Noble Savage. This stereotype of indigenous peoples has roots in the philosophy of seventeenth and eighteenth-century Europeans like Bartholome de las Casas, Michel de Montaigne, Jean Jacques-Rousseau and John Dryden, though only Dryden, who coined the term, used it explicitly. In contrast to the hostile and vicious images of indigenous people propagated since the European "discovery," this new conception in its variations essentially depicted American Indians as simple people, untainted by civilization, beneficent in nature, and morally upright in their "wild" state. In addition to having the Quileute shape-shifters similarly retain their "wild" nature, Meyer has conflated the Noble Savage myth with Quileute guardian spirit mythology, which I explore in the next two sections of this essay. While Western werewolves typically prey on humans, Meyer's creatures are in harmony with the human society that they exist to serve, like the Noble Savage of Caucasian fancy.

Meyer collapses the distinctions between werewolves, shape-shifters and lycanthropes through her inventive, though problematic, Quileute characters.

S.K. Robisch defines these three imaginative specters as three distinct types of creatures.[5] Shape-shifters transform through a collective social ritual, and their transformation is both "quest-oriented" and a means of community bonding. There are benevolent shape-shifters like the Northwest indigenous peoples' guardian spirits and wicked ones like the Navajo skin-walkers who embody a sinister transformation conjured by sorcerers. The benevolent shape-shifter eventually reaches an epiphany of the spiritual, non-human aspect of himself or herself. While not reaching an epiphany, Jacob, the other Quileute boys and Leah Clearwater eventually accept their wolf-selves. Werewolves, by contrast, are monsters of Western imagination: half-human, half-beast hybrids. They typically receive their affliction through another werewolf's bite, and anger or fear most often triggers their uncontrollable transformations. Lycanthropes, in contrast, are people who possess a psychotically pathological conception of themselves as werewolves. In fiction and actual documented cases from medieval times to the present, lycanthropes typically exhibit a clinically abnormal, id-driven association with wolves. Meyer's Quileute shape-shifters are a new creation: like the European werewolves they partially retain their humanity, and they exhibit the traits of mythical shape-shifters or guardian spirits, but they also display the mental afflictions of the lycanthrope. A closer look at Quileute and nearby indigenous peoples' shape-shifter rituals and ceremonies reveals how Meyer appropriates some American Indian beliefs, but in a manner that promotes the Noble Savage idea.

Northwest Coast Wolf Society Rituals and Guardian Spirits

Since Meyer loosely bases her Quileute characters on the actual Northwest Coast American Indians of that name, an overview of some Quileute customs will display how she has suited these to her fiction. The Quileute nation, numbering approximately 750 people, lives on the coastal La Push Reservation, about one square mile in size, roughly twelve miles west of Forks, Washington. These people share cultural characteristics with other Northwest Coast nations that include the Tlingit, Haida, Tsimshian, Kwakiutl, Nootka, Northern Wakashan, and the Bella people, and with nearby Coastal Salish groups such as the Makah, Hoh and Quinault.[6] Nevertheless, they are a distinct people with a language unrelated to that of any other people except for the Chimacum, who died at the hands of the Suquamish, led by Chief Seattle, in the 1860s.[7] Before the arrival of white settlers, the Quileute nation had some of the fiercest warriors in the area, and they provided perhaps the greatest resistance to early Russian and American explorers; archaeological and ethnographic evidence suggests that at one point they dominated the entire north Olympic Mountains region.[8]

In the past they subsisted primarily on whaling, fishing and seal hunting, but now they rely predominantly on a combination of fishing and tourism.

Meyer acknowledges that she chose Forks as the primary setting of her series because it is the rainiest, dimmest place in America, but serendipitously it is located in the center of a region with a long history of indigenous shape-shifting wolf mythology. In her website interviews, she acknowledges that the proximity of Forks to La Push was incidental, but explains that her great interest in Native American history led her to study Quileute history and culture.[9] *Twilight* initially focused entirely on the romance between Edward and Bella, and Meyer developed her shape-shifting characters in the sequels, at her editor's request, in order to add cultural complexity to the romance and potential for further volumes.

Although wolves were important animals in myth and ritual throughout the Northwestern region, Meyer's stumbling specifically upon the Quileute people was fortunate, offering a unique source to supplement her werewolf theme because of their legends, their Wolf Society and their Wolf Dance rituals. Also known as the Tlokwali or "Black Face," the Wolf Society was an elite group of warriors, and one of several Quileute dance societies which included the Whaler's, Elk Hunter's, Fishermen's and Shaman's societies.[10] Meyer ignores the fact that the Whaler's Society, not the Wolf, was traditionally the most prestigious and influential for the Quileute, as that tradition does not serve the purposes of her narrative.

Though in her series Meyer does not examine cultural issues irrelevant to her story, and she is vague in her interviews about the extent of her research into Quileute history and culture, certain scenes indicate Meyer's loose adaptation of Wolf Society rituals. In *New Moon* Jacob Black at first worries about other Quileute boys' unorthodox, cultish behavior. He tells Bella that it's as if Sam Uley has started a "gang" and the other boys have become his "followers" or "disciples," words that suggest a cult; Leah Clearwater also mentions that the boys call themselves "protectors."[11] If this were an actual Quileute cult, the Wolf Society is certainly the one they would have joined; the Quileute considered Wolf Society members to be the protectors of the tribe, so the boys' status as tribal guardians demonstrates that Meyer has applied some of what she learned about the Quileute traditions.

Meyer's series also indirectly reflects the physically intense aspect of the Wolf Society rituals, which functioned primarily to prepare the young warrior for the battlefield.[12] The initiation ceremony consisted of six days of dancing, fasting and performing other rituals, and at the climax, the young initiate ceremonially gouged himself with arrows, knives or harpoons in the back, arms, legs and/or upper lip. This self-flagellation demonstrated the novitiate's ferocity and strength, and it indicated his readiness to enter the Wolf Society. In the *Twilight* series, we often see such tolerance for pain among the young Quileute warriors. Jacob and Paul tear at each other fiercely when Bella first sees Jacob turn; Seth allows Victoria's newborn vampire lover to maul him in a feint to overthrow him; and Jacob endures vampire Bella's lashing after she discovers he has imprinted on her child Renessme.

The symbolic transformation that occurs during the Wolf Dance of the Nootka peoples, who include the Makah and southern Vancouver Island nations, also has some parallels with the Quileute transformations in *New Moon*. This suggests that Meyer researched beyond Quileute history and culture to incorporate other groups' customs into her story as well. Although the Nootka are a distinct people from the Quileute, with an unrelated language and separate history, anthropologists class them as within the larger Northwest Coast regional culture group, and they share some similar rituals and mythology. In the Nootka Wolf Dance rituals, the youths would be symbolically kidnapped by Wolf Society adults dressed as wolves and held captive for four to five days.[13] Alpha leader Sam Uley similarly coerces Quil, Paul, Jacob and other Quileute youths to leave their childhood friends and their innocence for his cult. While the real Nootka initiates would don wolf-skin jackets after their coming-of-age rites, the analogous act of the fictional Quileute was to cut their hair short after their transformations begin. According to Nootka beliefs, dead warriors become reincarnated into the world as wolves; thus, Nootka Wolf Society members wore wolf-skins to indicate their transformation. For many native peoples hair was a symbolic source of identity, and the cutting of their hair by an enemy indicated that they had lost their tribal status.[14] In the Western imagination long hair for men has also been associated with indigenous identity, thus the shortened hair of Jacob and the other Quileute boys' trimmed hair symbolizes an alienation from their indigenous selves that coincides with an adaptation to their wolf-selves. As newly initiated shape-shifters, the boys have begun to drift from their human selves. After the Nootka Wolf Ritual, the young initiates would be recovered, "tamed," and returned to "human society,"[15] and Meyer's Quileute elders similarly separate Jacob and the other Quileute boys from Bella and the people of Forks for a short period. They allow Bella back into the circle only after she forces the tribal secret from them.

Although Meyer presents the Quileute people positively throughout the series—for example, the Blacks are friends with Bella's family, and Jacob and Bella's interracial friendship is not considered taboo—Meyer's approach to incorporating Quileute warrior rites reveals her likely unconscious application of the Noble Savage stereotype. Before the shift in their beliefs caused by the turn-of-the-century Shaker religious movement, the Quileute warrior initiation ceremony, called Klukwalle-Kwat, functioned to connect the novice warrior with his Klukwalle-Tsit, or warrior spirit, an ally that he would bear into war. Wolves appropriately embody the warrior spirit because in nature these animals are courageous, free-roaming, and strategic fighters.[16] In *Breaking Dawn*, when Jacob challenges the Alpha, Sam Uley, he harnesses his warrior spirit; as he explains, "The primitive core of my wolf-self tensed for the battle of supremacy."[17] The word "primitive" here shows Meyer's subtle imposition of the Noble Savage myth onto her Quileute shape-shifters; at the heart of the Noble Savage stereotype is the belief that indigenous peoples represent an early or "primitive" stage of human social development. Western philosophers, writers and social-scientists from the seventeenth century to the twentieth century—and still today as the popularity of the recent film *Avatar* attests, though this is a subject for another essay—believed that due to their early developmental social state, indigenous peoples were closer to the animalistic side of human nature than "civilized" people, the latter having evolved from their primal selves. Ceremonies and rituals like those of the Wolf Society may have led Western thinkers to this conclusion, but they often misunderstood the purposes and meanings of these rituals.

Although Meyer's apparent familiarity with Quileute Wolf Society rituals is displayed in the explosive trembling of Jacob and other shape-shifters just before they turn, she changes a real-life symbolic transformation ritual into a magical shape-shifting rite of passage. During the real Quileute rituals the warriors would make wolf-like howls and whistles, and would wear wolf masks or actual wolf skulls. Four warriors would sing, one shaking a rattle shaped as the powerful trickster Raven, and they would circle the initiate who would shake violently, growl and then circle the fire, hunkered down in a wolf-like walk. At this point, the new warrior would symbolically become the wolf, and let the wolf spirit overtake him.[18] In Meyer's series, the Quileute boys shake before shifting only when they are young changelings, freshly initiated into their new abilities and about to become supernatural tribal protectors: noble werewolves.

The ceremonial masks of Northwest Coast peoples were essential for channeling the wolf spirit, and Meyer has not lost sight of this. However, while Quileute masks were traditionally intended to invoke the wolf, Meyer's masks serve instead to repress the human, as when Jacob lets his animal-side take over. Usually carved of wood, the masks represented a projection of the wolf-self—that is, the "ghostly" wolf of human imagination—rather than wolves as they actually exist. The ritual mask functions in two primary ways: first, "to provide intellectual and spiritual insight through role-playing, mimicry and shape-shifting," and second, to serve as a means of escaping "reality."[19] "Transcendence" occurs in the belief that "each mask represents at least two personae and a boundary separating them, the permeability of which makes poetry, shapes narrative."[20] Meyer gives this masking a metaphorical resonance. After Jacob starts shape-shifting, Bella observes that he "masks" his true feelings. He becomes less and less comfortable with complex human emotions like his frustration at the irrevocable changes he experiences and the pain caused by Bella's continual rejections, so he hides his vulnerabilities with wolfish grins. While ritually the mask was a catalyst for the shape-shifting Kwukwalle members of the tribe, Jacob's masking of his emotions serves as a symptom of his shape-shifting trauma. Ironically, he becomes most at ease when in his wolf form, and the "mask" helps him hold his human form steady.

Meyer's Quileute perform other rituals consistent with traditional Quileute beliefs, but also greatly shaped by her imagination as she adapts Quileute stories to suit her narrative's needs. For example, one reason the Whaler's Society was so revered by the Quileute is that they believed in an innate connection between whales and wolves. According to the legends, the Quileute wolves transformed into whales after jumping into the sea, and the black and white coloring of both animals serves as evidence of this connection. In *New Moon*, the cliff diving by the Quileute youths and later by Bella indirectly mirrors this legend. In actual Quileute mythology, after jumping into the sea to escape the Wolf People, the trickster creator Kwattee struggles with a monstrous whale. Similarly, when Bella mindlessly re-enacts the Quileute cliff dive into the tumultuous water below, she barely evades the monster that the vampire Victoria resembles. Fortunately, the wolf-man Jacob saves her, rather than letting her be consumed by the Victoria-Leviathan.

Unlike Western werewolves, who transform uncontrollably or with the full moon, the mythical guardian spirits of Meyer's story shape-shift when they or other people are in danger. American Indians of the Olympic region and Puget Sound area traditionally believed in the power of guardian spirits who could be called upon to protect them from demonic spirits or other threats.[21] When they were teenagers, native youths in this region, and in others like the Southwest and the Eastern woodlands, would go on a ritual "Power Quest" or "Vision Quest" to discover their spirit animal. In the Olympic region, this quest consisted of five days alone in the wilderness with little or no food, and the goal was to summon a vision of one's protective animal. In the *Twilight* series, the Quileute boys unwillingly begin to transform without first departing on a Power Quest, and for a long time Jacob is uncomfortable in his new skin. When he realizes the futility of pursuing Bella, though, he embraces his "inner" wolf and roams the far north in isolation; in this way he enacts his own Power Quest and eventually embraces his wolf-self.

Quileute Legends and Meyer's Revisions

Though her story shows that Meyer conducted some research into traditional Quileute mythology, the legends Bella hears are mostly Meyer's fabrications or legends elaborated through her own imagination. When asked about the source of her Quileute origin story, Meyer admits, "The werewolves' back story is something that I made up. Now the part that's true is the Quileute tribe, in their old legends, is that a magician turned a wolf into a man and that's how the tribe began."[22] The "magician" she refers to is actually the Quileute shape-shifter creator, Kwatee. While for the most part Meyer invents Quileute legends to serve her narrative, an investigation into several of the region's myths about Kwatee reveals many tribal motifs that she may have, whether consciously or unconsciously, incorporated into the series. Since she is vague about her research, however, some speculation about which myths she read will be necessary.

In *Twilight*, for example, Jacob tells Bella that the Quileute people believe themselves to be descended from wolves. This supports the tradition that the trickster creator Kwati formed the first Quileute from two wolves he found at the sacred site of their origins.[23] According to one legend, in ancient times all elks were people. One day the elk people decided to live in the woods, and to avoid being devoured by the wolves they invited them to a gift-giving ceremony called the potlatch, at which they burned them all except for the two wolves that had been left behind to guard their home.[24] Perhaps, these are the two wolves Kwati finds in the Quileute origin story. In the legend of the Olympic Peninsula peoples' origins, Kwati creates the nearby Queets from the dead skin of his hands; the Hoh, or "Up-side-down" people, by turning them over to walk on their feet instead of their hands; and the Ozette people from two dogs. The source of Quileute strength and courage derives from their descent from the two wolves— warrior animals— that Kwati encounters. Another tale, "Kwattee and the Monster in Lake Quinault," tells of the "Animal People," giant beings who could talk before Kwattee created humans. These are the guardian spirits of Quileute beliefs, and Meyer has retained their imposing magnitude in her Quileute shape-shifters' enormous size. They are so big that the people of Forks mistake them for bears, another animal traditionally associated with hunting and battle prowess.

The detailed origin story that Bella hears in *Eclipse* is clearly a retelling of the story, "Q'wasti' and the Wolves."[25] In the 1950s, anthropologist Ella E. Clark collected another version of this tale entitled "How Kwattee Made the River and the Rocks" from Levin Coe, a Quileute elder probably in his 70s, who claimed as his spirit guide the 950-year-old spirit of Kwattee, the creator. Although Meyer acknowledges that she read the Quileute origin myth and that her version is mostly from her imagination, there are some close parallels between her origin story and some Quileute versions of the myth.[26] In one version Kwattee beheads the murderer Chief Wolf when he's asleep. When the wolf family seeks Chief Wolf, Kwattee beguiles them with a song in which he confesses to killing the Chief, and then he deftly escapes from Chief Wolf's lodge. The Wolves pursue him, but he slows them down by forming a mountain when he drops his comb and creating a river by spilling his hair oil; as they tackle these obstacles he evades them by taking his canoe into the sea, at which point they give up the chase. An older version has Q'wasti' (Kwattee) hubristically playing with the chief's head before escaping after trespassing in his house. Yet another version of the tale includes the humorous detail of the wolf door-guards—derogatively called "testicle-eaters"—who bite each other in the mouth as Q'wasti' breezes by them. The story serves to display Kwattee's trickster craftiness while it also shows the futility of trying to outfox him. It warns of the consequences for transgressions like murder or overstepping one's territory, depending on the version told.

Meyer's retelling of "Q'wasti' and the Wolves" is more elaborate than any of the original tales, and it explains the origins of Quileute shape-shifting. Although she claims her origin tale is almost entirely made-up, a side-by-side comparison shows some interesting parallels between her story and the original. In *Eclipse*, she replaces Kwattee with her trickster, Utlapa, and Taha Aki is her version of Chief Wolf. While the original Kwattee is a powerful creator, Utlapa is one of Taha Aki's powerful spirit warriors. The basic storylines are similar in two ways: in the original myth Kwattee murders and decapitates Chief Wolf and in Meyer's story Utlapa removes Chief Taha Aki from human form, and both stories dramatize the origins of the Quileute and their powers.

Nevertheless, Meyer's story greatly differs from "Q'wasti and the Wolves" because it centers on her themes of self-sacrifice and good triumphing over evil, themes not relevant to the original myth. Whereas Kwattee transgresses by invading Chief Wolf's household, Meyer's Utlapa greedily desires to expand the Quileute lands by conquering neighboring peoples. In a clever twist on Chief Wolf's decapitation, Meyer has Utlapa possess Taha Aki's body and cut his own body's throat, thereby leaving Taha Aki with no human body to inhabit. Exiled from humanity, Taha Aki enters the body of a great wolf, and in this way he becomes the Quileute chief. While originally Kwattee forms the first Quileute from two wolves, in Meyer's story Utlapa indirectly causes Taha Aki to become a wolf-man when the rightful chief avenges Utlapa's murder of the innocent spirit warrior, Yut. (As in Meyer's series, actual Quileute chiefs inherited their status and reigned for life.) In the Quileute origin story Kwattee evades capture from the wolf people, but Meyer's Taha Aki vanquishes Utlapa when he becomes the Great Wolf: the first wolf-man and his people's true leader.

Although it is unclear if Meyer read it or not, another shape-shifter tale by the Stz'uminous First Nation (formerly the Chemainus Nation) of Vancouver Island, British Colombia, called "Wolf Family" (Stuqeeye'), resonates profoundly with wolf-man lore. In Donna Klockars' version, Wolf-Man, a shape-shifter made by the Great Creator Ha'als, falls in love with and marries a human girl called X'pey.[27] Like Jacob, Wolf-Man experiences alienation from his human society and yearns for a reconnection with it. Wolf-Man's story explores the consequences of his affair with X'pey. He comes to her village in human form to court her, but she paints his back in a way that leaves a visible mark when he resumes wolf form — much as Jacob's distinctive brown fur identifies him — and he leaves the village before the Stz'uminous people recognize him as a shape-shifter. When X'pey has a litter of wolf children, the people banish her from the village, and in sadness she raises her wolf-cubs alone. She eventually discovers their shape-shifting ability, however, which leads to a happy ending: Wolf-Man rejoins her, the people accept her again since she can explain her cubs' parentage, and the wolf family live peacefully and prosperously afterward. The story provides an alternate, happier outcome for a romance like that of Jacob and Bella; Bella ultimately chooses her mate from another supernatural clan, the "Cold Ones."

Totemism, Territoriality, and Reconciling the Dual Self

While Meyer's Quileute shape-shifters embody the Noble Savage, the figure of primitive humanity untrammeled by civilization's vices, the Cullens are a post-human tribe that have repressed their bestial instinct, the vampiric bloodlust, to retain some semblance of their human core.[28] As the nomadic vampire Garrett puts it, "These strange golden-eyed ones deny their very natures."[29] Meyer's vampire and shape-shifter mythology reconstitutes the Enlightenment dialectic of the mentally advanced and providentially dominant Europeans, and the primitive, though pure and noble, indigenous man. This becomes evident in *Breaking Dawn* when Carlisle, the Cullen patriarch and voice of scientific authority, informs Jacob that vampires have twenty-five chromosomes, while Quileute shape-shifters have only twenty-four. Vampires inhabit the inevitable progress of humanity — the next rung on the evolutionary ladder; they are the ultimate predator of humans. While in real life chimpanzees have one pair of chromosomes less than humans, Meyer's Quileute shape-shifters have one pair less than vampires, and her humans have one pair less than shape-shifters. This genetic inequality implies an evolutionary ladder with humans at the bottom, shape-shifters one rung up physically and psychically, and the nearly invincible vampires mentally and bodily at the top. Carlisle explains, however, that rather than sharing the evolutionary nature of the vampires' leap forward, the Quileute shape-shifters' divergence from Homo Sapiens has a mystical origin, "Magical, almost."[30] As the descendants of guardian spirits, they have magically evolved as beneficent protectors of humans in sharp contrast to the vampire predators. Vampires represent the dominating "civilized" advancement of humans, whereas shape-shifters embody the mystical human past.

Along with these biological differences, Meyer's vampires and shape-shifters have rooted cultural differences that mirror those traditionally perceived between Caucasians and indigenous Americans. The binaries between Jacob and Edward represent these social differences; Jacob is passionate, full of warmth and life, and tribe/pack oriented, while Edward is cool-headed enough to restrain his vampiric lusts, icily undead, and individualistic. (Though the Cullens are family-oriented, they can separate from each other at any time for self-preservation). Shape-shifters are tribally bound and must adhere to the Alpha leader's command, while vampires have autonomy. Edward explains this succinctly to Sam Uley, when Sam is confounded by Alice's desertion of the Cullens: "You are bound differently than we are ... *We* still have our freewill."[31] His assertion proves wrong, however, as Jacob later chooses to leave the pack; nevertheless, Jacob's separation renders him a tribal outcast. The distinction between Meyer's werewolves and her vampires reverberates with the anthropological contrast of communally-oriented indigenous peoples and individual family-based "civilized" societies. The shape-shifters' telepathy is both the advantage and often the bane of this community centered orientation. The *Twilight* series vampires, with the exception of Edward, are not bound to other vampires' thoughts in the way that shape-shifters are, but nor do they have the same kind of shared knowledge or lack of secrecy that is common among small close-knit tribal communities.

Nevertheless, while the Cullens live as "civilized" individualistic vampires, they also act together as a tribal unit, so the Quileute and Cullens could alternatively be viewed as neighboring tribes, each with their own totem. Nineteenth and twentieth-century anthropologists like J.F. McLennan, Scot W. Robertson Smith, and Scot James Frazer first developed the complex and controversial concept of the totem, which derives from the Ojibwe (Anishinaabe) concept "doodem."[32] Though definitions vary, according to anthropologist A.A. Goldenweiser the basic characteristics of a totemic clan include religious worship of a particular animal, plant or geological entity; belief in descent from their totem; a taboo against killing the totem animal or plant; a clan name often derived from the totem; and the custom of exogamy (the marriage of a tribal member, most often a young woman, to someone outside the tribe in order to support inter-tribal relations). "Totem" alternatively refers to an individual's guardian spirit animal. In the early twentieth-century, anthropologists like Franz Boas, A.A. Goldenweiser and Claude Levi-Strauss challenged the totem idea as an illusion, because communities vary widely in their "totemic customs" and few groups exhibit all of these beliefs.

Despite her fabrications of Quileute mythology, Meyer's Quileute young men retain their basic warrior totemic identification: the Wolf. Though the taboo against killing wolves is not explicitly present in the text, her Quileute, like the real Quileute, do believe themselves descended from wolves and revere them. Furthermore, in *Eclipse* Jacob gives Bella a carved wolf figurine as a protective charm, perhaps Meyer's adaptation of actual Quileute ceremonial wolf-head wands or representations of the violent guardian spirit Tabale.[33] Although the totem often indicated a group identity as with the Quileute, the totem as an individual's spirit animal also bears some pertinence to the series.

Invoking one's guardian spirit or totem animal, as the fictional Quileute do, has its risks, especially the danger of alienation from one's human self. As previously mentioned, after Bella's continual rejections of his romantic advances, Jacob assumes his wolf-self for long periods of time and roams the far north. Even while doing so, he takes measures to preserve his connection to human society; tying his shorts to his hind leg is the most visible symbol of his desire to preserve his humanity and his civility. Torn clothing and nudity are common tropes in werewolf legends, most often indicating the vulnerability of a werewolf's human side and, especially for the Omega wolf, a removal from human society. In carrying his clothes with him, Jacob maintains a connection to his humanity even as he trots through the forest, and he is always ready to rejoin human civilization after resuming manhood.

Like the Quileute werewolves, however, the Cullens and other vampires also have their own totemic spirit animals, each reflective of their personality. In *Twilight*, Bella repeatedly refers to the roving band of Victoria, James and Laurent as cat-like. She also describes Victoria, in *Eclipse*, as a "lioness" or "jungle cat," an appropriate totem for her powerful and solitary hunting, in contrast to the coordinated pack hunting and warfare of the Quileute.[34] While Victoria is a lioness, Bella describes Edward when he hunts as a lion, an animal that reflects his power and stealth. She associates the gargantuan Emmett with another war-like totem animal, the bear. All of these totems indicate fierce hunting and fighting abilities, and only through tribally designated domains could these "vegetarian" vampires and benign shape-shifters live harmoniously alongside one another.

The Quileute and the Cullens have co-existed peacefully for over a hundred years because of a treaty enforcing their hunting and settlement boundaries. Coincidentally, the real Quileute have been in treaty with Americans since the mid-nineteenth century. A brief look at Quileute history shows some echoes in Meyer's series. American settlers violated their treaty with the Quileute by squatting on their lands, taking over space; the Cullens also break their treaty with the Quileute, but they do so by transforming Bella into a vampire, taking over a person. Though it is likely an unconscious association by Meyer, the treaty violation caused by the American settlers' insatiable greed for land parallels the Cullen-Quileute pact breach caused by the creation of a new vampire feared to have an insatiable thirst for blood.

When Sam Uley's pack assaults the Cullens to punish them for the broken treaty and to destroy the being that Bella carries in her womb, Jacob's warning to Edward glaringly reveals Meyer's Noble Savage transposition on the Quileute shape-shifters. As he circles the Cullen stronghold in a protective perimeter, Jacob calls out, "circle the wagons, bloodsucker."[35] This metaphor implicitly associates the Cullens with nineteenth-century white pioneers, and the Quileute pack with "hostile Indians" attacking their settlement. Jacob, Leah and Seth act as American Indian allies with the Cullens in this scenario, with Jacob in particular becoming his tribe's intermediary between vampire and shape-shifter, white settler and Noble Savage.

By leaving the Quileute pack to protect Bella, Jacob plays the role of an assimilating Native American. He enters a state of limbo—no longer part of the pack, but also not a Cullen. This state echoes that of nineteenth and twentieth-century American Indian children, who were often caught between assimilating to mainstream white American society and adhering to their own people's traditional beliefs and customs. Most often these children returned to their people, but though most did not abandon their traditional beliefs completely, they almost never belonged as fully to the community as they did before they left. Many others never returned, abandoning their people and their beliefs, and assimilating to white culture. Jacob decides to leave the pack and join the Cullens, but like those assimilated kids of the past, he never completely surrenders his tribal identity.

When Jacob imprints on Bella's daughter Renesseme, however, he unwittingly forges an eventual alliance between the Quileute and Cullen clans. Meyer's version of imprinting is an ironic reversal of a natural phenomenon. She explains in an interview that imprinting derives from two sources: the natural bond of parents and their offspring and the impenetrable, irrevocable bond of dragons and their riders in Anne McCaffrey's *Dragonriders of Pern* fantasy books.[36] In reality, many young animals, such as wolf pups, imprint on their parents immediately after they are born, but the Quileute shape-shifters may imprint on mates of any age, even newborns. Furthermore, their imprinting is an unbreakable, supernatural bond that more closely resembles the connection between an individual and their guardian spirit—like McCaffrey's dragon-human bond—than that of child and parent. The new alliance that Jacob's imprinting causes, stronger than the former Quileute-Cullen treaty, unites the two groups into one. The most obligatory pack rule of the Quileute is to protect the subject of one of their member's imprinting, this rule even trumping the baby Remesseme's half-vampire status, so as a result both Sam and Jacob's packs, also allied in the end, now become the Cullens' protectors as well. The bond between Jacob and Renesseme is unbreakable, like that between the spirit man, Taha Aki, and his self-sacrificing human wife; although Renesseme is only a child—an unnaturally quickly aging child who will soon reach full maturity and stop aging at that point—Jacob can age as slowly as he wills, so that perhaps they will one day develop a matrimonial bond.

Ultimately the line between the human-self and animal-self fades for Jacob. Being a shape-shifter is about reconciling two selves, the animal and the human, about bringing euphony out of this dualism. When Jacob breaks from Sam's pack and unintentionally starts a new one with himself as Alpha when Leah and Seth choose to become his pack followers, he ponders, "I'd lived all-wolf for long enough that I knew how to be the animal completely, to see his way and think his way. I let the practical instincts take over...."[37] Rather than the schizophrenic schism of identity of the European and Euro-American werewolf, as a shape-shifter in tune with his protective spirit Jacob has merged both wolf and human selves into a harmonious whole while still being aware of his dual identity. One is reminded of the famous dream told by the ancient Chinese Taoist philosopher, Chuang Tzu:

> Once I, Chuang Tzu, dreamed I was a butterfly and was happy as a butterfly. I was conscious that I was quite pleased with myself, but I did not know that I was Tzu. Suddenly I awoke, and there was I, visibly Tzu. I do not know whether it was Tzu dreaming that he was a butterfly or the butterfly dreaming that he was Tzu. Between Tzu and the butterfly there must be some distinction. This is called the transformation of things.[38]

Jacob, like Tzu, is no longer purely human, nor has his mythical wolf-self entirely taken possession. He is neither and both simultaneously—a Noble Werewolf, a paradox, a shape-shifter.

Notes

1. Stephenie Meyer, *Breaking Dawn* (New York: Little, Brown and Company, 2008), 202.

2. Ibid., 705. The preferred usage for the plural of Quileute remains "Quileute."

3. Meyer may have borrowed the term "Children of the Moon" from the *Children of the Moon* series by young adult fiction writer, Lucy Monroe.

4. Sarah Higley, "Finding the Man Under the Skin: Identity, Monstrosity, Expulsion, and the Werewolf," in *The Shadow-Walkers" Jacob Grimm's Mythology of the Monstrous*, ed. Tom Shippey (Tempe: Arizona Center for Medieval and Renaissance Studies, 2005), 335–378. See also Stephen Glosecki's discussion of lupine shape-shifting in his article "Wolf" in *Medieval Folklore: An Encyclopedia of Myths, Legends, Tales, Beliefs, and Customs*, ed. Carl Lindahl, John McNamara, and John Lindow, Vol. 2 (Oxford: Oxford University Press, 2002), 1057–1061.

5. S.K. Robisch, *Wolves and the Wolf Myth in American Literature* (Reno: University of Nevada Press, 2009), 208.

6. Carol Sheehan, "The Northwest Coast," *Native American Myths and Legends* (New York: Smithmark Publishers Inc., 1994), 82–95.

7. Seattle is an anglicized version of the Duwaish name "Si'ahl." His name has also been spelled Sealth, Seathle, Seathl, and See-ahth, but the most common version is Seattle, as in the city named after him (see http://en.wikipedia.org/wiki/Chief_Seattle).

8. Jay Powell and Vickie Jensen, *Quileute: An Introduction to the Indians of La Push* (Seattle: University of Washington Press, 1976), 39–41.

9. "TheTwilightSaga.com's Q and A with Stephenie," *The Official Website of Stephenie Meyer*, http://www.stepheniemeyer.com.

10. George A. Pettit, "The Quileute of La Push: 1775–1945," *Anthropological Records*, 14 (Berkeley: University of California Press, 1960), 15–16.

11. Stephenie Meyer, *New Moon* (New York: Little, Brown and Company, 2006), 173 and 174.

12. In this essay, I will focus on Quileute and Northwest Coast rituals and beliefs of the past as defined by anthropologists, since Meyer adapts their traditional beliefs rather than their contemporary ones.

13. Norman Bancroft-Hunt and Werner Forman, *People of the Totem: the Indians of the Pacific Northwest* (New York: G. P. Putnam's Sons, 1979), 122–'124.

14. For example, see the testimony of nineteenth-century Lakota writer Luther Standing Bear on the traumatic assimilative process of cutting the hair of American Indian boarding school students in his autobiography, *My Indian Boyhood*.

15. Alan D. McMillan, *Since the Time of the Transformers: the Ancient Heritage of the Nuu-*

chah-nulth, Ditidaht, and Makah (Vancouver: University of British Colombia Press, 1999), 22–23.

16. Alice Henson Ernst, *The Wolf Ritual of the Northwest Coast* (Eugene: University of Oregon Press, 1952), 46–62.

17. Meyer, *Breaking Dawn*, 211.

18. Ernst, 46–62.

19. S.K. Robisch offers a detailed examination of the various wolf dance rituals of the Northwest Coast tribes including the Quileute, Makah, Kwakiutl, Haida and Nootka in Robisch, 236–237.

20. Ibid., 246.

21. Ella E. Clark, *Indian Legends of the Pacific Northwest* (Berkeley: University of California Press, 1953), 179–181.

22. "Stephaniesay's Journal," *LiveJournal*, http://stepheniesays.livejournal.com/3221.html#q5.

23. The name of the trickster Kwati is alternatively spelled Kwattee or Q'wasti.'

24. Manuel Andrade and Leo Frachtenberg, eds, *Quileute Texts* (New York: Columbia University Press, 1931), 120–121.

25. Several versions of this tale exist. Andrade and Frachtenberg include two different versions in *Quileute Texts* (see note 24).

26. "TheTwilightSaga.com's Q and A with Stephenie."

27. Donna Klockars, *Wolf Family* (Chemanius Tribal Council, Nanaimo, B.C. Pacific Edge Publishing Ltd., 1992).

28. For an explanation of posthumanism see Cary Wolfe, *What is Posthumanism?* (Minneapolis: University of Minneapolis Press, 2010) and Donna Haraway, *When Species Meet* (Minneapolis: University of Minneapolis Press, 2008).

29. Meyer, *Breaking Dawn*, 717.

30. Ibid., 237.

31. Ibid., 559.

32. For a comprehensive history of totemism, see Robert Alun Jones, *The Secret of the Totem: Religion and Society from McLennan to Freud* (New York: Colombia University Press, 2005).

33. For photos and further explanation of tabale see Powell and Jensen (note 8).

34 Meyer, *Eclipse*, 396 and 542.

35. Meyer, *Breaking Dawn*, 216.

36 "TheTwilightSaga.com's Q and A with Stephenie."

37. Meyer, *Breaking Dawn*, 314.

38. Chuang Tzu: *The Next Voice*, Http://www.chebucto.ns.ca/Philosophy/Taichi/chuang.html.

Abstinence, American-Style

ANN V. BLISS

The cover of *Twilight*, the first book in Stephenie Meyer's extraordinarily popular vampire series, shows a pair of pale, youthful hands cradling an excessively red apple, as if tempting the reader to participate in the prohibited practices described within. This particular forbidden fruit, though, remains untasted until the end of the series, an emblem of the layers of peculiarly American abstinence portrayed in the novels. The concept of abstinence underlies a number of stereotypical American mores that resonate throughout U.S. history. In particular, Puritanical moral values and anti-alcohol temperance movements contribute to the culture of the vampire community central to the novels. These values include not just abstaining from drinking human blood and engaging in pre-marital sex, but also from becoming a vampire, a sexualized act given its penetration imagery, and they are manifested in the relationship between the vampire patriarch, Carlisle Cullen, and his son, Edward, the first of Carlisle's vampire creations and the novels' male protagonist. Although Edward is the central male character of the series, Carlisle is its moral center, establishing the tenets of abstinence of all kinds in his vampire family. He passes these morals on to Edward, who becomes the new repository of conservative American practices. Until the end of the fourth book, *Breaking Dawn,* the vampire Cullen family refuses to embrace twenty-first century American sensibilities; instead they try to preserve a mythical U.S. culture of the past. This version of America, though, can only exist in isolation. It, like the Cullens, can never fully integrate into contemporary U.S. culture.

While the fundamental manifestation of abstinence in the *Twilight* series is the Cullen family's refusal to drink human blood, references to abstinence resonate throughout Edward's relationship with Bella. Rooted in a long history of abstinence that spread across much of the U.S., Edward's moral values reflect those of proponents of the nineteenth-century temperance movement. These movements did not confine their abstinence to just avoiding alcohol; in an attempt to attain Christian purity, they advocated abjuring from such activities as eating meat, drinking coffee and tea, and sleeping excessively. Jessica Warner sees America's commitment to abstinence as "a function of [its] commitment to an idiosyncratic and especially demanding strain of evangelical Protestantism."[1] Reflecting their historical roots, many twenty-first century evangelicals "are teetotalers, few use illicit drugs. Almost all continue to believe in premarital chastity."[2] While Edward's almost martyr-like self-control when he first encounters Bella is predicated on his vampiric desire for her blood, like a nineteenth-century temperance adherent he includes additional cravings in his personal inventory of prohibited behavior. Edward is tempted by layers of desire: he needs first to resist Bella's blood, then his sexual attraction to her, and finally her insistence that he turn her into a vampire. At the same time, he is compelled to protect her.

While Edward's persistent abstinence might seem martyr-like, abstinence confers its own kind of reward. Warner sees one attraction of abstinence being "its capacity to redefine pleasure in more exalted terms."[3] Abstainers "deny one pleasure in order to make room for one that is bigger and better.... People give up something tangible and short term for something ineffable and long term."[4] Edward embodies this concept; the exquisite pleasure he would get from drinking Bella's blood would be fleeting. Consuming Bella's blood is a never-to-be-repeated experience, whereas if he abstains from that drink, he can enjoy the somewhat masochistic pain he experiences when breathing her scent, as well as the erotic pleasure of touching only her face and hands. The need for sexual abstention, in part, stems from his belief that his extraordinary strength will result in him inadvertently harming, or even killing, Bella if he should indulge in any activity more vigorous than touching, or, later, kissing and embracing.

Edward's ability to resist Bella stems mostly from the group support of his vampire family, whose moral stance is established by Carlisle Cullen, the group's patriarch. Those who choose to abstain find that being accountable to a group is central to successful abstention. Warner suggests that abstainers enjoy "the sense of community it confers on those who make it a pillar of their lifestyle."[5] This sense of community is so highly developed in the Cullens that they have become a quasi-biological family in which the biological act of reproduction has been replaced by a male generative act of vampire creation.[6] The need for community fills the human need to belong. The Cullen family, as guided by the patriarch Carlisle, appears to replicate the beliefs, values and practices of the nineteenth-century abstinence movement and this behavior alienates them from vampire culture as much as their being vampires isolates them from fully participating in conventional contemporary society.[7]

Abstinence Movements in the U.S.

The U.S. has a long history of abstinence that reflects its equally long history of Christian evangelicalism. In her extensive study of abstinence, Jessica

Warner defines the practice as "a principled and unerring refusal to engage in a particular activity." For one who abstains, "if something is problematic on some occasions, then it is problematic on *all* occasions. Anything short of total victory is a form of defeat."[8] Jamie L. Mullaney defines abstinence as "not mere avoidance; instead, it entails a voluntary refusal to perform acts one can and is expected to do."[9] The Cullens' avoidance of human blood, then, clearly fits these definitions of abstinence. Indeed, any definition of "vampire" is inevitably going to include the consumption of human blood as a central identifying characteristic.[10]

The kind of abstinence practiced by the Cullens is quintessentially American. Warner links the beginning of the temperance movement to two significant political and religious movements: the shift from elite political control to a more populist democracy and the rise of evangelicalism with the Second Great Awakening.[11] However, Americans were not always so morally rigid. From the eighteenth century to the mid-nineteenth century, alcohol consumption increased significantly, as did tobacco use and excessive food consumption.[12] The mid-nineteenth century saw a shift in American attitudes towards excess consumption of almost anything, but especially alcohol, reflecting the moral values of evangelical Christianity in particular. Abstinence lost its "elitist trappings and became the virtue of the many."[13] Consequently, "moderation went from being a virtue to a vice."[14] The move from moderation to abstinence was reinforced in 1836 when the American Temperance Society became the American Temperance Union and its middle-class male leaders signed a teetotal pledge. For many of these men, committing to such a promise was not a sacrifice as few of those who renounced drink drank anyway, thus their lives were not dramatically changed by signing the teetotal pledge. However, the movement in general began to shift away from saving those who did not yet drink to saving those whose lives were already contaminated.[15]

Abstinence from consuming alcohol moved to a more general health reform in the mid 1800s as its practitioners began to abstain from a number of food and drinks deemed unhealthy. The goal of this extended temperance movement, according to Warner, "was to achieve purity on all fronts—physical, mental and sexual";[16] consequently, the health movement's relatively short-lived success was predicated not only on eliminating the consumption of alcohol, but also on controlling both sexual desires perceived as unhealthy (i.e. non-procreative sexual activity) and the consumption of animal products in order to achieve the movement's prime goal of alleviating the suffering of all people.[17] Lust was associated with eating meat, so meat became "morally objectionable" and disease became "a sin," brought on by the lifestyle choices of the individual; so one ought, therefore, to be able to control and overcome both.[18] The health movement extended from abstaining from perceived unhealthy foods to abstaining from "masturbation and sexual fantasies."[19]

The extreme asceticism of Carlisle Cullen's strictures on behavior mimics the dictates of the American health movement of the mid-nineteenth century. Carlisle does not only expect his family to refrain from consuming human blood, he also expects them to follow a moral code that appears to owe much to these nineteenth-century values. Edward's sexual restraint towards Bella reflects Carlisle's ethical standards.[20] Because Edward is doubly tempted by Bella, achieving these standards is more demanding for Edward than for his vampire siblings; he must resist drinking Bella's blood and also resist the sexual allure of her body. However, he is assisted in his goals by living with like-minded vampires, and this community-supported abstinence parallels nineteenth-century proponents of the health movement who believed that stimulants, including alcohol, "excited sexual desire."[21] Such practitioners of almost total (ascetic) abstinence fared best in communes of like-minded abstainers, much like that of the Cullens. Those who practiced broadly-defined abstinence considered the evils of "tobacco, alcohol and lust" virtually indistinguishable.[22]

Contemporary abstinence movements reflect more the individual's construction of identity than the accepted lifestyle of a particular social group. As Mullaney notes, abstinence within one of these nineteenth-century groups was no longer voluntary, but a requirement of group membership (much as refraining from expected vampire behavior is required by Carlisle of all the Cullens).[23] Twentieth- and twenty-first-century abstinence has become more a choice of a particular kind of abstaining (such as vegetarianism or not smoking, as well as belonging to groups such as Alcoholics Anonymous). Consequently, Mullaney sees contemporary abstinence as a "means of achieving a relatively high degree of identity control at a minimal cost."[24] For Warner, though, abstinence as practiced today has become "a protest against change rather than a force for it."[25]

One particular aspect of contemporary abstinence that relies in part on nineteenth-century abstinence values while situating itself firmly in twenty-first century culture is the evangelical Christian purity movement. This movement, which became prominent at the end of the twentieth century, promotes an abstinence-only approach to premarital sex. The movement was successful enough that in 1996 a sweeping welfare-reform law included funding for abstinence-only sex education in schools.[26] In 2000, government funding was made available to state and local organizations through the Community Based Abstinence Education program; much of this funding is received by Christian faith-based organizations.[27] Developing alongside these government-sanctioned programs, a number of evangelical Christian organizations promote abstinence through such programs as "True Love Waits" and "Silver Ring Thing" which require participants to sign a virginity pledge that echoes the abstinence pledge of early American temperance movements.[28] Unlike the early temperance movements, though, these programs are aimed at young women, from pre-pubescence through early adulthood. Edward's insistence on waiting for marriage before entering into a sexual relationship with Bella reflects nineteenth-century temperance values while referencing a twenty-first-century behavioral trend. While contemporary purity movements are invariably addressed to young women, the movement is increasingly encouraging participation from young men.[29]

Reading Abstinence in the Twilight *Series*

While it might seem unusual for characters in a twenty-first-century novel to follow nineteenth-century behavioral strictures, Stephenie Meyer's Mormon background provides a clue to understanding the centrality of morals that might otherwise be considered outdated. Established in the mid nineteenth-century, the Church of Latter-day Saints developed in the same geographic New England region where early temperance societies flourished.[30] Indeed, the Church Articles of Faith include the beliefs of "being honest, true, chaste, benevolent, virtuous, and in doing good to all men," and included in the revelations of Joseph Smith, founder of the Church of Latter-day Saints, is the edict known by the Church as "The Word of Wisdom," imparted to Smith in 1833.[31] This particular revelation instructs church followers "to eat healthy foods and avoid harmful substances, including alcohol, tobacco, tea, coffee, and harmful or habit-forming drugs."[32] Given the popularity of the American Health Movement during the same time period and in the same geographic location in which the Church of Latter-day Saints was evolving, it seems reasonable to suggest that the particularly American religion of Mormonism would reflect the values of the various American temperance movements. Meyer, as a professing and practicing Mormon, would be inculcated in such values. That her characters act out these values indicates the wide-spread influence of principles that have influenced American identity since the mid nineteenth-century.

The American Temperance Society, established in 1826, believed that "if a man wishes to have good done, to do it himself ... and to do it *now*."[33] Early temperance advocates refused to believe that "nothing could be done" about intemperance, while at the same time seeing a need to "protect the temperate few from the intemperate many."[34] This philosophy helps to explain Carlisle's actions and way of life, which he passes on to Edward. Just as early voluntary temperance societies promoted abstinence as a choice, the Cullens also consider the practice of self-denial a choice, and one that comes with associated risks. The risk from "the intemperate many" within the *Twilight* world is twofold. The Cullens are at risk of attack from vampires such as James (in *Twilight*) who do not share the Cullen belief in abstinence. At the same time, the larger community is at risk from these same vampires. Consequently, the Cullen's physical isolation from human and vampire communities protects both Cullens and humans alike.

Carlisle's high moral standards stem from his upbringing as the son of an Anglican pastor who actively sought to eliminate evil.[35] Therefore, being a Cullen comes with a certain innate responsibility. Having a family (albeit a non-biological, fictive family) is unusual for a vampire as conventionally portrayed in literature and film and, especially, in the world Meyer creates; Edward is willing to make the necessary sacrifices (by persistently abstaining from activities of which Carlisle does not approve) to remain in the family. This insistence on the centrality of family hearkens back to nineteenth-century mores. The idealized notion of the quintessential American family, according to family theorist Judith Stacey, consists of a "nuclear household unit made up of a married heterosexual couple and their biological or adopted children" and developed in the United States from nineteenth century industrialization which, Stacey notes, "turned men into breadwinners and women into homemakers."[36] Changes such as increasing divorce rates and falling birth rates during the latter years of the twentieth century have produced a cultural fear that this particular kind of American family is at risk, resulting in what Stacey calls "rampant nostalgia for the modern family system, or more precisely, for an idealized version of a 1950s Ozzie and Harriet image of the family, ... an increasingly potent ideological force in the United States." [37] When Edward contemplates fighting and possibly leaving the Cullen family over his pursuit of Bella, whom most Cullens consider an inconsequential human, he speculates about the possibility that he "might fight with [his] *family* over a human."[38] The emphasis on the word "family" indicates Edward's belief in its intrinsic value; the fallout from disrupting the family unit is greater than would result from sacrificing the life of one human, or, presumably, Edward's happiness.

Carlisle as Patriarch

The family as unit in these books is presented as inviolable, particularly because of Carlisle's patriarchal role. Carlisle's leadership is unquestioned, and while the younger generation of vampires is willing to take sides over Edward's involvement with Bella, Carlisle insists on the preservation of the family. Knowing that if the family remains located in Forks, Bella is likely to die, for Carlisle the only resolution is that the entire family move.[39] He counters Rosalie's offer to kill Bella without consuming her blood by emphasizing the value of the family unit to their chosen way of life; he wants "very much for [the] family to be *worth* protecting."[40] Carlisle refuses to entertain the idea of murder to preserve the family, for that action would destroy the moral center, and, therefore, the moral worth of the family. Any remaining hold these vampires have on humanity would be lost.

For Carlisle, maintaining a grasp on humanity, no matter how tenuous, is central to his ethos. Carlisle is the oldest of the Cullen clan; born in London in the 1640s, Carlisle embodies the values he promotes. He has never killed to fulfill the vampiric desire for human blood. In fact he has never tasted human blood. Even as a newly-created vampire, his self-control was so strong that he could resist this instinctive desire and only consume the blood of wild animals.[41] In particular, Carlisle's Anglican upbringing and his long existence reinforce his belief in God and, especially significant for a vampire, his belief in the Christian soul. Carlisle does not "doubt whether God exists in some form or the other," and he also believes "that there is still a point to this life," even for vampires. This belief extends to the hope that choosing a morally incorruptible lifestyle will result in "some measure of credit" in the afterlife.[42] While Edward shares Carlisle's belief in God, he does not concede the possibility of an afterlife for a vampire. Carlisle's faith, though, is inviolable; without it his existence has no direction and little point. Consequently, he chooses to live as if one day he will be redeemed.

Carlisle's patriarchal position, one that conveys paternalistic authority, situates him as almost Christ-like: he does not judge and is ready to forgive and love Edward, even if he should fail to follow Carlisle's example.[43] Conversely, Edward is wracked with guilt and remorse for even contemplating resisting Carlisle's edicts; even the idea of demonstrating his weakness to Carlisle fills him with misery. The revulsion he feels when confronted with the temptation Bella represents is not for the harm he might do Bella, but for himself. According to Warner, the abstinence movement grew out of the evangelists' "need to be on one's best behaviour, to cast aside any acquaintances and diversions that threatened to derail the believer's unblinking focus on God."[44] The only way to always "be on one's best behaviour" was to abstain from any kind of behavior that carried a risk. Like these nineteenth-century temperance adherents, Edward believes that the only way to avoid any potentially dangerous behavior is to abstain entirely, and the benefit of such abstention is to himself rather than his potential victims. By continuing to abstain, he will not revert to his monstrous self, one that he has fought hard to overcome. For Edward, giving in to his cravings will undo eighty years of asceticism, and this fear translates into self-loathing for potentially disappointing Carlisle.[45] Edward views his attraction for Bella as counter to Carlisle's prohibition. In contrast to Carlisle's strength and morality, Edward sees himself as weak and cowardly.[46]

Edward's initial interest in Bella is provoked by his inability to hear her thoughts as he can with everyone else. Not until he gets close enough to smell her blood does he experience an immediate and seemingly insatiable desire for her, and his resolve to maintain his chosen lifestyle is very nearly undone. He is so tempted by Bella that he believes his remaining traces of humanity are extinguished and he is in danger of becoming completely monstrous; he barely maintains control by seeing what he considers this monstrosity reflected in Bella's eyes.[47] However, what actually prevents Edward from killing everyone in the room so he can enjoy Bella is the thought of Carlisle. When a breath of air carries Bella's scent away, Edward immediately thinks of Carlisle, comparing his own monstrous self with his mentor and role model. In Carlisle, Edward sees wisdom, compassion and patience — all qualities he desires but feels he is in danger of losing entirely when faced with the temptation of Bella.[48] While the guilt instigated by imagining disappointing Carlisle is enough to prevent Edward from killing Bella, he cannot fully embrace Carlisle's beliefs. Although Edward follows Carlisle's model, he cannot subscribe to Carlisle's faith in the possibility of redemption for vampires through abstinence. Through his relationship with Bella, and her belief in the existence of the vampire soul, Edward finally accepts this position as an ideological possibility.

Edward's Behavioral Shift

After wrestling with his conscience and invoking Carlisle's moral code, Edward's desire for Bella undergoes a shift. He no longer sees her as tempting his lust for human blood, but rather as a test of his resolve not to succumb to this particular temptation. The focus of Edward's struggle with Carlisle's moral code has shifted from Bella to himself. He is not struggling with violating Bella, but with violating the moral code. The result of this shift is that he is no longer attracted to Bella's blood, but to her body — an equally problematic attraction and one that also violates the Cullen code of conduct.[49] Mullaney suggests that those who choose to abstain will deliberately put themselves in the path of temptation, permitting themselves "to engage in acts that allow them to feel the heat of the flames. They welcome temptation, as such moments allow abstainers to see if they can approach the fire and escape without burns."[50]The change in Edward's attraction to Bella gives him plenty of opportunity to "approach the fire" as he repeatedly seeks out her company. Recognizing this new temptation, Edward once more seeks solace in Carlisle, who is again positioned as the wise and trusted patriarch to whom Edward can confess his initial desire for Bella's blood.[51]Although Edward feels ashamed when admitting to Carlisle what he perceives as a weakness, Carlisle's trust in Edward is reinstated after Edward rescues Bella from being crushed by a truck in the school parking lot. Carlisle tells Edward that rescuing Bella was the right thing to do.[52] Edward now is acting much like Carlisle; he is choosing to do what is right over giving in to his baser desires. It is as if Carlisle has conferred onto Edward the ability to make the correct choice.

The immediate consequence of Edward's change in perception is that he can increasingly bear the pain of being in proximity to Bella. The pain has morphed from the pain of resisting the desire of consumption to the more predictable emotions associated with romantic love and sexual desire. Edward considers his new-found desire to simply touch Bella's face unsafe on many levels. While his desire for her blood remains, it is superseded by a more conventional concern that his sexual attraction to Bella will result in him not behaving as a gentleman. His moral code does not simply prohibit him from drinking human blood, but, like the temperance movement, it also prohibits sexual activity outside of marriage.[53]Adding a layer of sexual attraction between Edward and Bella imbues all Edward's comments about the need for caution around Bella with sexual innuendo. His constant reiteration that she is not safe around him and that her proximity to him now puts her at risk carries the implied additional risk of inappropriate sexual desire.[54] Indeed, it becomes increasingly difficult for Edward to distinguish between desire for Bella's blood and his increasing sexual attraction to her as demonstrated by him wanting to "wrench her into [his] arms and crush her [throat] to his teeth." [55] While overtly he is talking about his craving for her blood, the language is sexually charged. His earlier desire for her blood is expressed in his plans to kill everyone in the classroom so he can then feast on Bella. He calls himself a monster, and the description of the planned killings is confined to physical violence. In contrast, the language Edward employs to describe his ongoing desire for Bella's blood is reminiscent of a romance novel.[56]

The Rewards of Abstinence

Throughout much of the *Twilight* series, Edward's abstinence seems to have little immediate reward for Edward himself. Although Bella's life is spared, enabling Edward and Bella to fall in love, Edward does not allow himself to fully enjoy Bella in any way until he changes her into a vampire in *Breaking Dawn* in order to save her from death. Even then, the Cullen clan is threatened by the ruling Volturi vampire family, and Edward and Bella's long-denied pleasure looks to be short-lived. But the rewards of abstinence are not meant to be immediate. As Warner puts it, the central goal of abstaining is that the Christian abstainer "can conquer sin."[57] Within the *Twilight* series, the means to conquer sin can be found in Carlisle's persistence in doing "the right thing." Warner notes that "abstainers do not look to society to fix their problems: they look to themselves,"[58] and, as Edward says, "Carlisle always chose the right way."[59] The unintended benefit of such a choice, though, is that Carlisle maintains a sense of humanity while most vampires have long forgotten that they were once human.

Eventually, Edward is able to embrace the concept that the Cullen lifestyle enables those who are no longer human to persist nevertheless in their humanity. This realization, though, is activated by Bella, not Carlisle; without Bella, Edward would never fully understand the importance of abstaining. A particularly telling example of Edward's move towards acknowledging his latent humanity through Bella can be seen in the self-control he evinces after he rescues Bella from being attacked in Port Angeles. Edward's instinct is to hunt down and kill the men who threatened Bella, partly to prevent them from hurting anyone else, but mostly as revenge and as a way to assuage his anger which he calls "a lust for slaughter."[60] This time, it is not consideration for Carlisle that prevents Edward acting on his instincts, but the belief that if he returns to killing humans, however justified he believes that act to be, Bella will be so horrified that she will be "out of ... reach forever."[61] Instead, he turns again to Carlisle for help, and in doing so, demonstrates—according to Carlisle—the very human characteristics of "compassion" and "control."[62]

This burgeoning sense of humanity in Edward leads to his acknowledgement of the possibility of the existence of the vampire soul, again through interaction with Bella. At the end of *New Moon*, when Bella has agreed to marry Edward, and Edward has agreed to change Bella into a vampire after they are married, he tells her that she is "eager for eternal damnation."[63] Bella shows Edward that he actually believes in Carlisle's version of eternity. She points out that in Volterra, when confronted with the very-much-alive Bella, he believed they were both dead and exclaimed that "*Carlisle was right,*" indicating a belief in the afterlife.[64] As the only witness to this comment, it necessarily has to be Bella to awaken Edward to his own belief, a role Carlisle has long been aware that Bella played in Edward's existence.

The rewards of abstinence, though, are much more significant and far-reaching than the individual belief in the soul and redemption. Abstinence confers upon the Cullens the kind of power that could potentially disrupt the vampire world and supplant the evil ruling Volturi with the benevolent way of life practiced by those who follow Carlisle. Warner considers the abstainer's ability to acquire a new identity "one that sets him apart from those who have yet to make the same sacrifices," and she argues that this concept of superior identity accounts for those who are powerless, such as nineteenth-century African Americans, embracing abstinence, as it confers upon them a degree of power.[65] The relationship between abstinence and power becomes apparent at the end of the fourth book in the series, *Breaking Dawn*, when the abstaining vampires and their followers trounce the Volturi, by comparison a remarkably degenerate group. The Volturi not only consume human blood, but the cruelty with which they do so—by rounding up unaware tourists, for example—indicates the pleasure they experience in inflicting pain. They are also an ancient and powerful vampire family who impose their rule on the global vampire community. Their authority has not been challenged for thousands of years.[66]

The climax of *Breaking Dawn* (and, arguably, of the entire *Twilight* series) is the confrontation between the ideologically different factions of vampires. The Volturi represent the accepted vampiric existence, dependent on the consumption of human blood, while the Cullens and their supporters represent an alternative existence predicated on Christian values and morals evinced through abstinence. Significantly, not all those who stand in support of the Cullens practice abstinence themselves; yet despite the disparate nature of the Cullen supporters, the dramatic confrontation between the two groups—Cullens and Volturi—assumes an atmosphere of a tent revival or a mass conversion. In particular, those conventional vampires who stand with the Cullens do so as witnesses. Here the word takes on the connotation associated with Christian witnessing, beyond its denotative meaning of observation. These supporters of Carlisle do more than simply observe the proceedings of the meeting between the Cullens and the Volturi. Garrett, a Cullen supporter, accuses the Volturi of seeking to eliminate the free will of those under their control, and he actively proselytizes for Carlisle and his beliefs. In particular, he references the denial inherent in the Cullen lifestyle, a reference that alludes to Christian self-denial, a key tenet of evangelical Christianity. Garrett's speech is a public affirmation of the power of the Cullens—and of Carlisle in particular—that stems directly from their choice to abstain from consuming human blood.

The recognition in such a public arena of the significance of the sacrifice the Cullens have made initiates a potential shift in power away from the Volturi, and it suggests an ideological change in the supernatural *Twilight* culture that exists in tandem with the real world. In order for the Volturi to retain power, they must reinforce the need for the protective obscurity of secrecy. The Volturi's power is predicated on fear, and if that fear proves groundless, then their control of the vampire world is undermined. Edward and Bella's hybrid vampire-human daughter, Renesmee, represents what the Volturi dread most: a threat to their control through the negation of fear. The Volturi suggest that Renesmee poses a risk to vampire obscurity, but Garrett argues that the Volturi's "true purpose" in confronting the Cullens is "to erase what they perceive as the competition."[67] Garrett's speech illustrates the central difference between the Cullens and the Volturi: while the Volturi are a "coven," the Cullens are a "family." The Cullens' strength comes not from fulfillment of the desires of the individual, but from the benefits of an existence based on sacrifice rather than greed.[68]

This confrontation between the two vampire factions shows both sides how "the vampire world was changing" in a way that weakens the Volturi.[69] When faced with the evidence of this impending change through the existence of Nahuel, another vampire-human hybrid, the Volturi witnesses vanish, leaving the now vulnerable Volturi aware of their dissipating power. The shift in power from Volturi to Cullens can be seen in the last interaction between Carlisle and Aro; Carlisle now addresses Aro in the imperative, telling him to leave and to refrain from hunting in their territory. Most significantly, though, Carlisle has the last word, a clear indication of the new hierarchy of power.

Perhaps the predicted relationship between the werewolf/shapeshifter Jacob Black and Renesmee—a relationship that will presumably culminate in marriage—indicates a new kind of family in the *Twilight* world. While the intrinsic values and morals remain the same, the structure of the family will come to reflect a more heterogeneous U.S. culture. If humans, vampires and werewolves can successfully intermarry and reproduce, then perhaps the *Twilight* series is suggesting a twenty-first century approach to integration where moral and ethical values are preserved and where abstinence confers benign power on those who practice it.

Notes

1. Jessica Warner, *The Day George Bush Stopped Drinking: Why Abstinence Matters to the Religious Right* (Ontario: McClelland & Stewart, 2008), xii.
2. Ibid., xii.
3. Ibid., 4.
4. Ibid., 4.
5. Ibid., 6.
6. While it is possible for female vampires to create other vampires (Jasper, for example, was created by a female), in the Cullen family, only Carlisle, a male, has done so.
7. Chronologically, within the context of the novels, neither Carlisle nor Edward date from nineteenth-century America. Carlisle was born in seventeenth-century England, and while Edward is American, he was born at the beginning of the twentieth century. However, as I argue later, neither of these characters espouse the values of their chronological ages; nor do they promote twenty-first-century sensibilities. Instead, their fictional construction enables them to embrace values endemic to both nineteenth- and twenty-first-century abstinence movements.
8. Warner, xi.
9. Jamie L. Mullaney, *Everyone Is NOT Doing It: Abstinence and Personal Identity* (Chicago: University of Chicago Press, 2006), 2.
10. The *Oxford English Dictionary*, for example, defines a vampire as one who "seek[s] nourishment, or [does] harm, by sucking the blood of sleeping persons." Oxford English Dictionary, http://www.oed.com/.
11. Warner, 10–11.
12. Ibid., 31.
13. Ibid., 36.
14. Ibid., 37.
15. Ibid., 52, 55, 58.
16. Ibid., 73.
17. Warner notes that this movement, initiated in the mid–1830s, was all but over by the mid–1850s. Ibid., 92.
18. Ibid., 73
19. Ibid., 79. Richard H. Shryock notes in his discussion of Sylvester Graham's health movement that Graham lectured to thousands of followers in the mid-nineteenth century who were known as Grahamites. While the movement only lasted a few years, it attracted a large number of adherents. Richard H. Shryock, "Sylvester Graham and the Popular Health Movement, 1830–1870," *The Mississippi Valley Historical Review* Vol 18, (1931), 172–183 http://www.jstor.org/stable/1893378?seq=8.
20. Stephenie Meyer, "Midnight Sun," *The Official Website of Stephenie Meyer*, http://www.stepheniemeyer.com/pdf/midnightsun_partial_draft4.pdf.
21. Ibid., 86.
22. Ibid., 90.
23. Mullaney, 66.

24. Ibid., 69

25. Warner, xiii.

26. J. Shoshanna Ehrlich, "From Age of Consent Laws to the 'Silver Ring Thing': The Regulation of Adolescent Female Sexuality," *Health Matrix: Journal of Law Medicine,* Vol 16 (2006), 173, http://search.ebscohost.com/login.aspx?direct=true&db=f5h&AN=20614181&site=ehost-live, 173.

27. Ibid.

28. Ibid., 179. Stephanie Rosenbloom explains the virginity pledge in "A Ring That Says No, Not Yet," *The New York Times*, December 14, 2005, Fashion section. The True Love Waits Commitment Card, from the *Lifeway* website, asks the signer to "make a commitment to God, myself, my family, my friends, my future mate, and my future children to a lifetime of purity including sexual abstinence from this day until the day I enter a biblical marriage relationship." This language is rhetorically similar to early nineteenth-century temperance pledges. One such pledge states: "We hereby solemnly promise, God helping us, to abstain from all distilled, fermented and malt liquors including wine beer [sic], and to employ all proper means to discourage the use of, and the trafic [sic] in, the same." Both pledges use extensive lists and promises to God; both pledges include space for those pledging to sign. Significantly, the purity pledge directs the promise to a specific audience while the temperance is unclear to whom the promise is addressed. "True Love Waits Commitment Card," *Lifeway: Biblical Solutions for Life,* http://www.lifeway.com/tlw/students/card.asp. "Our Temperance Pledge," http://www.frontierfamilies.net/family/Miller/E5JM/Jacob_Miller_Temperance_Pledge.htm.

29. Members of the popular music band the Jonas Brothers, for example, have signed purity pledges and wear purity rings. "Jonas Bros talk about Purity and Purity Rings on television interview," *Purity Rings,* http://purityrings.com/blog/2009/06/jonas-bros-talk-about-purity-and-purity-rings-on-television-interview.aspx.

30. There are many resources available that provide the history of the Mormon faith; the information used here is found in the *Encyclopedia of American Religions.* J. Gordon Melton, *Encyclopedia of American Religions* (Detroit: Gale, 2003) 7th ed. Electronic book. Also, see Sarah Schwartzman's discussion of Mormonism and *Twilight* in this collection.

31. "Obey the Word of Wisdom," *The Church of Jesus Christ of Latter-day Saints,* http://www.mormon.org/mormonorg/eng/basic-beliefs/the-commandments/obey-the-word-of-wisdom.

32. "Obey the Word of Wisdom."

33. qtd. in Warner, 34. Original emphasis.

34. Warner, 46–47.

35. Stephenie Meyer, *Twilight* (New York: Little, Brown and Company, 2005), 331.

36. Judith Stacey, *In the Name of the Family: Rethinking Family Values in the Postmodern Age* (Boston: Beacon Press, 1996), 38–39.

37. Ibid., 45 and 47.

38. Meyer, "Midnight Sun," 78.

39. Ibid., 80. Bella has witnessed Edward's inhuman speed and strength; the chance of her talking about what she saw poses a risk to the anonymous existence of the Cullen vampire coven. In order to protect the family, Rosalie suggests she kill Bella.

40. Ibid., 82.

41. Meyer, *Twilight*, 337.

42. Stephenie Meyer, *New Moon* (New York: Little, Brown and Company, 2006), 36–7.

43. Meyer, "Midnight Sun," 13.

44. Warner, 18.

45. Meyer, "Midnight Sun," 17.

46. Ibid., 25.

47. Ibid., 10.

48. Ibid., 13.

49. While Carlisle does not explicitly forbid pre-marital sex, his conservative values and the structure of the Cullen family imply this prohibition. The novel suggests that, with the exception of Edward, all the Cullens are married: Carlisle to Esme, Emmet to Rosalie and Jasper to Alice.

50. Mullaney, 125.

51. Meyer, "Midnight Sun," 51.

52. Ibid., 64–5.

53. Indeed, even when Bella and Edward are married, he is reluctant to engage in sex as he fears he will hurt her.

54. Meyer, "Midnight Sun," 44, 46.

55. Ibid., 71.

56. This excerpt from Elizabeth Walker's 1989 novel *The Court*, describing how the male protagonist kisses his mistress, offers one example, typical of many: "He bent his head, pushed her hair aside and pressed his mouth to her neck. Violent, sustained kisses, sucking at her flesh." (London: Knight, 1989), 151.

57. Warner, xii.

58. Ibid., 3.

59. Meyer, "Midnight Sun," 54.

60. Ibid., 174

61. Ibid., 176.

62. Ibid., 215.

63. Ibid., 546.

64. Ibid., 546. Original emphasis.

65. Warner, 60.

66. The complete scene explaining the power of the Volturi can be found in Chapter 37 of *Breaking Dawn*.

67. Stephenie Meyer, *Breaking Dawn* (New York: Little, Brown and Company, 2008), 717.

68. Ibid., 717–8.

69. Ibid., 73.

Is *Twilight* Mormon?

SARAH SCHWARTZMAN

Nearly every interview with Stephenie Meyer mentions her religious affiliation with the Church of Jesus Christ of Latter-day Saints, more commonly known as the LDS or Mormon Church.[1] Why are there such frequent references to Meyer's faith? One probable reason for popular interest in Meyer's religion is her openness with readers and fans, and her willingness to "out herself as a Mormon writer in a way other writers don't."[2] A second reason is the common perception of Mormonism as an exoticized and "set apart" religious community. Meyer herself has been surprised to see the media's interest in her faith and agrees that it has to do with Mormons being stereotyped as different. In one interview she comments, "It seems funny that [my Mormon faith] is still a story ... you didn't hear people saying, 'Jon Stewart, Jewish writer,' when his book came out. I guess being a Mormon is just *odd enough* that people think it's a real story" (italics added).[3]

The "odd enough" quality of Meyer's Mormonism is one probable reason for the public interest in her faith. However, the media's interest also reflects a general wariness on the part of American readers about religion or allegory being snuck into mainstream, presumably secular reading. For *Twilight* readers, this wariness intensified as the series increasingly took on hot-button ethical issues, such as teenage sex and pregnancy, traditional family values, and abortion. Meyer's decision to write about these issues led some readers to question whether a Mormon treatise for conservative religious and social values was concealed within the romantic entanglements of Meyer's characters.

This essay responds to the title question, "Is *Twilight* Mormon?" in three sections. The first section explores how Mormon beliefs can be seen in the *Twilight* novels. Meyer herself recognizes that despite not purposely addressing religion, her religious faith does work its way into her writing. Religious elements are particularly noticeable when examining the Cullen family in relation to Mormon beliefs, specifically those pertaining to eternal families, free choice, and the virtue of sacrificial lifestyles.

The second section of the essay shifts the focus from Mormon beliefs to Mormon culture, analyzing how the novels establish specific gender and sexual mores as normative. Especially ripe for analysis is the series' treatment of key cultural values regarding abstinence and chastity, traditional family structure, and motherhood as a part of female purpose.

The third and final section takes a brief look at responses to the series from Mormon and other Christian readers, asking whether or not they see the novels as "Mormon." It is necessary to understand what is meant by this line of questioning: "Is *Twilight* Mormon?" First, it implies that Meyer wrote the books to deliberately function as religious allegories or narratives. Second, it implies that the books are explicitly intended for the spiritual edification or reflection of Mormon readers, or to expose and convert non–Mormon readers to the Mormon faith. In response to the first implication, Meyer has been frank in interviews that she wrote and published these novels with no intention of them being considered Mormon novels. (She is, however, currently working on a book that she does consider a Mormon Young Adult novel, and has expressed concerns about how her non–Mormon fans and their families will respond.) In response to the second implication, there is very little reason to suppose that the *Twilight* books were written or marketed to promote Mormonism. In order to explore whether or not readers perceive the series as promoting religious values, the third section of this essay takes a look at how readers have responded to the series in articles, blogs, and reviews. These reactions were written mostly by Mormons, by other Christians, and by fans and critics unconcerned with religion. Their differing reactions help to problematize any simplistic attempts to label the books as explicitly "Mormon." These responses also demonstrate how the books might be interpreted from diverse religious contexts, and not exclusively through a Mormon one.

When talking about religion in literature, it is helpful to think about religion as providing concepts, narratives, and symbols that communities use to understand the world around them.[4] Meyer, as a practicing Mormon, uses in her writing those systems common to her faith—concepts of agency, narratives of sacrifice, and ideas about eternal family. Meyer told one profiler that her religious faith was "part of the fabric of the book the way it is part of [me]."[5] Based on this recognition, an important distinction needs to be made: the *Twilight* books should not be viewed simplistically as a "Mormon series," as if they were religious tracts or allegories seeking to grapple with or promote Mormonism. However, we can explore the "fabric" of these books—especially their emphases on specific values and norms—as informed by and reflective of Meyer's religious beliefs and culture.

Mormon Beliefs in Twilight

Family and Marriage

One of the clearest ways to discuss the role of Mormonism in the series is to look first to the family. The nuclear family can be thought of as the smallest and most basic unit of organization in the modern Mormon Church.[6] The Church teaches that spirits exist in a premortal realm and come to Earth in physical form, working towards perfection and a divine future. Creating families is a sacred duty, since reproduction provides the opportunity for more spirit children to enter physical form and continue their spiritual journeys. It is expected that families regularly come together for church activities and weekly Family Home Evenings, and they are also generally expected to model certain behaviors based on traditional gender roles. Gender is viewed as an essential part of individual identity, and therefore family roles and responsibilities are often sharply divided according to gender.[7]

The Cullen family represents an idealized Mormon family. Although they are not biologically related to one another, each vampire lives in the traditional family arrangement with marked gender roles. Carlisle is the admired and respected patriarch who works and earns a living, and whose judgment and leadership set the example for the family; in Bella's words, he is "their creator, their center, and their guide."[8] Esme is the loving wife, homemaker, and mother to the five Cullen "kids." These kids—Edward, Alice, Jasper, Rosalie, and Emmett—are respectful and obedient, and strive to live up to the value system set by their "vegetarian" parents: that despite being vampires, they will resist the temptation to drink blood and will live lives of a higher moral order. When the Cullens convert others to their vegetarian way of life, as they did with Tanya's coven, that coven becomes part of the Cullens' extended family. The coven is referred to by using the same language of extended kinship that is common between non-related members of the Mormon Church.

The relationship between Bella and Edward also models traditional family roles. Edward is persistently responsible for protecting and caring for Bella, while her primary concern is simply to be at his side, a priority that she values over college, career, or other personal interests. Once married, Bella and Edward begin their own family with the birth of Renesmee.[9] Edward quickly begins to assume the fatherly exemplar role that Carlisle has modeled, and Bella eagerly accepts her role as devoted wife and mother whose foremost concern is the wellbeing of her family.

The series highlights not only a Mormon belief in the importance of families, but also a conceptualization of families as eternal. The Book of Mormon teaches that a couple married in the temple is "sealed" to one another, believed to be married "for time and eternity ... together forever."[10] Sealed marriages are considered a goal of every Latter-day Saint since the marriages lead to exaltation (the attainment of the kind of divine eternal life lived by the Heavenly Father). Bella and Edward repeatedly use language of eternity and immortality when talking about their relationship, and they regularly discuss how their relationship will continue to the end of their existences. For example, Bella says to Edward, "You are ... well, not exactly the love of my life, because I expect to love you for much longer than that. The love of my existence."[11] Once they are both vampires, Bella and Edward have literally ended their mortal lives and are continuing on as an eternal family in their afterlives. Another Mormon teaching seen here is that spirits are separated from bodies at death and then reunited in the resurrection, at which time spirits receive perfected immortal bodies. This teaching resembles Bella's own process of transformation. Her heart stops beating and she momentarily dies, immediately to be resurrected as a vampire. She then awakens with a newly perfected body — one that is still hers as she was when human, and yet is made perfectly beautiful and virtually immortal.

Agency and Restraint

Although the "eternal couple" may be one of the most conspicuous symbols of Mormon beliefs in the text, Meyer feels that the series' most prominently religious themes deal with free agency and sacrifice.[12] Mormons believe that agency (or human responsibility) is an eternal principle that transcends physical and mortal existence. Life on earth is a time to be tested in one's faith and choices, to find out if one is worthy of becoming like God, or achieving Godhood. This focus on agency can be seen in Mormonism's unique interpretation of the story of Adam and Eve, explained as a moment not of original sin but "as a necessary step in the plan of life and a great blessing to all mankind."[13] The Fall of Adam and Eve led to humans being given mortal bodies, the right to choose between good and evil, and the chance to earn eternal life and Godhood. (Susan Jeffers explores this theme in more detail in her essay in this book.)

Multiple times in *Twilight*, Bella's decision making is symbolized by the image of Eve choosing to take the apple. Both the novel's opening epigraph from Genesis 2:17 and the apple on the cover are references to the Fall and its symbolism of free choice. Meyer has described the apple on the cover as "an offer.... Are you going to choose to take that apple?... Is Bella going to find out about this other world or is she happier the way she is?"[14] Metaphorically, the link between Bella and Eve has to do with her decision to learn about the vampires (taking the apple), her moral agency in responding to this knowledge (choosing between good and evil), and her resulting experience of supernatural love and immortal transformation (earning a kind of "eternal life"). The apple as a symbol of free choice was also kept in the film of *Twilight*. When Edward first approaches Bella in the cafeteria, she drops a red apple which he catches and returns to her. In the book, when Bella sits next to Edward, she wonders at his revulsion, thinking, "He didn't know me from Eve."[15] All of these references to Bella as Eve highlight Meyer's emphasis on free choice, a theme further reiterated by the decision to set the story in the aptly-named town of Forks.[16]

For practicing Mormons, free choice is directly connected to the importance of disciplined living and abstention from a variety of practices. This includes avoiding alcohol, caffeine, drugs or stimulants, and eschewing impure behaviors related to sexuality, the media, and social activities.[17] Self-control is a dominant theme in the Cullens' vegetarianism, a way of life based on abstention. The Cullens refuse to drink human blood despite the enormous physical pain that refusal causes them, both because they value human life and because they see blood as a defiling substance. To drink human blood is discussed as a slip-up, an urge that they try carefully not to indulge. Edward explains that drinking it makes vampires feel and behave less like humans and more like monsters. At the end of *Breaking Dawn*, Garrett defines the Cullens' abstention from blood as central to their sacrificial lifestyle, something that allows them to live peacefully and as a real family.[18] This diet also leaves the Cullens with eyes of liquid gold rather than bloodthirsty red, highlighting the sense of purity that comes with their conscientious avoidance of defiling substances and actions.[19]

Self-restraint is portrayed as a heroic quality throughout the series. Carlisle is revered by his family for his unwavering ability to be near exposed human blood without ever succumbing to temptation. Edward's heroism is also seen in his admirable self-control. Meyer makes many references to the intensity of Edward's restraint with Bella, describing his "Herculean effort" and the acute physical pain that Edward feels when resisting Bella's blood.[20] Aro, a leader in the Volturi clan, has the ability to know every thought a person has ever had upon touching them. When he touches Edward, he exclaims about Edward's incredible self-control: "But *your* restraint!... I did not know such strength was possible. To inure yourself against such a siren call, not just once but again and again."[21] Readers are frequently reminded that Edward is only able to be with Bella through this deeply self-sacrificing love. His intense thirst and desire is clearly symbolic of sexual temptation, and the books portray him as heroic for his virtuous efforts to master these impulses.

Restraint as a virtue is even further highlighted when Bella is transformed into a vampire. Most vampires in the Cullen family have a kind of natural gift or talent, and Bella's gift is her incredible self-control. She shocks the Cullen family by her almost immediate ability to be in the presence of humans without killing them, and by her ability to stop in the middle of a hunt and return to a rational, controlled state of mind. This exceptional restraint is also part of her talent as a shield, a gift which could otherwise be understood as sovereignty over her own mind, even when external pressures try to control, manipulate, or sway her thinking.

Another "Mormon" aspect of the Cullens' way of life is that it sets them apart from other vampire communities. Sometimes this difference is dangerous for the Cullens, but more frequently it is the unifying force that makes them powerful as a family. Scholars of religion have written that religious abstentions largely contribute to a sense of belonging and solidarity within communities. Mormons follow abstentions laid out in the Word of Wisdom, a scriptural health law proscribing alcohol, coffee, tea, and tobacco. Conscientious avoidance of these substances, which are commonly consumed among non–Mormons, can function as important reminders to Mormons that they are "a peculiar people, a group set apart, who live in the world but are not of the world."[22] One scholar writes that the Word of Wisdom "makes Mormons uncomfortable at cocktail parties, coffee breaks, and other such gatherings" that act as meeting grounds for much of American society.[23] This subtle mark of difference helps maintain their religious identity as a distinctive and set apart community. The Cullens' vegetarianism certainly functions in parallel ways to mark them as a group apart. It marks them apart from other vampires through their unusual eyes, eating habits, and residential lifestyle. Simply by virtue of being vampires, they were already marked apart from humans through their graceful movement, impressive beauty, and superhuman abilities. While still able to blend in with communities around them, the Cullens are marked by their way of life, unified but a people apart.

Sacrifice

The Cullens' way of life should also be understood as one of sacrifice. On one level, this can be seen in their fundamental willingness to sacrifice pleasure by resisting the temptation to drink blood. On a deeper level, however, the characters are repeatedly willing to sacrifice their lives for others whom they love. For example, Bella is willing to die in place of others in each novel in the series. *Twilight* opens with Bella facing death, thinking to herself that it was a good and noble way to die, "in place of someone else, someone I loved."[24] Then in *New Moon*, she runs to Volterra to save Edward, knowing that she is risking her life at the hands of the Volturi. In *Eclipse,* Bella tries to emulate the Quileute story of the third wife's sacrifice, a story of a wife and mother who kills herself to distract a vampire and protect her family. Finally, in *Breaking Dawn*, Bella is prepared to die in childbirth to ensure that her baby survives, thereby becoming a "classic martyr" in Jacob's words.[25] At the very end of the series, Bella fights the Volturi expecting to die, but hoping she might first protect the lives of her daughter, family and friends.

The final battle in *Breaking Dawn* can be seen as a defense of the values of sacrifice and agency. The Volturi are described as those who "seek the death of our free will."[26] In other words, they try to destroy the sense of agency and choice that Mormons consider sacred. The Cullens, their vampire friends, and the pack of Quileute werewolves are willing to fight, even if it means sacrificing their lives. In the first part of the confrontation, they come together to witness on behalf of Renesmee. Witnessing is a regular practice in Mormon churches. Every month, believers are asked to serve as witnesses who can testify to the truth of the Church. In *Breaking Dawn*, the witnesses gather to testify on behalf of the miracle baby, Renesmee, and on behalf of the virtues upheld by the Cullens.

Mormon Culture in Twilight

In addition to examining how Mormon religious beliefs can be seen in the books, it is worthwhile to explore the ways in which the books depict Mormon cultural norms and values. This section will focus specifically on how Mormon communities encourage women to uphold chaste values regarding sex, gender, and motherhood. Part of this process includes identifying ways in which certain values are glorified, especially those dealing with a "culture of life": those views that highlight messages about abstinence until marriage, pro-life principles, and emphasis on motherhood as part of female purpose.

Abstinence and Chastity

One of the most commented upon qualities in this series is its ability to be simultaneously arousing and chaste. Critics have commended Meyer for the difficult achievement of having "made abstinence sexy."[27] Gail Collins of the *New York Times* suggests that the success of *Twilight* has to do with the gentlemanly but hunky vampire hero who will be faithful to Bella forever, even though they cannot have sex. Instead, they "spend all their time kissing and cuddling and talking about their feelings."[28] The series is full of sexually arousing situations, but the physical dangers of Bella becoming too intimate with Edward are always good enough reasons for Edward to interrupt Bella's sexual advances. His body temperature is so cold that cuddling requires a protective blanket to serve as an insulating barrier between them. Edward's intense thirst for Bella's blood and his sharp, venom-coated teeth make any kind of passionate kiss a real danger to Bella's safety. Also, Edward's strength is so great that he could accidentally hurt Bella just by getting a little carried away during an embrace. Indeed, when the couple does have sex for the first time, she awakens the next morning — much to Edward's horror — with bruises all over her body. In addition to all of these physical obstacles to the couple's intimacy, Meyer also makes clear that Edward is old-fashioned and gentlemanly. As such, he is determined to protect Bella's "virtue," as well as his own.

Meyer acknowledges that she wrote these books to be "clean," a word used to acknowledge literature, media, and entertainment considered appropriate to be enjoyed by Mormons.[29] She describes her own childhood and adolescence as one in which she was a "good girl" in a community where such behavior was the norm.[30] She does not include drinking, drugs, gossiping, or graphic sexuality in the series. The first time sex does happen is after Bella and Edward are married, and Meyer emphasizes Bella's nervousness leading up to the moment. The scene portrays Bella as feeling intensely vulnerable before sex, wondering how people could be sexually intimate with "less than the absolute commitment Edward had given me?"[31] Also, their sexual interactions are still very dangerous to Bella, and it is not until she is transformed into a vampire — allegorically, until her soul is in the same state as Edward's and the couple is made spiritually compatible and "sealed"—that they can fully relax and enjoy the experience. One message conveyed is that sexual relations before a sealed marriage can be both unnerving and dangerous.

This emphasis on abstinence is reinforced by sexual mores woven into the dialogue. When Bella and Edward tell Charlie about their plans to wed, Edward comments that he and Bella are going to move across the country together, which he would like to do the "right way" by marrying her first. Explained as characteristic of Edward's old-fashioned morals, Edward's loaded reasoning reinforces the idea that cohabitation before marriage is immoral. As Bella imagines Charlie's response, we are given an equally loaded reaction: "What could he say? *I'd prefer you live in sin first?*"[32] What is implied is that there are only two options for Bella and Edward: living as a married couple *or* living in sin by cohabitating unwed.

One Mormon reader and blogger, Natalie B., argues that the series introduces several of the contradictory sexual messages with which Mormon women are frequently faced. She argues that the *Twilight* series reinforces a belief taught to Mormon young women, that marriage to an eternal companion is their one and only way to salvation. She also writes that the central romantic fantasy of the series is "deeply Mormon in its trajectory" for the way it juxtaposes sexual ignorance with an almost pornographic eroticization of the idealized, chaste man.[33] Although *Twilight* includes no overtly pornographic sexual details, Natalie B. argues that it nonetheless fosters an arousing romantic fantasy that establishes unrealistic and objectifying images of men. To add to the fantasy of Edward's unquenched desire for Bella, every other young male also wants to be Bella's lover. Natalie B. discusses the inability of males to be "just friends" with Bella as typical of the ways that Mormon women are conditioned to perceive men: only as potential or taken husbands. She suggests that these aspects of *Twilight* show a few of the ironic sexual messages that Mormon young women often face, "balanc[ing] enforced sexual ignorance with the fact that it is through marriage, and hence sex, that she becomes exalted."

Coupling and Marrying Young

It is taken for granted in the series that every "good" person would find a happy ending through being satisfactorily settled in a heterosexual relationship. Being paired off is one means we are given to understand that the series is ending happily for everybody: the Cullens, Bella's parents and high school friends, and most of the Quileute werewolves. Even the villainous vampires usually are coupled, like Victoria and James or the Volturi and their wives.

There is also something notable about the frequent youth of so many of these couples. Edward and Bella are married right after high school when she is eighteen and he is seventeen (or so he will always appear). Many of the

Quileute boys have imprinted by their teenage years. Even "parents" Carlisle and Esme appear to be in their mid-twenties. This youthfulness reflects a cultural reality among Mormon communities in that people commonly choose mates and marry at a relatively young age. Church activities, that include separate church services for young singles, are designed to help young people find marriage partners. Brigham Young University campuses are also considered ideal places for young Mormons to meet and marry. One study specifically investigated this trend of Mormon couples having short courtships and young marriages. The couples interviewed offered two common reasons: first, they felt ready to marry, and second, since marriage requires moral purity (which prohibits sexual experimentation or cohabitation), young couples did not want to suffer excessively prolonged temptation.[34] Parents were also very supportive of fast courtships, respecting their children's moral agency in choosing whom and when to marry. In the *Twilight* series, then, the relative youth of so many of these immortal or imprinted couples could be understood as a reflection of Mormon culture. Also common are the supportive reactions that Bella's and Edward's parents had, both to the young couple's decision to marry and to their very brief engagement.

Female Power in Motherhood

Another way in which normative social values are written into the texts has to do with how the novels promote marked gender roles, specifically relating to women and motherhood. Bella is responsible for many of the domestic responsibilities traditionally encouraged of Mormon women. She regularly prepares meals for Charlie, and doing so is always described as making "Charlie's dinner" rather than "our dinner." The deliberateness of Bella's cooking *for Charlie* highlights the expectation that women should prepare meals for the men in their families. This gender expectation is also evident among the Cullens (Esme and Rosalie prepare food for Bella, but Carlisle, Jasper, and Emmett never do) and the Quileute (Emily prepares food for the pack of werewolf boys, and Sue Clearwater cooks for Charlie after Bella leaves).

Bella is also the stereotypical damsel in distress for much of the series. She is repeatedly described as clumsy and accident-prone, so she relies on the various men in her life to keep her safe. As a result, there is a paternalistic quality to nearly all of Bella's relationships with men. Arguably, the first time Bella is *more* than a frail human dependent on men to save her is after she has become a mother, which coincides with her new supernatural vampire strength. The new powers that Bella claims surrounding childbirth reinforce an idea that female strength is connected to one's ability to be a mother. Even as a vampire, her abilities are notably maternal in that they are not aggressive but shielding, enabling her to protect her family from harmful outside forces.

Mormon women are strongly encouraged to become mothers. Men, who are ordained as priests, are thought to be responsible for carrying on the *spiritual rebirth* of the family, while women are considered responsible for the *physical birth* and nurturing of the family. In this way, mothers and fathers are seen as equal partners in raising families, although they have different responsibilities. This sense that motherhood is not only a gift, but also part of a woman's divine purpose and power, becomes a central issue for many of the female characters in the book.[35] Vampire women seriously struggle with their inability to bear children. For Edward's sister Rosalie, the inability to have children is what makes her envy Bella and value human life. She even comments on how her attraction to Emmett is in part because of his resemblance to a son she hoped to have.[36] For Esme, the death of her baby led her to attempt suicide by jumping off a cliff, the event that led to Carlisle finding and transforming her.[37] As a vampire, Esme deals with her inability to have children by "adopting" the children that Carlisle has "fathered," and by allowing those relationships to serve as a kind of substitute motherhood. The discussions of Immortal Children also reinforce how desperately vampire women have wanted to be mothers. They turned infants into vampires which resulted in terribly strong monster babies. Nonetheless, when the Immortal Children were destroyed, it deeply traumatized the vampire world, especially the mothers who had created them. Further, Leah Clearwater, the only female werewolf, also expresses concerns that she may have lost the choice to become a mother.

The suffering of these women who are unable to be mothers provides the backdrop to Bella's own dangerous pregnancy. The result is a setup that strongly endorses a pro-life message. It emphasizes Bella's pregnancy as a miraculous gift, one that is envied and wished for by all of the women around her. Abortion is an absolute impossibility in Bella's newly empowered (motherly) mind. Even when the baby is killing her and when Edward wants to terminate the fetus, Bella and Rosalie consider it their sacred maternal responsibility to protect the baby. Despite the grim improbability of her survival, Bella has a kind of religious faith that she will live to be a mother to her baby. Edward is "converted" to Bella's faith once the baby is born. Multiple passages discuss the religious and reverential ways he looks down at his miraculously born baby. Bella's conviction throughout her pregnancy reinforces the impression that motherhood is part of her purpose and her destined plan. Becoming a mother empowers her both emotionally and physically, and it is the circumstance needed to complete her "sealing" to her new eternal family. After the baby is born and Bella's motherhood is fully realized, Edward injects Bella with his venom. He then licks Bella's skin with each bite, causing the skin to literally "seal" the venom inside Bella as she is reborn into her glorified, immortal condition.[38]

Religious Readings of Twilight

The previous sections were devoted to exploring the ways in which Mormonism can be seen in the *Twilight* series, both through its focus on key beliefs regarding marriage, agency, and sacrifice, and through its inclusion of cultural norms regarding gender roles, coupling, and motherhood. After having examined how these beliefs and cultural norms are noticeable in the series, I also felt it was important to explore a variety of readers' responses to religious elements in the texts. In poring through newspapers, blogs, reviews, and religious websites, I have found radically mixed reactions from religious readers: there are both those who see *Twilight* as religious allegory and fodder for Bible Study, and those who see it as blasphemy.[39] Meyer herself has had concerns about reactions from her own religious community, and admits to being asked fairly frequently, "What's a nice Mormon girl like you doing writing about vampires?"[40]

The series has received ambivalent responses from the Mormon community. Some readers have expressed concern about the series' focus on vampires, as well as its eroticism and its exploration of teenage intimacy. One Mormon strongly opposed to the series contended that the books are "the antithesis of Mormon doctrine and should be disturbing to any faithful active member," largely for their provocation of erotic thoughts and feelings.[41] Other Mormons have defended Meyer by arguing that it is unfair to scrutinize the books for their adherence to or promotion of Mormonism, especially since the books do not claim to be Mormon novels. A third response by Mormon readers was to advocate the series, arguing that it is "clean" reading which promotes chastity until marriage, highlights solid family values, and emphasizes the importance of choosing to live virtuously. These mixed reviews have been controversial enough for the bookstore chain owned by The Church of Jesus Christ of Latter-day Saints, Deseret Book, to stop carrying the *Twilight* series. Likely in reaction to what some considered mature romantic content, Deseret Book issued a company statement explaining, "When we find products that are met with mixed review, we typically move them to special order status."[42]

Other Christian groups have latched onto the series, however, using its popularity as a means of outreach to engage young church members. Several Christian organizations have lauded the books for their emphases on supernatural love, chaste relationships, avoidance of temptation, and concern for the soul's welfare in the afterlife. One evangelical magazine, *Christianity Today,* posted along with its movie review of *Twilight* a list of discussion starters to accompany Bible Study. The questions ask teenage church members to think about the books' values in relation to selected Biblical passages. For example, one question refers to verses in Matthew, Mark, and Romans, and follows up with the question, "How are Edward's attempts not to give in to his evil desires like the life of a Christian?"[43]

John Mark Reynolds, an Orthodox professor at evangelical Biola University, also writes that *Twilight* addresses Christian morality and concerns about salvation. Reynolds commends the series for suggesting to readers that divine mercy and grace are available to all, since "even a vampire may have a soul and escape damnation."[44] His primary critique of the book is that it encourages a recklessly unchecked love—one that is directed passionately towards another human being rather than towards God. Another Orthodox reader, John Granger, responded to this critique by suggesting that Reynolds is not fully accounting for the allegory in *Twilight*'s romance, which should wholly be understood as the Spiritual love between God and Man, a "Mormon *Pilgrim's Progress* or *Commedia* wrapped inside a Harlequin romance."[45] Reynolds and Granger are two examples of many readers who found the themes in *Twilight* speaking to broadly Christian issues, rather than exclusively Mormon ones.

Of course, other readers have interpreted the novels in radically divergent ways. The series has faced vitriolic backlashes by some fundamentalist groups similar to those experienced by J.K. Rowling's *Harry Potter* series: namely critiques that the books deal with Satanic subject matter (like vampires, blood-drinking, and supernatural powers). At the other extreme, some readers have contended that the books are a form of Mormon proselytism which, according to one blogger, functions to "till the soil in the hearts of young LDS women" to prepare them to accept key religious values. This blogger goes on to suggest that the books introduce non–Mormon readers to a sanitized version of LDS theology, made glamorous and cool by its mainstream popularity.[46] This concern with sneaky Mormon proselytism has been written about both by impassioned Christians and secularists, but consistently without substantive reasoning. Usually such claims are loaded with derisive anti–Mormon rhetoric and demonstrate ill-informed and unwieldy biases on the part of their proponents.

Conclusion

There is no doubt that Meyer's active membership in the Mormon Church has a significant influence on her writing. Her religion should be understood as informing her writing, laying the foundations for what it means to be an eternal couple, a vegetarian vampire, and an empowered mother. However, understanding that religion shapes Meyer's storytelling—in terms of the concepts, narratives, and symbols she uses—should not be confused with saying too simply that *Twilight* is a Mormon series. Meyer's intentions in creating and promoting these books, the deeply mixed reactions among Mormons to the series, and the series' ability to be interpreted religiously through various Christian lenses all contribute to debunking generalized claims that *Twilight* is Mormon.

Notes

1. The use of the term "Mormon" is controversial. In years past, the church has indicated that it was inappropriate to refer to the Church of Jesus Christ of Latter-day Saints as "Mor-

mon," saying that "Mormon" should only refer to the scriptural Book of Mormon. However, the church's position has shifted in recent years so that the term "Mormon" is acceptable, although "Latter-day Saints" is generally preferred. In this essay, I am following the lead of Richard N. and Joan K. Ostling who suggest it is reasonable to use the term "Mormon" because of its common and unbothered use by many members of the community of Latter-day Saints, and also because the term is so ingrained in everyday usage that it is unlikely to be avoided in public discourse. In interviews, Stephenie Meyer has not shied away from self-identifying as a Mormon, and academic works on this religious community frequently use the term. Therefore, in order to avoid the wordiness of stating the full name of the Church of Jesus Christ of Latter-day Saints at every turn, I will follow the Ostlings' lead in occasionally using the church's full name, while more frequently relying on the term "Mormon" to refer to members of this church and its teachings, practices, and culture. See Preface of Richard N. and Joan K. Ostling, *Mormon America* (New York: HarperOne, 2007), x–xi.

2. Jana Reiss from Publishers Weekly is credited with identifying these two reasons for the public's interest in Meyer's religion: her openness about it, and the exoticised minority status of Mormonism. See Irwin, Megan. "Charmed: Stephenie Meyer's Vampire Romance Novels Made a Mormon Mom an International Success." *Phoenix New Times News*, July 12, 2007, under line break beginning "One thing that hasn't changed," http://www.phoenixnewtimes.com/2007–07–12/news/charmed/.

3. Carol Memmott, "'Twilight' author Stephenie Meyer unfazed as fame dawns," *USA Today*, July 30, 2008, http://www.usatoday.com/life/books/news/2008-07-30-stephenie-meyer-main_N.htm.

4. My understanding of religion as a system of words, narratives, and stories told to make sense of the world around us is largely influenced by religion scholar Reza Aslan. For more on this understanding of religion, see various interviews with Reza Aslan posted online, or Reza Aslan, *No God but God* (New York: Random House, 2006), xxv.

5. Robert Sullivan, "Dreamcatcher," *Vogue*, ed. for Style.com, March 2009, http://www.vogue.com/feature/2009_March_Stephenie_Meyer/.

6. For more information about the family as the fundamental unit of Mormon church organization, and the role of gender within that organization, see Marie Cornwall, "The Institutional Role of Mormon Women," in *Contemporary Mormonism*, ed. Marie Cornwall, Tim B. Heaton, and Lawrence A. Young (Urbana: University of Illinois Press, 1994).

7. Gender is described in Mormon scripture as "an essential characteristic of individual premortal, mortal, and eternal identity and purpose." For more information on this teaching, see "The Family: A Proclamation to the World" read by President Gordon B. Hinckley on September 23, 1995. Proclamations given by church presidents, who are considered modern-day prophets, become part of Latter-day Saint scripture. The full text of this proclamation can be found at the official website of the Church of Jesus Christ of Latter-day Saints. See The Church of Jesus Christ of Latter-day Saints, "The Family: a Proclamation to the World, " http://www.lds.org/library/display/0,4945,161-1-11-1,00.html.

8. Stephenie Meyer, *Breaking Dawn* (New York: Little, Brown and Company, 2008), 32.

9. Based on the emphasis on intergenerational families, Mormons are also encouraged to keep detailed family records and genealogies. This effort to maintain recorded connections to past generations can be noted in Bella's decision to name Renesmee. The baby's full name is Renesmee Carlie, named first for Bella and Edward's mothers (Renee and Esme) and second for Bella and Edward's fathers (Charlie and Carlisle).

10. The Church of Jesus Christ of Latter-day Saints, *Gospel Principles* (Salt Lake City, Utah: The Church of Jesus Christ of Latter-day Saints, 1988), 222. Latter-day Saints make a distinction between marriages that take place inside or outside a Mormon temple. Temples are sacred places reserved for ceremonies and rituals and which may only be accessed by practicing and observant Saints. Marriages are one such ceremony that must happen within a temple in order for a couple to be sealed.

11. Stephenie Meyer, *Eclipse* (New York: Little, Brown and Company, 2007), 143. The sense

of the eternal couple is also evident in the experience of imprinting that happens among the Quileute werewolves. To imprint is a condition in which a male and female are perfectly matched for one another. For example, when Sam imprints on Emily, it is described as an instantaneous moment in which he became entirely focused on her; Emily became the center of Sam's world. The idea of existing apart from one's destined companion is both painful and unthinkable for one who has imprinted.

Imprinting is made particularly problematic in the *Twilight* series because the werewolves are much older boys who sometimes imprint on very, very young girls. The most charitable reading of this would be to see these couples as "predestined," a common theme in Mormon literature. Based on the Mormon belief in premortal life, predestined coupling supposes that couples know each another in a premortal life and then come to earth with lingering commitments. In this case, the couples are born at different ages, but they are fulfilling commitments made prior to coming to earth, before there was an age difference to be concerned with. For more about premortal coupling in *Twilight* and as a theme in Mormon literature, see Eric W. Jepson, "Saturday's Werewolf: Vestiges of the Premortal Romance in Stephenie Meyer's Twilight Novels," *Reading Until Dawn* 1, no. 2 (2009), http://www.motleyvision.org/readinguntildawn/ojs/index.php?journal=readinguntildawn&page=article&op=viewFile&path[]=5&path[]=33.

As an aside, there are those who have attempted to link Mormonism to the books' disturbing discussions of imprinting on very young girls. To clear up some confusion, it would be extremely problematic to associate Meyer's writing about imprinting on young girls with the scandals of underage marriage that have arisen in the FLDS church. The Fundamentalist Church of Jesus Christ of Latter-day Saints (FLDS) is a denomination that broke off from the mainstream Church of Jesus Christ of Latter-day Saints (LDS). The FLDS Church is not recognized by the LDS Church. FLDS communities have received a lot of media attention for illegal marriages of underage females to significantly older men. Because of popular misunderstandings that conflate the FLDS church with the LDS church, many members of the LDS (mainstream Mormon) church have had to fight misconceptions about its marriage practices. The LDS Church does not allow underage marriage (or polygamy, which is another common misconception), and its marriage practices should not be confused with those of the FLDS church.

12. See William Morris, "Interview: *Twilight* author Stephenie Meyer," *A Motley Vision*, interview posted October 26, 2005, http://www.motleyvision.org/2005/interview-twilight-author-stephanie-meyer/.

13. The Church of Jesus Christ of Latter-day Saints, *Gospel Principles*, 31.

14. Transcript of Book Signing Q&A with Stephenie Meyer, "The Breaking Dawn Concert Tour-Seattle Q&A," Twilight Lexicon, http://www.twilightlexicon.com/?page_id=1323.

15. Stephenie Meyer, *Twilight* (New York: Little, Brown and Company, 2008), 24

16. One complicating factor to Meyer's emphasis on free agency is the process of imprinting, an experience in which two people meet and their entire world is said to shift. (See footnote 13 for more on imprinting.) Meyer insinuates that her characters still have the right to choose their imprinted partner, but the imprinting experience is so strong that their choice is a foregone conclusion. Even characters who do not technically imprint still experience a similar sense of predestined coupling (i.e., Bella and Edward, Carlisle and Esme, and Alice and Jasper.) One Mormon writer argues that although this concept of the predestined couple complicates values about free agency, it is still relatively common to Mormon literature. It relies on a belief in premortal life, and an idea of lingering commitments meant to be fulfilled on earth. For more of this analysis, see Jepson article cited in note 11 and for another kind of imprinting, see Jensen's article in this volume.

It is possible that Meyer was unaware of this theme in Mormon literature. She has written that her interest in imprinting was inspired by two other sources: imprinting that happens in nature between ducklings and their parent ducks, and imprinting in Anne McCaffrey's series of books about dragons, in which humans and dragons bond in extreme ways. She writes that her interest in imprinting was based on wanting to further explore this kind of "life-changing and compulsory relationship." See Stephenie Meyer, "New Moon: The Movie. TheTwilightSaga.com's Q and A with Stephenie Meyer," *Stephenie Meyer Official Website*, http://www.stepheniemeyer.com/nm_movie_qanda.html.

17. As a note that is insignificant but interesting, there is one small passage in *New Moon* that may be seen as indicative of the LDS abstention from caffeinated beverages. On the plane ride home from Rome, Bella is determined to stay awake and orders a Coke from the flight attendant. "'Bella,' Edward said disapprovingly. He knew my low tolerance for caffeine." (New York: Little, Brown and Company, 2007), 494.

18. Meyer, *Breaking Dawn*, 718.

19. The self-discipline required by the vampires should not be devalued as a simple decision to only drink animal blood. Meyer has explained the extent of pain that a thirsty vampire feels. She has written that a vampire who refuses to drink blood can feel thirst in the way that an anorexic will feel starvation; however, since the vampire is immortal, that pain will simply continue to intensify over time with no end. She writes that according to her own vampire mythology, a vampire who abstains from blood is in "acute physical pain ... literally crazy for relief—beyond thought." Despite drinking animal blood, a vampire's avoidance of human blood causes "constant pain" and is an act of intense physical endurance. "Personal Correspondence 12," Twilight Lexicon, entry posted May 20, 2007, http://www.twilightlexicon.com/?p=360.

20. Meyer, *Eclipse*, 18.

21. Meyer, *New Moon*, 472.

22. Christie Davies, "Coffee, Tea and the Ultra-Protestant and Jewish Nature of the Boundaries of Mormonism," in *Mormon Identities in Transition*, ed. Douglas J. Davies (London: Cassell, 1996), 38.

23. Dean L. May, "Mormons," in *Mormons and Mormonism*, ed. Eric A. Eliason (Urbana: University of Illinois Press, 2001), 72–74.

24. See Meyer, *Twilight*, 1, for the first quote about Bella's sacrifice. For references to her sacrifice in Volterra or to the Quileute story, see (respectively): *New Moon*, 436; and *Eclipse*, 252–260.

25. See Meyer, *Breaking Dawn*, 187.

26. See Meyer, *Breaking Dawn*, 719.

27. Lev Grossman, "Stephenie Meyer: A New J.K. Rowling?" *Time*, April 24, 2008, http://www.time.com/time/magazine/article/0,9171,1734838-1,00.html.

28. Gail Collins, "A Virginal Goth Girl," *The New York Times*, July 12, 2008, under Op-Ed, http://www.nytimes.com/2008/07/12/opinion/12colllins.html.

29. One instance of Meyer's deliberate attempts at making her work "clean" is that the films could not be so graphic as to be R-rated. Meyer has never seen an R-rated movie and knows that such a rating would be off-limits to many of her fans who are also part of the Mormon community.

30. See interview in Gregory Kirschling, "Stephenie Meyer's 'Twilight' Zone," *Entertainment Weekly*, July 5, 2008, http://www.ew.com/ew/article/0,,20049578,00.html.

31. See Meyer, *Breaking Dawn*, 83.

32. See Meyer, *Breaking Dawn*, 16–17.

33. This entry was posted on a well-known website for Mormon bloggers. See Natalie B., "Reading Twilight through the lens of my Mormon youth," By *Common Consent* (BCC), entry posted January 1, 2009, http://bycommonconsent.com/2009/01/01/reading-twilight-through-the-lens-of-my-mormon-youth/.

34. Thomas B. Holman, "Commitment Making Mate Selection Processes among Active Mormon American Couples," in *Mormon Identities in Transition*, ed. Douglas J. Davies (London: Cassell, 1996), 129–130.

35. Interestingly, this emphasis on motherhood frequently appears in discussions of Meyer herself. She is often described as a mother to her young female readers, and has thrown Proms and slumber parties for her readers to attend.

36. Meyer, *Eclipse,* 167.
37. Meyer, *Twilight*, 368.
38. Meyer, *Breaking Dawn*, 355.
39. There were a couple of reasons for the decision to research reader responses through online blogs and comment boards. First, it allowed me to view the wide array of reader responses, and to gauge the relative popularity or dismissal of some interpretations over others. Second, I spent time with blogs because I was specifically interested in Mormon reader responses, and blogging has become a common way for Mormons to gather online and share ideas. Mormons have been encouraged to use the internet to blog and share the gospel, and it has been an overwhelmingly popular activity—a means of extending an already-very-alive emphasis on record keeping among Mormons. For a great discussion of the rise of the "Mormon Bloggernacle," see related articles and comments in *Religion Dispatches.* Specifically see Krista Kapralos, "Birth of the Bloggernacle," *Religion Dispatches*, February 24, 2009, http://www.religiondispatches.org/archive/mediaculture/1148/ and Krista Kapralos, "Mormon Bloggernacle is No Choir," *Religion Dispatches*, March 4, 2009, http://www.religiondispatches.org/archive/mediaculture/1179/.
40. Barnes & Noble Books, "Meet the Author," under "Good to Know" heading, Barnes & Noble website, http://search.barnesandnoble.com/Eclipse/Stephenie-Meyer/e/9780316160209#TABS.
41. Opinions by strongly offended Mormon readers were posted on the blog "Mormon Matters," within an entry exploring whether or not *Twilight* should be considered a Mormon text. See entry by Hawkgrrrl, "Twilight and 'The Great Mormon Novel,'" Mormon Matters blog, posted November 24, 2008, http://mormonmatters.org/2008/11/24/twilight-and-the-great-mormon-novel/.
42. Statement published in Ethan Thomas, "'Twilight' loses luster with Deseret Books," *Deseret News*, April 23, 2009, http://www.deseretnews.com/article/705299108/Twilight-loses-luster-with-Deseret-Book.html.
43. Bible study discussion starters followed a *Twilight* film review that was posted on the website for *Christianity Today*. See Todd Hertz, "Twilight," *Christianity Today*, entry posted November 21, 2008, http://www.christianitytoday.com/ct/movies/reviews/2008/twilight.html?start=1.
44. See John Mark Reynolds, "Twilight's Flawed Faith," *The Scriptorium*, entry posted July 31, 2009, http://www.scriptoriumdaily.com/2009/07/31/twilights-flawed-faith/.
45. See John Granger, "John Mark Reynolds on Twilight," Forks High School Professor personal blog, posted August 7, 2009, http://fhsprofessor.com/?p=131.
46. See personal blog of Amie Charney, "Twilight preaches Mormonism," posted November 22, 2008, http://writetools.wordpress.com/?s=twilight.

Bella and the Choice Made in Eden

SUSAN JEFFERS

Introduction

In their article titled "*Vampire-Dämmerung*: What Can *Twilight* Tell Us About God?," Peter S. Fosl and Eli Fosl argue that there is no God in the *Twilight* series, and that all the characters are involved in a quest for existential self-actualization.[1] I suggest that for a series of books with no God, this one is permeated with theology. Stephenie Meyer is a member of the Church of Jesus Christ of Latter-day Saints,[2] and evidence of the relatively unique beliefs of that faith is present throughout her series. Among the many points of LDS doctrine possible to address,[3] I will discuss specifically how Latter-day Saint doctrine on the Fall, moral agency, and the afterlife appear in these books. The story of the Fall involves the actions of Eve, and the struggles of Bella Swan are reminiscent of Eve's life-journey as expressed by Latter-day Saint theology. I am not suggesting that Stephenie Meyer intended for Bella to represent Eve, but the notion of Eve as a hero is so ingrained in Mormon culture that the connection between Bella and Eve exists regardless of authorial intent. Therefore, a consideration of Eve's place within LDS culture and theology can add insight into Bella Swan's character.

Some readers see Bella Swan as wholly submissive, dependent on male authority, acquiescent to traditional gender roles, and in general weak in mind, body, and character. She is viewed as the stereotypical oppressed female and the four *Twilight* books as tools that reify tyrannical social systems. The reading provided by this essay, however, offers a different way of understanding Bella. As viewed through the LDS lens, rather than being a co-dependent victim of an oppressive patriarchal structure, she is in fact an active agent in her own life who insists on redefining the terms by which others understand her. The agency exercised by both Bella and Eve during their journeys demonstrates the kind of self-empowerment prized by feminism.

Although in a curious way they are moving in opposite directions, both Eve and Bella follow a typical heroic trajectory. They each leave what is familiar and safe to explore the unknown, and as they experience life, they make choices and learn. In Mormon theology, Eve moves from a state of innocence and perfection to one of fallen mortality in order to embrace her personal, eternal progression, her moral agency, and the good of her family. In the Garden, Eve exists in an unblemished state of ease, but there her mode of being is incomplete and therefore imperfect, so she progresses through mortality to achieve a final state of completion and perfection. Bella achieves a similar state of happiness as her experiences move her from a vulnerable, mortal, corruptible state towards one of everlasting perfection. She moves, one might say, from a fallen Eve to an Eve redeemed, becoming a fictional "Second Eve."[4] Bella's persistent passivity and relative impotence sometimes frustrate readers, but when read in light of LDS doctrine on the Fall, her position is one that actually embraces agency.

Eve and Bella as Heroes

While Eve is never presented as an actively malignant figure, much Christian discourse at least implies, through the notion of original sin, that her gullibility and vanity led to the damnation of all humankind. If only she had been wiser, if only she had been content with her place in the Garden, the reasoning goes, everyone would be happy now.[5] Latter-day Saints, though, have an opposing view of the Fall. They believe that mortality is a necessary condition for progression, and that mortality was only made possible by the Fall. They believe that a plan for human existence, personal progression, and mortality existed before Creation, and in this plan provision was made for the Fall through the Atonement. Because the Fall was necessary to bring to pass humans' mortal condition, Bruce R. McConkie describes it as a fall "downward and forward and onward."[6] Although somewhat neglecting Eve's agency here, he further considers the Fall as "Adam's gift to man," explaining that "the gift of God would be eternal life through Jesus Christ our Lord. Thus, existence came from God; death came by Adam; and immortality and eternal life come through Christ."[7] Since the Atonement redeems all humanity from the so-called "original sin," and since the Fall ushered in the next phase of humanity's collective development, Latter-day Saints see any negative consequences of the Fall as either nonexistent or necessary for people's continuing progression. Without the Fall, a mortal existence would be forever denied not only to Adam and Eve, but to the entire human family — and in Latter-day Saint theology, to be denied mortality would be the real tragedy.

The Fall was less a punishment than a natural consequence of Eve and Adam's *deliberate* choice, and so Eve is a hero for her part in forwarding humanity's progress. Without the choice she made, according to LDS theology, no one would ever have been born. She chose to give up the ease of stasis, the privilege of speaking with God face-to-face, and the Paradise of the Garden; and in exchange for this, she was promised sorrow and pain, but also goodness, peace, and joy. What is more, she made the choice willingly. While Satan introduced her to the idea of eating the fruit, she knew that by so doing she would be cast out of the Garden of Eden. She may not have known exactly how difficult and heartbreaking mortality could be, but given the choice between stasis and growth, she chose growth. Joseph Fielding Smith (the 10th President of the Church of Jesus Christ of Latter-day Saints, not to be confused with his great-uncle, Joseph Smith) applauds her, saying:

> Adam and Eve could have remained in the Garden of Eden; they could have been there to this day, if Eve hadn't done something. One of these days, if I ever get to where I can speak to Mother Eve, I want to thank her for tempting Adam to partake of the fruit.... If she hadn't had that influence over Adam, and if Adam had done according to the commandment [not to eat the forbidden fruit], they would still be in the Garden of Eden and we would not be here at all.[8]

At one point in *The Pearl of Great Price* (one of the books of Mormon scripture) Eve says "Were it not for our transgression we never should have had seed, and never should have known good and evil, and the joy of our redemption, and the eternal life which God giveth unto all the obedient."[9]

Eve rejoices in the happy consequences of her choice, and Latter-day Saint women are encouraged to pattern themselves after her and to think of themselves in similarly positive ways.[10] For Latter-day Saint women, Eve represents themselves. Because of her representative status as a template for all women, it is possible, first, for the template of Eve to influence Meyer's creation of the character Bella, and second, for Bella to be read as Eve. Like Eve, Bella makes a difficult choice to leave behind the relatively safe life with which she is familiar and progress on to something new and potentially dangerous, and Bella's choice, like Eve's, ultimately brings happiness to almost everyone involved. Her desire and ultimate decision to become a vampire reflects her pioneering character, but there are other ways in which she makes difficult choices that require her to explore new communities, lifestyles, and friendships. As she redefines her own existence, her choices have far-reaching effects on others as well as herself.

Bella's yearning for something better and her determination to achieve her goals make her heroic in the same way that Eve is heroic, and not just by LDS standards of heroism. Carol Pearson and Katherine Pope argue for a definition of female heroism that can be applied to many characters in Western literature.[11] In constructing their argument, they look at Jane Eyre and Bertha Rochester from *Jane Eyre,* Tess Durbeyfield in *Tess of the D'Urbervilles,* and Kate Brown in *The Summer Before the Dark,* among many others. Female heroes, just like male heroes, they say, act with "bravery, strength, and wisdom."[12] Pearson and

Pope point out that any heroic journey "is a psychological journey in which the hero escapes from the captivity of her conditioning and searches for her true self."[13] They further observe that for female heroes, the captivity is often represented by some kind of enclosed space, and that leaving this physical space also involves a mental and emotional rejection of the mother, which is the first step on a journey towards both psychological freedom and self-actualization.[14] Although another quest may be involved as well, the hero, male or female, goes out to gain experience from the world. Pearson and Pope argue that for female characters this departure often involves the need to find a male authorizer, but sexual autonomy is what marks a female hero's triumph over this particular hurdle.[15] As the female hero discovers and accepts her own identity, she confronts her rejection of her mother and instead embraces her mother and the mother within herself.[16] In Pearson and Pope's view, the reward at the end of the female hero's journey is herself, her true self, viewed without the entrapments of her enculturation. They use Jane Eyre as an example of this, observing that "when Jane learns to be her own mistress, Bertha dies, Thornfield burns down, Rochester is maimed, and Jane inherits money."[17] All of those events are outward signs of Jane's inner change. While she is rewarded with both money and an egalitarian marriage, Jane's true reward is the independence and freedom of choice she has gained. As a result of her bravery, the female hero, whoever she is, can "know the joy of independence or of a loving community between heroic equals.... In the comic mode, the hero returns and becomes part of a rejuvenated human community. In tragedy, she finds community in the spiritual realm. In both cases, she values herself and therefore is not dependent on social approval or on a male figure to complete and validate her."[18]

Pearson and Pope's description of the female heroic journey applies equally well to that of both Eve and Bella as both leave their homes to confront themselves. In the Mormon understanding of her story, Eve goes out into the world to experience all that mortality has to offer. Likewise, Bella willingly sacrifices the sunny familiarity of Phoenix for life in rainy Forks, and once there she embraces the experiences of love, fear, joy, and tragedy that confront her. As a part of their respective experiences, Eve and Bella experience sex, sensuality, and new physical sensations. Eve finds joy in her role as First Mother, and Bella also finds an unexpected joy in her own eventual status as a mother. Latter-day Saints believe that Eve is among the blessed and has a secure place in Heaven, participating in a spiritual (and, according to LDS thought, physical) community. Likewise, Bella enjoys a happy existence with her nearly immortal family at the end of her heroic journey. Careful reading reveals Bella's growing independence and self-determination throughout the series, so that by the end of *Breaking Dawn,* Edward is her companion, not her master, and Bella is able to recognize and employ her own gifts and strengths. Her trip to Seattle to secure documents for Jacob and Renesmee is one example of her acting independently.[19] Just as Eve rejoiced in her new life in mortality and in her family, so too does Bella find self-fulfillment in her life with her new family after she becomes a vampire. These experiences are closely tied to each woman's physical condition, for without becoming mortal Eve would never have become a mother; without becoming a vampire, Bella would have died in childbirth, and without being mortal, she would never have had children. Bella's physical being influences the kind of experiences she is able to have, just as Eve's influences hers, and for each their physical state is essential to their experience and progression.

The happiness Eve and Bella find in their families that comes from their physical being exemplifies and extends third-wave feminist theories which valorize the physical aspects of womanhood. Some contemporary feminists, such as Elizabeth Grosz, are working to reclaim the female body as a symbol of empowerment rather than as an obstacle to be overcome.[20] Grosz argues that a woman's physical experience can be as valid a way of knowing, as valid a form of philosophy, as traditional forms of reasoning.[21] This dovetails nicely with Eve's decision to enter mortality to gain knowledge and experience that is accessible in no other fashion. According to LDS theology, one condition of mortality is the physical body in which all humans find themselves. People are meant to learn to control their bodies and learn from the experiences gained from corporeality. The assumption is that people need to understand hunger, lust, broken bones, all the difficulties of being mortal, in a more than merely theoretical fashion.

Grosz's theory also supports many of Bella's decisions; Bella's certain knowledge of the connection between herself and Edward, her decision to become a vampire, and her choice to keep her baby, are related to impressions, desires, and actions rooted in bodily functions. It is no great logical leap to say that if women's lived experiences have epistemological value, and if women's lived experiences occur within a physical female body (as they must), then those experiences that come from being in a female body have value pedagogically for personal development and even fulfillment. By extension, this line of reasoning implies that Eve and Bella's experiences and personal growth are tied to their corporeality. From an LDS theological standpoint, it is impossible for anyone to progress without a mortal body. Eve's progression is dependent upon the Fall and her mortality, and the emphasis in *Breaking Dawn* on Bella's physicality and the consequences of her physical actions show how essential corporeality is to having the experiences narrated in that novel.

Eve and Bella can also be considered examples of feminist reclamation by their rejection of patriarchal systems. Eve's position as a hero within LDS culture is a strong refutation of oppressive attitudes that seek to undermine women's authority. LDS theology suggests that Eve should be applauded for her carefully considered action. She acts initially as a self-interested agent by partaking of the fruit, deciding for herself that wisdom is better than innocence. She does not consult or seek authorization from anyone else, nor does she indicate any craving for male approval. Her decision, and the fact that she makes it on her own to benefit herself, demonstrates her individuality and status as an agent. While she does choose to share her wisdom with Adam, and while her actions do benefit the whole human family, she first of all acts in her own self-interest, and according to Mormon doctrine she is free to do so. There is no significant attempt to control her, nor is there any indication of any kind of oppressive action or attitude that would otherwise prevent her action. Bella's decision-making process is similar to Eve's. In *Twilight* she says, "Making decisions was the painful part to me.... But once the decision was made, I simply followed through."[22] While Bella's ability to make choices will be discussed in greater depth in the following section, it is worth noting here that, like Eve, Bella does make decisions on her own based on her own desires and reasoning. She is also subject to the consequences—good or bad—of those decisions, also like Eve, like all of us.

Bella rejects the violence inherent in a patriarchal system as well. One way she does this is by refusing to be an object in a homosocial triangle.[23] Some readers may see Bella's need to choose between Edward and Jacob as a classic manifestation of patriarchal oppression. In this reading, Edward and Jacob are trying to negotiate their relationship, supremacy, and potency with each other by using Bella as an object signifying those things; whoever possesses or "wins" her would therefore be more powerful than the other. There is evidence to support this reading, particularly in *Eclipse,* where Edward and Jacob literally hand Bella off to each other. While this is an understandable reading, it is one that completely disregards Bella's own choices and status as an agent. Bella refuses to allow Edward and Jacob to remain rivals, and she engineers circumstances that require them to put their differences aside and work together. She insists that they find common ground, first in their mutual affection for her, and second, in their mutual need to protect their families from outside forces. When Bella marries Edward and Jacob imprints on their child, Edward and Jacob are forced to renegotiate their relationship themselves, and Bella and Renesmee are facilitators in this negotiation, rather than being objects signifying the power of their male partners. The birth of Renesmee thus precipitates the crisis that forces Edward and Jacob to reconsider and express their feelings about their relationship to each other. By the end of the series, Bella has restructured the homosocial triangle into a family circle in which everyone is valued and secure in their place. Her concern for those she loves, for her "family" (even as constructed by herself), and her heroic efforts to achieve it and protect it, may be compared to Eve's.

Eve and Bella as Agents

Agency is crucial to the purpose of life and human progression, according to LDS theology. "Agency" and "agents" are words that have also become very popular with literary theorists and critics lately, and the meaning of these words can be somewhat fluid. However, when Latter-day Saints speak of agency, they have a very specific meaning in mind. D. Todd Christofferson suggests that true agency contains at least the three following elements:

> First, there must be alternatives among which to choose.... Second, for us to have agency, we must not only have alternatives, but we must also know what they are.... Third [there must be] the freedom to make choices. This freedom to act for ourselves in choosing among alternatives is often referred to in the scriptures as agency itself.[24]

In other words, to truly have agency, people must know what they are doing and what is involved in their choices, and be free to act on that knowledge. If people lack any one of those three elements, then they lack agency. According to Mormons, the ability of humans to make choices is the one thing with which God never interferes, though He may try to influence the choices they make. Agency is important in LDS theology in part because being human is the means whereby people learn and progress. Without agency, human existence would be purposeless.

Eve is the prototypical agent. While Latter-day Saints believe that human agency is an eternal principle, that people had agency before mortality and can continue to have it in the afterlife, Eve is the first figure in scripture who demonstrates it. According to Christofferson's definition, for Eve to have been an agent, she must have had options from which to choose, knowledge of her choices, and the freedom to act on those choices. A quick review of her story, according to LDS doctrine, reveals her status as an agent. First, Eve did have options from which to choose. When Adam and Eve were placed in the Garden of Eden, they were commanded to "be fruitful, and multiply,"[25] a commandment Mormons believe could not be carried out while Adam and Eve remained in the Garden. The *Book of Mormon* explains that without the Fall, "all things which were created must have remained in the same state in which they were after they were created; and they must have remained forever, and had no end. And they [meaning Adam and Eve] would have had no children; wherefore they would have remained in a state of innocence, having no joy, for they knew no misery; doing no good, for they knew no sin."[26] Eve's choice was between two good commandments, to be fruitful and multiply or to avoid eating the forbidden fruit and remain forever in the Garden. She also had knowledge of both choices. God spoke directly to her when he gave her and Adam the commandment to have children.[27] She also acknowledges that she understands the consequences of her choice, and in eating the fruit Eve demonstrates her freedom to make that choice. Furthermore she uses her position as an agent to help others, sharing the wisdom she gained with Adam — rather than using her greater wisdom to try to control him. Latter-day Saints argue that Eve demonstrated care for the entire human family by choosing wisdom and keeping the commandment to have children, rather than choosing to avoid the fruit.

Agency is important throughout the *Twilight* series. As Edward explains to Bella, just because vampires are subject to certain impulses or desires, "it doesn't mean that [they] can't choose to ... conquer the boundaries of a destiny that none of [them] wanted."[28] Exercising agency is how the Cullens retain their humanity and how Bella attains her goal of becoming a vampire. Among Bella's many choices, four seem especially significant. First of all, Bella chooses to come to Forks, setting in motion the events of *Twilight*. Second, she chooses Edward — again, and again, and again — against seemingly impossible odds throughout the series. Thirdly, she chooses to become a vampire. Finally, she chooses to keep her baby when she becomes pregnant. Each of these major choices depends on her previous choices. The angst of the series lies in the negotiation of her second and third choices and on her insistence that her choices be recognized. As she makes each choice, Bella becomes more free to make other choices. For each of these four choices, Bella has options, obtains knowledge about her choice and its consequences, and, eventually, gains the freedom to exercise that choice.

Each choice merits particular attention, beginning with Bella's move to Forks. She considers the consequences of this action and prepares accordingly. This decision does not make her happy, but her authority to make it is never in question; instead, her mother merely makes it clear that she is not making Bella leave. This journey is Bella's choice, and in this regard she is a fully authorized agent. The major consequence of Bella's decision to move to Forks is her introduction to Edward Cullen. Bella chooses Edward as her life partner — repeatedly — but with other young men in the picture this is not her only option. A relationship with Edward, though, is the only one that would require both partners to change in order for the relationship to be viable. While I would not go so far as to say that Bella is conscious of this factor in her decision-making process, I do think the opportunity for progression is part of Edward's appeal to her on a meta-novel level. If Bella remained single and dated a "normal" human like Mike Newton, or even chose to be with Jacob instead, she would not have to change at all. Her choice, therefore, is the same as Eve's — to stay with what is comfortable, familiar, and easy, or to try something new, challenging, and exciting.

In some ways, the love affair between Bella and Edward may seem fated. Bella says herself that she is unsure if she ever really had a choice.[29] Alice's visions of the future further reinforce this sense of destiny, as though the fate of Bella and Edward has been decided and all that is left for them is to go through the motions of romance. Yet, for a love affair that is clearly destined to have a happy ending, a lot of "choosing" happens. After a genuine attempt to give Bella up for her own good, an attempt that almost destroys himself, Bella, and the entire Cullen family, Edward chooses not to live without her. Bella likewise chooses Edward, first in *Twilight*, but again in *Eclipse, New Moon,* and *Breaking Dawn*. She has ample opportunity to leave him, but at every crossroads she chooses Edward. Again, once Bella has decided on a course of action, she stands by it.[30] She has agency when it comes to her love life because she knows her options and is free to act on that knowledge.

Bella's choice to become a vampire is one that she spends the entire series trying to implement. As far as options go, Bella has plenty of opportunities to remain mortal, but each time she chooses to go forward with her initial resolve. Really, each time she chooses Edward, she is choosing immortality. Eventually the issue becomes not one of whether she will or she will not, but of when and by what means. Bella decides at the end of *Twilight* that she is ready to move on to this new state of being,[31] and she recommits herself to that decision in *Eclipse*.[32] While tired of being saved and putting others in danger, she is also informed about what her decision to become a vampire means. Starting, as most of us do, at Google, she looks up vampires, and then moves on to real life experience. She hears different points of view on vampirism and sees first-hand the charity of Carlisle, the exploitative cruelty of the Volturi, and the selfishness and carelessness with which most vampires regard human life and each other. Bella's time with the werewolf pack of the Quileute allows her to hear from others who are familiar with vampires, and whose very existence is a rejection of them. At the time of making her choice, she could not know any more about vampires without being one herself.

Bella is not, however, entirely free to act on her choice to become a vampire initially; she gains this freedom over the course of the novels. Edward himself is her greatest obstacle, and his behavior towards Bella for the first three books is frightening in many ways. Over the course of the series, he watches her sleep, constantly tells her she is absurd, and tries to control who she sees and who her friends are. This abusive behavior is rooted in his inability to recognize Bella's agency, his inability to acknowledge that she can decide for herself what she needs. His refusal to allow her to become a vampire is further evidence of that paternalism. The three later novels focus both on Bella's becoming a vampire and Edward's dawning recognition of Bella's status as an agent. Just as Bella continues to choose him over the course of the series, and just as she remains determined in her resolve to become a vampire, so Edward makes progress in recognizing Bella's agency. At the end of *Twilight,* they are at an impasse, with neither party yielding, and at that point Bella is powerless to do anything about her wishes. At the end of *New Moon,* Edward is similarly resolved against Bella becoming a vampire and against her friendship with the werewolves, but Bella has demonstrated that she can get what she wants without him. Edward's controlling behavior continues in *Eclipse,* but he is able to make some meaningful compromises. At the end of *Eclipse,* he finally says, "I've clung with idiotic obstinacy to my idea of what's best for you, though it's only hurt you.... I don't trust myself anymore. You can have happiness your way. My way is always wrong."[33] Though Bella's decisions in *Breaking Dawn* are difficult for Edward to support initially, he realizes that she is going to do as she pleases with or without his permission. While his decision to change her into a vampire is an act of desperation made to save her life, it is also clear in *Breaking Dawn* that Bella plans on someone changing her at the birth of her child regardless. Edward's willingness to change her rather than let her die indicates the change in how he views both the idea of Bella as a vampire and the idea of Bella as an agent. Bella has to fight and negotiate with Edward for the freedom to act on her choice to be a vampire, but she does secure that freedom.[34]

After Bella becomes a vampire, she and Edward are better partners. Bella describes their first sexual experience after her change as one entirely different from their previous relations: "No caution, no restraint. No fear — especially not that. We could love *together*— both active participants now. Finally equals."[35] Adjectives such as "caution," "restraint" and "fear" characterize the nature of their physical relationship while Bella was mortal. After Edward's change of heart, Bella can be his physical equal, and with Bella's physical change, their relationship is able to progress and become purer emotionally as well. As Meyer describes it, their relationship can then be characterized as one of togetherness and equality.

Finally, Bella chooses to carry her baby to term in spite of the fact that it may harm her. This choice is significant for the analogy with Eve. In LDS doctrine, Eve finds motherhood to be a balm for the sorrows of losing Eden and the difficulties of mortality. Likewise Bella's fierce love for her unborn child makes her willing to experience potential alienation from Edward, possibly death itself, and even a friendship with the previously hostile Rosalie. Edward, Jacob, and others concerned for her life would have liked for Bella to have an abortion, but her body is her own, as are her experiences, her life, and her freedom of choice. Bella's choice in this matter is truly her own, for now she acts as a completely independent agent, more than ever before — in fact, fiercely. Though she depends on the help of those around her, she asks for aid only from those people she is certain will support her decisions. As in the case of Eve's choice, Bella's choice results in a great change for the better for her family as her "death" and Renesmee's birth eventually forge peace between Edward and Jacob. Bella's transformation also, unequivocally, aids her family in their defense against the Volturi, but more importantly, it brings bliss to Bella, Edward, and the rest of their family, extended now to include the werewolves. Bella even manages to preserve her relationship with Charlie after her transformation.

Bella's choice to leave behind her safe mortal life, to be Edward's partner, and to have her baby are all evidence of a fully empowered woman, and not, as some might feel, evidence of submission to a traditional patriarchal mindset. Bella is confident in her own personhood and can embrace her being as a female. Her choice to continue to nurture her family, just as she always has, to protect them, love them, and otherwise care for them, is just that — a choice. Bella's choice to care for her child reflects the kind of third-wave corporeal feminism advocated by Grosz and many others. In order to be respected or to be a feminist or to forward the cause of women, it is not always necessary to emulate masculine role models. Bella, like Eve, exemplifies this emphasis both on personal choice and on joy in one's female qualities.

While Bella's choices may be objectionable to some, her desire to become a vampire is almost the least shocking of her desires. Her marrying Edward at such a young age and then deciding to carry her child to term even at the probable expense of her own life has provoked criticism. However, when Bella's choices are read with LDS theology as well as third-wave feminist theory in mind, it appears that she is in control of her life much in the manner that Eve had control over her own destiny, and by the end of the series Bella is surrounded by those who have agreed to honor her agency.

Bella and the "Forever Family"

In the *Twilight* series, Stephenie Meyer has Bella finish the story that began with Eve. Eve made choices that brought her from a state of perfection to mortality, and Bella's choices take her from mortality back to a kind of perfection. Some readers might find uncomfortable the apparent glorification of vampirism in *Breaking Dawn*, but when read with LDS theology in mind, this glorification actually describes something very like the LDS version of heaven. Since not all vampires live like the Cullens, it is clearly not vampirism itself that might be compared to a heavenly existence, but the Cullens' particular practice and the way it involves approaching others in compassionate, non-exploitative ways. This attitude reflects the LDS heaven called "the Celestial Kingdom," a place where people have glorified, perfected, resurrected bodies.[36] They live in family groups and continue to produce offspring into the eternities.[37] God, Christ, and the Holy Ghost all abide there,[38] and it is a place of perfect peace, harmony, and joy. People even continue to progress there, even in heaven, because for Latter-day Saints, progression should be eternal.[39] Furthermore, Adam and Eve are there too; Eve's transformation into an exalted being is acknowledged by Latter-day Saint theology. In *Doctrine and Covenants*, Eve is seen beside Adam (and Abel and Seth) in a state of paradise prior to her resurrection,[40] and their exalted status in the Celestial Kingdom is further confirmed elsewhere in the Mormon scriptures.[41] Bella's transformation and early experiences as a newborn demonstrate one way of imagining the Celestial Kingdom. When Bella first sees herself after her transfiguration, she is amazed by her own beauty. She still looks like herself, but herself more beautiful than she ever thought she could be. Her characteristic klutziness is gone, replaced with grace and strength; as a vampire, she is finally able to realize her best possible corporeal self. Physically speaking, Bella as a vampire might fit in nicely with any other resurrected beings found in the LDS version of heaven.

Another correlation between Bella's vampiric state and the Celestial Kingdom is that she continues to dwell with a family. Latter-day Saints believe that the family is (or can be) an eternal unit, and Bella enters her immortal existence safely (ok, dramatically) in the arms of those she cares about. She leaves her human existence surrounded by her family and wakes surrounded by them also. Not only that, but because of her actions while mortal (like her determination to marry Edward and her insistence on keeping her baby), she is able to continue to raise children after she has left human mortality.

A final element of the Celestial Kingdom that I will mention here is the eternal marriage. It stands to reason that if one is to have a family forever and to raise progeny in the afterlife, then one must have an eternal partner. Eternal marriage with such a partner is characterized by, among other things, mutual respect, unconditional love, and unity of purpose. An eternal marriage, or celestial marriage as it is sometimes called, embodies the true union of two disparate souls. Given the fact that resurrected beings have bodies and are expected to produce progeny, one could conclude that this relationship will involve physical intimacy as well. Bella and Edward are able, by the end of the series, to experience this sort of union. While Edward recognizes Bella's status as an agent increasingly throughout the novels, he is able to acknowledge her agency fully, with both words and actions, only after her mortal body is transformed into a vampiric one and they have become physical equals. As discussed earlier, this physical equality indicates inward equality as well. Edward recognizes Bella's inner strength when she resists her "natural desire" to feed on humans and is almost immediately able to interact with her child, her father, and other mortals—an achievement that is all the more impressive because it is so unusual among newborn vampires. Now Edward sees her gifts and values them in a non-exploitative way, recognizing that he and Bella are partners and companions, and he ceases his attempts to control her.

True union occurs between Edward and Bella not when they have sex or marry, but when Edward fully acknowledges Bella's status as an agent and participates with her as an equal in actions designed to help their family. The first time Edward ever sees Bella *truly* naked is after the final battle with the Volturi. When Edward has acknowledged her agency and Bella is able to trust him, she pushes her shield away and allows him to read her mind and to understand her completely. At that moment, neither hides anything from the other; instead, they are united in love, purpose, and joy. This is characteristic of the LDS idea of eternal marriage: such a marriage, like Bella's and Edward's, would involve equal partners knit together, forever dwelling in a state of bliss and pure, open-hearted love.

Conclusion

Bella can be read reductively as one more silly female protagonist in a typically angsty teenage romance, but reading Bella in light of Latter-day Saint theology and third-wave feminism reveals a nuanced character dealing with themes of eternal importance, a character in this respect much like Eve. Eve is a strong, decisive, wise figure in LDS culture and thought who chooses to enter mortality to the benefit of herself and others, and as a result of her experiences in mortality, she experiences a joy unlike any she had ever known before. Bella is similarly a determined agent working out the terms of her own existence, and, in refusing to live without love, to settle for second best, or to acquiesce to what others want for her, she makes decisions about her own life that have far-reaching effects on her family. Eve, as a result of her decisions, moved from a state of perfection to mortality, and Bella, also exercising her ability to choose, finishes the cycle by moving from mortality to a blissful eternal state. The heroism of Bella and Eve (according to LDS doctrine) is consistent with the feminism that valorizes female agency — even when exercised in ways that some readers might not choose for themselves. While there remains much more to be said about the evidence of LDS theology in the *Twilight* Series and about how the series might comment on LDS culture, even this preliminary reading of Bella's desires and motivation in the light of that theology offers a fuller, less superficial understanding of her strong character and role in these popular novels.[42]

Notes

1. Peter S. Fosl and Eli Fosl, "*Vampire-Dämmerung:* What Can *Twilight* Tell Us about God?" in *Twilight and Philosophy: Vampires, Vegetarians, and the Pursuit of Immortality,* edited by Rebecca Housel and J. Jeremy Wisnewski (Hoboken, NJ: John Wiley & Sons, Inc. 2009), 63–77.

2. The official name is The Church of Jesus Christ of Latter-day Saints. In this essay it will be referred to as the LDS Church or Mormonism, and its followers will be called Latter-day Saints, LDS, or Mormons.

3. For further exploration of some LDS doctrines that may or may not be present in the *Twilight* series, see Sarah Schwartzman's essay, "Is *Twilight* Mormon?" also in this volume.

4. In some Christian thought, Adam was the first man and brought about the Fall. Since Christ redeems humanity from the consequences of the Fall, he is sometimes referred to as a "Second Adam" or "Second Man." While Bella is clearly not a Christ-figure, her story may be read as completing the one that began with Eve.

5. Consider, for example, Mattox's description of Eve's "fall into sin" and Eve's status as "inferior" to Adam's after the Fall. (Mickey L. Mattox, "Luther on Eve, Women, and the Church," in *The Pastoral Luther: Essays on Martin Luther's Practical Theology,* edited by Timothy Wengert, 251–270 [Grand Rapids, MI: William B. Eerdman's Publishing Company, 2009].) or the words of Luther himself that Mattox references. Mattox's claim in this article is not that the pains of mortality are Eve's fault, but this is an assumption on which he (like Luther) rests part of his argument. These cultural assumptions are evident among non-scholars as well. Typical examples of this include websites such as "Eve: Bible Woman: God, Adam, the Serpent and the Garden of Eden" (www.womenin thebible.net/1.1.Eve.htm), or this Sunday School lesson on Eve, provided by Kathryn Capoccia, titled "A Woman Who Helped Her Husband Sin" (www.biblebb.com/files/kss/kss-eve.htm). Christian scholarship in recent years has moved away from this negative portrayal of Eve, taking instead a more skeptical stance towards her supposed fault, inferiority, sinfulness, and effect on humanity. However, traditional understandings continue to prevail and contemporary scholarship is still influenced by previous negative interpretations.

6. Bruce R. McConkie, "Christ and the Creation," *Ensign* (June 1982), under "Gospel Library" then "Magazines," http://lds.org/ldsorg/v/index.jsp?hideNav=1&locale=0&sourceId=5ed347f765adb010VgnVCM10004d82620a____&vgnextoid=f318118dd536c010VgnVCM1000004d82620aRCRD.

7. Ibid.

8. Joseph Fielding Smith, "Gospel Classics: Adam's Role in Bringing Us Mortality," *Ensign* (January 2006), under "Gospel Library" then "Magazines," http://lds.org/ldsorg/v/index.jsp?hideNav=1&locale=0&sourceId=bdd6e2270ed6c010VgnVCM1000004d82620a____&vgnextoid=f318118dd536c010VgnVCM1000004d82620aRCRD. (Joseph Fielding Smith, 10th president of the Church of Jesus Christ of Latter-day Saints, should not be confused with his great-uncle, LDS founder Joseph Smith.)

9. *The Pearl of Great Price*, Moses 5:11

10. Joseph Campbell sees Eve as an archetype as well, and his view happens to agree with Mormon theology. He suggests that she is "God's daughter Eve, now ripe to depart from the idyl of the Garden." For Campbell, Eve represents the call to adventure, the promise of "danger, reassurance, trial, passage, and the mysteries of birth." In Joseph Campbell, *The Hero with a Thousand Faces* (Princeton, NJ: Princeton University Press, 1968), 52.

11. Carol Pearson and Katherine Pope, *The Female Hero in American and British Literature* (New York: R.R. Bowker Company, 1981).

12. Ibid., 6.

13. Ibid., 63.

14. Ibid., 79.

15. Ibid., chapter 5

16. Ibid., chapter 6.

17. Ibid., 227.

18. Ibid., 226.

19. Stephenie Meyer, *Breaking Dawn* (New York: Little, Brown and Company, 2008), chapter 33, "Forgery."

20. There are many feminists who are concerned with the way the female body interacts with the socially constructed concept of "woman." In addition to Grosz, cited below, interested readers could consider the following sources for more information: Susan Bordo, *Unbearable Weight: Feminism, Western Culture, and the Body* (Berkeley and Los Angeles: University of California Press, 1993); Judith Butler, *Bodies that Matter: On the Discursive Limits of "Sex"* (New York: Routledge, 1993); Janet Price, and Margrit Shildrick, eds., *Feminist Theory and the Body: A Reader* (New York: Routledge, 1999). Virginia Tech also provides an admirable reading list on this topic on their website at http://www.cddc.vt.edu/feminism/bod.html.

21. Elizabeth Grosz, *Volatile Bodies: Towards a Corporeal Feminism* (Indianapolis, Indiana: Indiana University Press, 1994).

22. Stephenie Meyer, *Twilight* (New York: Little, Brown and Company, 2005), 140.

23. According to Eve Sedgwick's notion of the "homosocial triangle," when two men compete for a woman, it is not about the woman at all. Because men cannot speak about their feelings for each other, they have to negotiate their relationship through a third object, in this case, a woman. In a homosocial triangle, the woman has no meaning in and of herself, but is merely an object through which men demonstrate their power to other men.

24. D. Todd Christofferson, "Moral Agency," *Ensign* (November 2009), under "Gospel Library" then "Magazines," http://lds.org/ldsorg/v/index.jsp?hideNav=1&locale=0&sourceId=108f56627ab94210VgnVCM100000176f620a____&vgnextoid=2354fccf2b7db010VgnVCM1000004d82620aRCRD.

25. Genesis 1:28.

26. *The Book of Mormon*, 2 Nephi 2:22–23.

27. Genesis 3:3.

28. Meyer, *Twilight*, 307.

29. Ibid., 139.

30. Ibid., 140.
31. Ibid., 497–498.
32. Stephenie Meyer, *Eclipse* (New York: Little, Brown and Company, 2007), 435.
33. Ibid., 617.
34. Because I am comparing Bella to Eve, some readers may wonder about parallels between Adam and Edward. I do not find Adam and Edward particularly comparable because, for one thing, Adam never questions Eve's status as agent. He accepts her as his equal without reservation. Furthermore, Edward is one of Bella's choices, whereas Adam is a given in Eve's life, so Adam and Edward do not have the same status in their respective narratives.
35. Meyer, *Breaking Dawn*, 482.
36. *Doctrine & Covenants* 76:64–65.
37. Ibid., 131:4.
38. Ibid., 76:62.
39. "Eternal progression" is not usually explicitly defined in Mormon discourse, but it is a term with which almost all Latter-day Saints are familiar. It includes, as the referenced verses indicate, living forever in Heaven with God the Father, Jesus Christ, and the Holy Spirit. It also involves spending eternity with one's spouse and other family members and having more children in the afterlife. The idea of progression also includes basic character development, such as acting with more compassion or being more patient over time. Latter-day Saints believe that people's basic characters are pretty much set after their mortal lives, but it is still possible for change to occur — it is just more difficult. People continue to learn, to grow, to set goals and achieve them in the afterlife just as they do here. See *Doctrine and Covenants* 132:19–20.
40. Ibid., 138: 39.
41. Ibid., 137:5.
42. I would like to thank Dr. Mikee Deloney of Abilene Christian University, whose encouragement and support made this essay possible.

Bella and Boundaries, Crossed and Redeployed

KERI WOLF

In the *Twilight* series, Stephenie Meyer constructs a world containing boundaries that are geographical, physical, and social. These borders are apparent from the beginning of the first novel, where Meyer maps out the location of Forks, a town seemingly removed from the rest of the world by virtue of its remote location in the Olympic Peninsula of Northwest Washington State. The very name of the city, moreover, connotes the images of geographical areas being separated from each other as forks in a road or a river divide places and lead one to new territories.[1] After Bella, the outsider who calls Phoenix her home, enters this world she terms an "alien planet,"[2] she gradually discovers the boundaries between human, vampire, and werewolf, learns to transcend them, and finally becomes a creator and user of boundaries in a spectacular way.

Bella also deals with social borders apparent in physical placement within the microcosm of the Forks High School campus. Plagued with balance problems, Bella exhibits a clumsiness that prevents her from excelling in any of the typical areas—such as sports or dancing—that might make a teenage girl "fit in" in high school. She is also severely directionally challenged. She admits that she needs guidance to find her way around, and she is literally led around by others on her first day of school at Forks High. In a remark she makes before she ventures out on a walk into the forest beyond her father's house, Bella refers to her sense of direction as "hopeless."[3] She later demonstrates the truth of this statement when visiting the nearby town of Port Angeles where she inadvertently wanders in the wrong direction and encounters four dangerous men intent upon accosting her.[4] While Bella may possess no sense of direction, however, she does have an acute awareness of positioning. Although Bella does not fit in with stereotypical models of beautiful heroines who never struggle with self-esteem, her awareness of boundaries and her ability to negotiate between them disrupt power relationships and give this heroine a powerful autonomy in a world constructed around physical and social perimeters.

In both a physical and mental sense, Bella defies stereotypes and has never been able to "fit in" anywhere, an experience she views negatively and attempts to change upon moving to Forks. Her mental acuity and sense of responsibility prevent her from being relegated to the category of a "normal teenager." She is a daughter who looks after her mother and a teenager who, according to her mom, "was born thirty-five years old."[5] As she leaves Phoenix, Bella is concerned with who will take care of her mother, thinking of the older woman much as a mother would a child and questioning how she could abandon someone so erratic and flighty. Bella rationalizes that, since her mother is married now, her new husband Phil would most likely ensure that the bills would be paid, that the refrigerator would be stocked with food, that the gas tank would be filled, and that her mother would have someone to call should she become lost. But Bella still expresses concern about her mother's ability to fend for herself without her daughter's guidance.[6] Similar to how Bella's maturity causes her to assume the role of a mother, she also does not conform to other social expectations for young women. As Bella admits, she has difficulties relating to other people[7] and suffers from a lack of tactfulness.[8] At school in Arizona, she was not a part of the popular crowd because she was not wealthy and did not play sports or go out on dates with boys. Furthermore, her pale skin defies the stereotype of what a girl from the sunny state of Arizona should look like,[9] and she lacks interest in making up her face and hair perfectly as well as in dressing in the latest fashions.

Aware that she does not fit in, Bella tries her hardest to remain inconspicuous when arriving in Forks. On Bella's first day at Forks High School, she does not want to draw undue attention to herself as the obvious newcomer to a small community, but her hopeless sense of direction forces her either to rely on others to guide her to her classes or to depend on a map. Concerned that she will not be able to find her way around the campus, she arrives early and visits the school's front office to get directions. The woman inside provides Bella with a map of the campus, highlighting the best route to each of the young woman's classes.[10] Bella, again attempting not to stand out, studies the map intently in the cab of her old second-hand truck, so that she will not become even more conspicuous by walking around the campus and continually taking out the map to consult it.[11] Fortunately, she finds her first class, English, without trouble, and other students take over guiding her around campus for the rest of the morning classes. As she says, students braver than the rest inevitably approach her and, after introductions, attempt polite conversation by asking her about her initial reactions to Forks. Aware of her difficulties with diplomacy, Bella gives the socially appropriate responses although these entail lying. She endures this questioning, conceding that these awkward niceties at least ensured that she did not need the map.[12]

Though poor in geographical positioning, Bella is, nonetheless, aware of the nuance of placement. At lunch, Jessica, a girl from her Spanish class, seats

Bella at the end of a table already filled with her friends.[13] From this position, Bella first observes the Cullens—Edward, Emmett, Alice, Rosalie, and Jasper—and notes that they sit in the corner of the long cafeteria hall as far from her location as possible.[14] She notices them because, like her, they are different from the rest. Not only does their beauty distinguish them from the remainder of the student body, but they also sit at their own table, and none of the other students interact with them. When Bella learns that they recently had moved to Forks from an unidentified place in Alaska,[15] she feels a kinship with the strange group, simultaneously experiencing relief for herself and pity for them.[16] Her relief stems from two things: first, the Cullens are also "outsiders" who are not originally from the small town of Forks, and second, their obvious physical beauty draws attention away from her. The sympathetic sense of pity that Bella feels for them derives from the fact that they are obviously not accepted into the Forks community. She can relate to them because she imposes a similar "outsider" status on herself, even though the other students attempt to include her.

The next day is easier for Bella because she knows what to expect: her new acquaintance Mike sits next to her in English and walks her to her next class, and at lunch, he "intercepts" her and Jessica to "steer" them to his table.[17] Bella observes the rather territorial layout of the cafeteria and is glad to be welcomed to Mike's table and not to have to sit by herself in a physical display of her otherness. In sum, Bella spends her first and second days at Forks High School literally being led around the campus by others. But she shows she is not a mere follower: her geographical disorientation does not impede her autonomy by causing her to conform to and rely on socially dictated norms.

While she initially seems rather passive, Bella demonstrates an acute awareness of social boundaries that are expressed physically and territorially. It is in this area of social perimeters that Bella turns her inability to fit in into a powerful force of autonomy. Although she laments the fact that she does not "belong" anywhere, the very fact of her being an outsider gives Bella the ability to transverse physical borders that confine the other main characters of the novels, as well as to cross physical boundaries that determine the extent of people's social interactions.

This physical restriction experienced by others is displayed, for instance, by Bella's father Charlie, the visiting vampire Laurent, and the local vampire Edward. As the police chief of Forks, Bella's father Charlie is responsible for enforcing the law only within the boundaries of the city limits; although he can be called in to assist other communities, his scope of authority does not extend into the forest or the nearby Indian reservation. The vampires observe similar boundaries in their feeding habits. Even Laurent, the itinerant vampire who interrupts the Cullen family as they play baseball in their carefully selected field, inquires about the limits of their hunting grounds. Upon learning the answer of Edward's adopted father, Carlisle Cullen, Laurent assures him that they will not encroach upon the boundaries of the Cullens' territory.[18] Furthermore, the prohibition against vampires entering the land of the Quileute prevents Edward from accompanying the group of Forks High students to the beach at La Push.[19] Edward also expresses his concern about his relationship with Bella primarily in terms of proximity and distance, exclaiming that he does not know how to be close to her or even know if he has the ability to do so without harming her.[20] Edward even warns her about being close to him, directly telling her that she should stay away[21] and castigating himself for wanting to be with her.[22] She proves, however, to be the only one who can reach him, both physically and mentally, for even among his closely knit family, Edward is, according to Esme, the "odd man out," alone in the crowd.[23]

From the start, Bella chooses her movements carefully, according to her own will. Although she is led around Forks High on the first few days, she makes the conscious decision to follow other students in order to blend in and be as "like" her peers as she can, despite her knowledge that she does not really ever connect with anyone else. Her agency extends from such broad geographical moves as those from Phoenix to Forks and back to Phoenix, to the more seemingly mundane movements within the school cafeteria, to transversing the boundaries between the reservation, Forks' city limits, and the Cullen home. When Edward assumes that Bella's mother sent her to Forks, Bella immediately corrects him by adamantly declaring that her mother did not send her, that instead Bella actually sent herself[24]; thereby, she alerts Edward to her own ability to move autonomously. In the beginning of the series, Bella also emphasizes how it was her own decision to stay with her father in Forks. Before she leaves her mother in the Phoenix airport, Bella reveals to the reader that she is exiling herself to Forks despite her extreme and intense dislike for the town.[25] Nevertheless, while she views her move to Forks as a type of exile, it is a voluntary one. Bella makes this choice out of selflessness in order to allow her mother time with her new husband, Phil. Despite her mother's assurances that Bella's presence will not encroach upon the newlyweds' relationship, Bella believes the couple should begin their marriage with some time to themselves, and she acts upon this belief by going off to Forks.

In the smaller cosmos of Forks High School when Bella observes the social implications of seating, she is able to cross group boundaries as well as to manipulate seating arrangements to her advantage. She is acutely aware of the positioning not only of herself but also of others. When Edward saves her from Tyler's oncoming van in the school parking lot, Edward claims he was standing right next to her[26] and was thus able to push her out of the way of the careening vehicle, but Bella knows that he was standing precisely four cars away from her.[27] She thinks that no one noticed him there because no one was as aware of him as she is,[28] but in truth, she has a unique awareness of positioning, as she demonstrates in her descriptions of the classroom layouts, the seating in the cafeteria, and the later seating arrangements in vehicles when she and her friends travel to the beach.

On that beach trip, for example, Bella knows that Mike is interested in her, yet she does not return his interest and perceives that Jessica longs for his attentions. With Jessica's feelings in mind, Bella ensures that, in the car bound for the beach, Mike has the opportunity to sit next to Jessica rather than her.[29] On another occasion back at school, she and Jessica enter the cafeteria later than the others, who are already seated. As an aside, Bella notes that she intentionally avoided the available seat next to Mike and instead took the one beside Angela. She then noticed that Mike held the chair out politely for Jessica, causing Jessica's expression to light up.[30] Although Bella records this event as somewhat of an afterthought, it reveals that she is extremely spatially aware.

In the cafeteria, Bella is likewise able to transverse different social spheres that are expressed in the physical seating arrangement. On a day following the accident with Tyler's van, Edward takes an empty table in the cafeteria and motions for Bella to join him. Breaking away from her own normal seating arrangement, she approaches him. Recounting her next move, she relates that she reaches the chair across from Edward and stands there until he suggests she sit with him that day. Bella automatically sits, but she regards Edward with caution even though he has delivered his suggestions with a smile.[31] In choosing to go to Edward and sit with him, Bella accomplishes something no other student at Forks High School has done. She has entered into his social sphere. Of Edward, Bella observes that he does not belong to the same world as the other students from their school, even before she realizes that he is a vampire.[32] Yet when still unaware of how different his world is, Bella herself has begun to make her way between their different "worlds." While physical and social boundaries do not constrain her as they do the other prominent characters in the book, perhaps more importantly, entering one sphere does not prohibit her from crossing back into a previous one. Although Bella does go to sit with Edward in the school cafeteria, for example, she also remains able to sit with her other friends at their usual table. Mike later welcomes her back to sit with his group of friends in the cafeteria, insisting that, as his friend, Bella can sit with them despite the fact that another one of his friends, Lauren, has been rather disdainful of what she perceives to be Bella's inconsistencies.[33]

Bella likewise transverses the larger physical boundaries between the Indian werewolves on the Quileute reservation and the Cullen family grounds outside of the city boundaries. In her old pickup, she roars through the town of Forks, crossing onto the reservation and the Cullen's land without anyone ever challenging her access. Both her Quileute friend Jacob Black and the Cullens, however, have their physical movement restricted by a firm pact between the two factions. On the beach at La Push, Jacob tells Bella that the vampire family of Cullens is not permitted to come onto the reservation lands,[34] and he outlines the boundaries set out by the old treaty between the Quileute and the Cullens. According to legend, he explains (not himself believing it for a moment at the time), the vampires, or "cold ones," are the traditional enemies of his wolf ancestors, known to humans as werewolves. But because of the Cullen vampires' "vegetarian" lifestyle, Jacob's great grandfather, a tribal elder, made a truce with them when they first arrived upon the werewolves' territory years ago. According to this treaty, the vampires would stay off the land of the Quileute and not attack any humans, and in exchange, the Quileute agreed to keep silent about their knowledge of the Cullens being vampires.[35]

Bella, in contrast, has absolute freedom to come onto the reservation despite her association with Edward, a relationship about which the Indians are gravely concerned. Jacob and Billy's care for the young woman is not diminished by her friendship and eventual marriage to one of their enemies, but they are required to express their concern without encroaching upon the territorial boundaries set out by the treaty. For instance, Jacob and his father Billy Black come to visit Charlie with the express purpose of warning Bella to stay away from the Cullens. When Edward sees them, he mutters that their actions are "crossing the line."[36] Billy cannot go to the Cullens' territory to tell them to stay away from Bella: he has to go to the more neutral place of Bella's home and talk to the girl who is herself able to cross these boundaries. With his "insider" knowledge of the Cullens' species, Billy makes attempts to warm Bella of the Cullens without revealing why. Later, he even sends Jacob to the school dance to talk with Bella because of his perception that it is "neutral ground," a "safe place" for him to caution her about literally and symbolically getting too close to Edward and his family.[37]

Similar to how she can go upon the reservation lands unimpeded, Bella is welcomed within the protected "safe zone" of the Cullen home. According to Edward, their house is the only place they have in which they never have to hide from others.[38] Whenever they depart from their home, they must put on an act of trying to blend in as ordinary humans, an act not unlike Bella's. Even their choice of cars reflects this act, for Edward explains that the siblings normally drive the Volvo to school because Rosalie's red convertible demands attention.[39] Hidden outside of town on an unmarked, unpaved road that one can scarcely discern amid the surrounding ferns,[40] their home escapes the scrutiny of the citizens of Forks and allows them to have a permanent residence as long as they do not venture onto the territory of the werewolves or hunt humans. Yet they risk the entire life they have carefully constructed for themselves in Forks by allowing Bella to enter into their isolated home. Once she is inside, the Cullens do not limit her to spaces conventionally designated for entertaining. Rather, they expose the most personal and intimate sections of the dwelling to her. She goes through the rooms in the house, examining all the fixtures and furniture not only in the central living room but also in the private upstairs quarters of Carlisle's office and the individual bedrooms. She familiarizes herself completely with all aspects of their living situation and their history, asking questions about how they carry out daily functions.[41]

Because Bella is a human being rather than a supernatural creature, her obvious physical inferiority would appear to subordinate her to the vampires who easily could force her to conform to their wishes. Initially, it seems that they literally push the human girl around, beginning with the moment when Edward throws Bella out of the path of Tyler's out-of-control van careening through the school parking lot. The language that Bella uses to describe other encounters with members of the Cullen family intensifies the impression that she is a toy to be physically manipulated. Bella, for example, explains that Edward towed her to his car after her fainting incident in their Biology class.[42] Then after running with her on his back, Edward pulls her around and cradles her as one would hold a small child[43]; later, he picks her up by the tops of her arms and sits her on her bed next to him.[44] In other instances, his hands grasp her wrists like shackles,[45] and he tosses her upon his shoulder to carry her.[46] Similarly, when attempting to escape James, Emmett pulls Bella out of her seat in the truck and tucks her to his chest,[47] and soon thereafter, Esme carries Bella up the stairs and dresses up the girl in her own clothes like a doll.[48]

Although the vampires initially exhibit control over Bella's body, they cannot, however, control her mind, which is dark even to the mind-reading Edward. As a result, Bella's decisions direct the action of the final portion of *Twilight*. In order to protect her father from James, who is stalking her, Bella plans to stage an outburst with her father and demand to go back to Phoenix. This act, she hopes, will draw James away from her and will also keep him from harming Charlie. But James does find out where she is, and when she arrives in Phoenix and finds that James has apparently captured her mother, Bella outmaneuvers the Cullen vampires Emmett and Alice and escapes their protective custody in the airport. Once Bella has made the choice to die if she must in order to save those she loves (both her human family and the vampire Cullens who could be destroyed by protecting her), she acts upon the path that she has set for herself,[49] and the others lose physical control over her even though she is a mere human.

Ultimately, Bella's ability to transcend boundaries disrupts power relationships, although the way her mind perceives things frightens her. She asks Edward why he thinks he cannot hear her thoughts as he can do with every other human. In response, he murmurs that he does not know for certain, but he guesses that her mind works differently than most humans' minds do, likening the difference to that between AM and FM radio frequencies.[50] Instead of taking her ability as a gift, Bella reacts emotionally to his assertion that she is different and again expresses her dismay that she does not "fit in." She bursts out with the concern that her mind does not work correctly, assuming that Edward must think of her as "a freak." As an aside to the reader, she admits that her emotional outburst stemmed from embarrassment at having another person confirm what she had suspected for years, that her mind functions in ways others cannot comprehend.[51] But while Bella struggles with being dissimilar, her "differentness" is exactly what enables her to emerge as an autonomous woman.

Despite Edward telling her that she does not see herself clearly,[52] Bella has the ability to see apparently invisible social relationships. Her unique awareness of positioning and spatiality essentially gives her the ability to do what Edward continually struggles with — to transverse boundaries. The entire way of life of Edward and the Cullens is based on their attempt to cross the ethical boundary between what they believe is their nature as vampires and what they perceive to be morally right, not feeding on humans. Commenting on the nature of vampires and his choice to be a "vegetarian" vampire, Edward says, "Just because we've been ... dealt a certain hand ... it doesn't mean that we can't choose to rise above — to conquer the boundaries of a destiny that none of us wanted. To try to retain whatever essential humanity we can."[53]

Boundary lines exist everywhere, but Bella is the only character whom they do not inhibit in a physical and social sense. She is the character who can move into different physical and social worlds, often disrupting carefully negotiated power relationships that derive from the control of others over their specific areas. In *Twilight* and the novels that follow, power is expressed spatially through control over territory. But Bella, in not being confined or limited to a territory, does not ever become a possession of those who claim a particular territory as their own. Instead, her abilities to move between various kinds of physical boundaries give her a powerful autonomy.

Although this essay deals primarily with the novel *Twilight*, I will close by proposing that Bella's awareness of positioning and her ability to transverse boundaries even as a human forms the foundations for who she becomes as a vampire later in the series. This special spatial awareness is the human trait that Bella takes with her when she is transformed into a vampire; it becomes her "gift." According to Edward, many vampires possess such gifts. As he explains, Carlisle has a theory that, after they are transformed, some vampires bring elements of their strongest human traits with them and that these traits become even more intensified in their new lives as vampires. For example, Carlisle surmises that, as a human, Edward was likely perceptive about the thoughts of people around him, and that Alice, when human, had a gift of precognition that converted into her stronger ability to foresee events as a vampire.[54] When Bella becomes a new-born vampire, she has no particular desire for human blood, and this absence puzzles Edward, leading him to speculate that her lack of blood-lust may be Bella's unique vampire "gift."

But Bella's true gift — and perhaps the most spectacular of all the vampires' gifts — is her ability to create her own zone of influence, actually creating a mental boundary and projecting it over her friends and family. She thus interferes with the other "bad" vampires' special powers in the final confrontation with the Volturi in *Breaking Dawn*. In this defining moment, Bella describes how, against their powers, her shield becomes almost a tangible, though invisible, boundary that she can throw out from herself and use to cover others from danger. She explains how she adjusts this impenetrable object "into a low, wide dome"[55] that she fits over her entire group, and then she continues to describe the situation in spatial terms: "sharp plumes of light"[56] designate the places where her family and friends stand, and strangely, each plume has a different flavor that Bella feels she will be able to recognize as she practices using her shield. Next, she describes how, with concentration, she is able to pull the "elastic armor"[57] of her shield around each of those individuals she knows and wants to protect. Carlisle, who stands the farthest from Bella and the closest to the enemy, is encapsulated within Bella's shield first as she wraps it "as exactly to his body"[58] as she can. Quickly learning how to manipulate her shield, Bella manages to ease it around Carlisle so that when he moves to stand by Tanya, "the elastic stretched with him, drawn to his spark."[59] Continuing to experiment with her abilities, Bella "tugged in more threads of the fabric, pulling it around each glimmering shape that was a friend or ally. The shield clung to them willingly, moving as they moved."[60] As these final moments illustrate, Bella's agency stems from her spatial awareness, and she chooses to use it to protect those she loves and unite them to her, covering them within her own sphere of influence. Thus, the *Twilight* series leads us through an exceptional progression of the protagonist. From the seemingly frightened young girl needing protection but highly aware of social boundaries and placement, Bella emerges as a confident woman, prepared and able to direct the course of her life and having the special gift of her shield with which she can extend protection over her loved ones.

Moreover, by means of her unique gift, Bella even "transgresses" the boundary of genre in her story.[61] The series has been building in a predictable manner to an apocalyptic final confrontation where the side opposed to the protagonist will be defeated and likely completely decimated. Drawing on our knowledge of Bella's bloody encounter with James in *Twilight*, we expect a type of inverted rematch between "good" and "bad" in which Bella, now a nearly physically indestructible being, can match the brute strength of the vampires rather than be pummeled virtually to death. Since she is no longer limited by human frailties, we envision Bella exacting revenge for the wrongs done to her when an innocent young girl by obliterating the forces of "evil." Activating her shield, however, Bella redeploys boundaries, transforming the passive barrier around her own mind into an invisible, but nonetheless real, projectile that she can engage and maneuver into a protective border between her loved ones and the forces that seek to destroy them. Because Bella's superhero power is this shield instead of a more physically violent device, that gift that so alarmed and intrigued the Cullens when she first arrived in Forks, now greatly intensified, allows Bella to successfully thwart both the Volturi and our expectations of a violent outcome.

Notes

1. In answer to the question of why she selected the title of *Twilight*, Meyer explains that the process of titling the book was not easy and that she originally called the first novel *Forks*

when initially sending out queries to publishers. Stephenie Meyer, *The Official Website of Stephenie Meyer*, http://www.stepheniemeyer.com/twilight_faq.html#title.

2. Stephenie Meyer, *Twilight* (New York: Little, Brown, and Company, 2005), 8.
3. Ibid., 136.
4. Ibid., 157.
5. Ibid., 106.
6. Ibid., 4.
7. Ibid., 10.
8. Ibid., 31.
9. Ibid., 10.
10. Ibid., 14.
11. Ibid.
12. Ibid., 17.
13. Ibid.
14. Ibid., 18.
15. Ibid., 21.
16. Ibid., 22.
17. Ibid., 30.
18. Ibid., 378.
19. Ibid., 123.
20. Ibid., 278.
21. Ibid., 84, 266.
22. Ibid., 187.
23. Ibid., 368.
24. Ibid., 49.
25. Ibid., 4.
26. Ibid., 57.
27. Ibid., 56.
28. Ibid., 69.
29. Ibid., 114.
30. Ibid., 146.
31. Ibid., 87.
32. Ibid., 102–103.
33. Ibid., 112.
34. Ibid., 123.
35. Ibid., 124–125.
36. Ibid., 349.
37. Ibid., 490.
38. Ibid., 329.
39. Ibid., 199.
40. Ibid., 320.
41. Ibid., 322–347.
42. Ibid., 103.
43. Ibid., 280.
44. Ibid., 297.
45. Ibid., 302.
46. Ibid., 315, 363.
47. Ibid., 399.
48. Ibid., 401–402.
49. Ibid., 430, 440.
50. Ibid., 181.
51. Ibid.
52. Ibid., 245.

53. Ibid., 307.
54. Ibid.
55. Stephenie Meyer, *Breaking Dawn* (New York: Little, Brown, and Company, 2008), 702.
56. Ibid., 703.
57. Ibid.
58. Ibid.
59. Ibid., 703.
60. Ibid.
61. I would like to thank Marijane Osborn for first noticing Meyer's redeployment of the theme of the epic battle and drawing it to my attention.

Sleeping Beauty and the Idealized Undead: Avoiding Adolescence

JANICE HAWES

In Chapter 20 of *Breaking Dawn* (the final book of Stephenie Meyer's *Twilight* series) the heroine Bella awakes to a new world. Having just endured the agony of a horrible childbirth involving broken ribs, a broken spine, and vast internal bleeding, and finally culminating in her human death, Bella opens her eyes as a vampire—an immortal with perfect beauty and grace. But the three days that Bella lies still and helpless during her transformation is just one example of sleep and sleep-like states in the novels. In fact, Bella spends much of her time asleep, and her dreams are a response to her waking world, a world in which her human teenage self is usually portrayed as helpless as is her counterpart "Sleeping Beauty," a nickname Edward actually gives to Bella as she is suffering from jet lag upon their return from visiting Bella's mother back in Florida.[1] Like the sleeping princess who awaits her prince, Bella often must be rescued from situations she cannot control herself. Moreover, just like the fairy tale heroine whose sleep isolates her from the rest of the world, Bella's feelings of inadequacy and helplessness isolate her from the real challenges of everyday maturation. When she is not passively awaiting her prince Edward, she is actively avoiding the dancing, dating, shopping, and bickering of the social whirl that is high school. Her sleep is symbolic of her own avoidance of the everyday rituals associated with adolescence and of a desire to escape, rather than confront, her insecurities.

In this, she is not unlike the heroines of European fairy tales that developed during the latter part of the Middle Ages. As Heide Göttner-Abendroth has shown, earlier folklore reflecting a "matriarchal world view" underwent a transformation that increasingly reflected stronger patriarchal values:

> [T]he active, young princess was changed into an active hero; matrilineal marriage and family ties became patrilineal; the essence of the symbols, based on matriarchal

> rites, was depleted and made benign; and the pattern of action that concerned maturation and integration was gradually recast to stress domination and wealth.[2]

This process is illustrated, for instance, in the contrast between the canonical eighteenth and nineteenth century versions of the adventures of the helpless heroine Little Red Riding Hood and the oral story "The Grandmother's Tale" where the heroine is comfortable with and in control of her sexuality and where she undergoes an initiation into the adult world, as illustrated by the agency she uses to save herself.[3]

Unlike the Red Riding Hood oral stories that were later transformed into written tales with codified bougeousie standards of female behavior, the original Sleeping Beauty tale already reflected these rigid gender norms: the end of the process of patriarchy. The earliest record of this tale is the fourteenth-century *Frayre de Joy e Sur de Placer.* Later, the tale appears as "Troylus and Zellandine" in the sixteenth-century French prose romance *Perceforest.* Giambatista Basile based his seventeenth-century version in *The Pentamerone* on the French version: a young woman is condemned to eternal sleep after pricking herself while spinning flax. She is subsequently raped and impregnated in this helpless state, and, having given birth in her sleep, she awakens when her hungry baby, mistaking the flax chip for her nipple, sucks it off and thus rescues his mother from her passive sleep. Basile's version was likely a major inspiration for the eighteenth-century "La belle au bois dormant" by Charles Perrault, who was also responsible for many of the "canonical" versions of European fairy tales, including "Cinderella." The Grimm brothers, who added the famous kiss, relied heavily on Perrault's version for their own "Brier Rose," and it is this nineteenth-century version that became the basis for the version we know today. Unlike the earlier versions, now it is a prince, not the heroine's infant, who saves her.[4]

The final awakening of the princess that occurs in Meyer's series is a gothicization of this scene, as described by Jacob, who watches in horror as Edward transforms the dying Bella: "Where his tongue washed the venom over her skin, it sealed shut" to keep the venom in her body.[5] It will take Bella three days to wake up, but it is Edward and his vampire kisses that allow her to wake up, now no longer human. She has finally been granted her wish.

Through Bella and her fairy tale, the audience may also experience vicarious wish fulfillment. The *Twilight* series is known for its appeal to a broad audience, and part of this appeal is Meyer's incorporation of fairy tales. We may associate "Cinderella," "Little Red Riding Hood," "Snow White," and "Sleeping Beauty" with childhood, stories that we tell our children before they go to bed. But we forget that childhood, in the particular form we give it now, is, according to many social theorists, a very recent cultural construct in Western societies.[6] Likewise, oral folk tales, which often served as the basis for written fairy tales, originated in a tradition created by and for adult culture (children would, of course, have been part of the listening audience).[7] Thus, if it is true that fairy tales encode certain behaviors (for example, a young girl faces the dangers of the wolf by herself, or a young girl becomes the passive victim of her own violation of taboos and is eaten by the wolf), then these messages had and continue to have a varied audience. Moreover, part of that audience, the adults who distribute that information to children, helps to encode that information further, transforming the teachings to suit the norms of the current audience's society. As Maria Tatar notes, "Fairy tales do not merely encode arrangements from the past, but also participate in their creation for the present and future."[8]

Many scholars agree that power and oppression have always been major concerns of fairy tales, whether as an attempt to subvert power in some way or to enforce the status quo that allows that power. Jack Zipes, among others, discusses the rigid social norms of the society in which the "fairy tales," as opposed to earlier folk tales, originated:

> We must remember that the fairy tale for children originated in a period of absolutism when French culture was setting standards of *civilité* for the rest of Europe. Exquisite care was thus taken to cultivate a discourse on the civilization process through the fairy tale for the benefit of well-raised children. [...] The behavioral standards were expressly codified in books on manners and civility. This means that the individual symbolic act of writing the literary fairy tale expressed a certain level of social consciousness and conscience that was related to the standard mode of socialization at that time.[9]

Although the European fairy tale, as opposed to the folk tale, is usually considered a literate genre, the distinction between oral and written versions of folkloric tales is difficult: the tales were told, condensed, expanded, and retold in both traditions. In other words, an oral tale may well influence a written tale, but a written tale may in turn become part of the oral culture.[10] Thus, the "behavioral standards" that Zipes discusses are reinforced by both oral and literate culture. This encoding of "proper" behavior is not just a thing of the past, as Roberta Trites discusses in her study of power dynamics depicted in literature for young adults: "Adolescent literature is itself an institutional discourse that participates in the power and repression dynamic that socializes adolescents into their cultural positions."[11] As the histories of the "Red Riding Hood" and "Sleeping Beauty" stories illustrate, discussion of fairy tales and works like the *Twilight* series that utilize their messages is a complex endeavor.

In his landmark (and controversial) psychoanalytical study of fairy tales *The Uses of Enchantment*, Bruno Bettelheim offers a psychoanalytical approach to the "meaning" of fairy tales. His discussion of the Sleeping Beauty story is useful for our purposes:

> While many fairy tales stress great deeds the heroes must perform to become themselves, "The Sleeping Beauty" emphasizes the long, quiet concentration on oneself that is also needed. During the months before the first menstruation and often also for some time immediately following it, girls are passive, seem sleepy, and withdraw into themselves. [...] After the period of inactivity which typically occurs during early puberty, adolescents become active and make up for the period of passivity: in

> real life and in fairy tales they try to prove their young manhood or womanhood, often through dangerous adventures. This is how the symbolic language of the fairy tale states that after having gathered strength in solitude they now have to become themselves.[12]

For Bettelheim, the heroine's state of sleep symbolizes that time of retreat often observed in young people first entering adolescence. This withdrawal allows for a period of inner growth after which the young person will emerge stronger and more active, even to the point of engaging in hazardous behavior: their "adventures." In other words, Bettelheim's analysis of the tale suggests that Sleeping Beauty experiences what Jack Zipes refers to as "the fruitful sleep."[13] Bettelheim's analysis has been criticized for its tendency to be "overdetermined": Maria Tatar, who actually employs many of Bettelheim's ideas, notes that it is wrongheaded to find sexual symbolism in everything.[14] Bettelheim's interpretations have also been criticized for not allowing for distinctions of class, sex, or ethnicity in children who make up the audience of the tales. Scholars who critique Bettelheim's approach note that children from various backgrounds are not likely to interpret characters and events in the texts in a uniform fashion.[15] With these caveats in mind, it is arguably possible to read the Sleeping Beauty story in a broadly symbolic way that cautiously employs Bettelheim's approach without falling into the trap of reading too much into every specific detail or assuming that a particular association will speak to all audiences. Bettelheim's reading of the story is one possible reading and *use* of the tale. If Bettelheim's "Sleeping Beauty" represents a waking into adolescence, however, Bella's sleep represents an avoidance of adolescence, with all of its awkwardness and challenges.

Before her monstrous transformation, Bella is confronted throughout her adventures with the frailties of her humanity, frailties of which she is ashamed. Edward's presence in her life allows her to address but not work through her insecurities about these perceived flaws through fantasy. Bella, whose name is obviously allusive, consciously casts herself as a fairy tale heroine. When she is abandoned by Edward in *New Moon*, Bella considers how to salvage a life without the ideal fairy tale: "The prince was never coming back to kiss me awake from my enchanted sleep."[16] She spends the first four months after his departure asleep to the world (metaphorically speaking), as is demonstrated by Meyer's including chapter headings for those months but no text and therefore, no story.[17] Bella's growing relationship with Jacob indicates that she is capable of being somewhat adaptive. She does gradually begin to wake up, but always with a sense of not being whole. That there is a persistent sense of incompleteness in her life despite her strengthening attachment to Jacob is illustrated by her reaction to the homecoming of her true love Edward. She triumphantly notes that her "fairy tale" has resumed: "Prince returned, bad spell broken."[18]

The setting of Bella's fairy tale, the woods (where, among other things, the Cullens live), invades her dreams. It is a landscape that Bella, who is from

Phoenix, Arizona, initially has trouble accepting. In fact, at one point, Edward overhears her complaining in her sleep that it's "'too *green*.'"[19] It is a place of strange beauty, but also of danger, and Bella is the fragile heroine warned against straying off of the path: Edward warns Bella in the first book of the series not to enter the forest by herself.[20] When Bella does venture into the forest alone to find the enchanted meadow she once visited with her true love Edward, she feels vulnerable without a protector by her side. In fact, like Little Red Riding Hood, Bella is vulnerable alone in the woods, as the fact that she gets lost and almost loses her life at the hands of the vampire Laurent illustrates. She notes that the woods are "creepier today," like something out of her "most recent nightmare," but it's due to her being "alone."[21] As long as she is with her prince, however, she is safe, and her connection to the forest becomes so intense that, faced with the possibility of having to leave for good, she mourns its potential loss, convinced that she would miss "the green, the timelessness, the mystery" of the forest.[22] The forest becomes a central part of Bella's preferred fairy tale world, but it's the connection to Edward, along with the security that he represents, that matters most.

Her vulnerability when without her prince, however, is not limited to the fairytale landscape of the forest; for Bella, the entire world is a forest where she feels overwhelmed and in constant danger. Visiting the small, low-crime rate, town of Port Angeles with two of her classmates, Bella gets lost and discovers to her horror that she is being hunted ("herded" is the word she uses) by a group of men. As in any good fairy tale, however, Edward comes to the rescue (in his sport car rather than on a horse).[23] The natural and ingrained vulnerability of his beloved is only emphasized by Edward's words to the heroine upon his return from a hunting trip, recalling his warning before he left for her not to "fall in the ocean or get run over" and explaining that he "was distracted" with "worrying" while he was gone.[24] Bella's awkwardness casts her as the helpless damsel, and ironically, she thinks this is one of her most appealing qualities at the same time that it endangers her. Refusing to see any other attractive qualities in herself, Bella comes to the conclusion that the male attention she gets at her high school must be due to her clumsiness, which encourages a protective response in young men who find her awkwardness "endearing," and who thus see her as "the damsel in distress."[25] Despite her occasional complaints when Edward becomes overly protective, Bella seems to be comfortable in her role as she becomes increasingly more dependent on her prince. Her mother's concerned words about her daughter illustrate the intensity of this dependent bond she has with Edward. She compares Bella to "a satellite" which "orient[s]" itself to the pull of another body (Edward), as if by the attraction of "magnets" or "gravity."[26]

The comparisons between Bella and fairy tale heroines (including Sleeping Beauty) intensify this image of dependency. Jack Zipes describes the implied norms enforced by Sleeping Beauty's plight:

> [S]he is expected to be passive and patient for a hundred years until a prince rescues and resuscitates her. Her *manner* of speech is such that she charms the prince, and he marries her. Then she must demonstrate even more patience when the ogress takes her children from her. Such docility and self-abandonment are rewarded in the end when the prince returns to set things right.[27]

Zipes' discussion of Perrault's version of the tale, with the ogress tale at the end, illustrates the potentially repressive nature of the story.[28] As noted earlier, Perrault was writing at a time in which French society was stressing "standards of *civilité*." Part of this "civilizing process" involves knowing how to enact one's gender, to follow the social norms expected of one's biological sex. Although these codes of behavior arguably change over time, social codes preserved in oral and written lore are often transferred from era to era.[29] Maria Tatar contends that "the choice of catatonic Snow White and Sleeping Beauty as the fairest and most desirable of them all may offer a sobering statement on folkloristic visions of the ideal bride."[30] But their popularity today also suggests much about twenty-first-century Western society and our assumptions about gender behavior. Our codes of behavior may be reinforced by the messages we receive in popular tales like the fairy tales under discussion. The transmission of these messages in turn is aided by the possibilities of modern media, "expanded through radio, film, theater, opera, and the Internet to communicate and debate notions of gender, comportment and violence management."[31] Bella as a character, in fact, may be a reflection of our own anxieties and confusion about our specific roles in society. The depiction of Bella as a helpless female who is dependent on her vampire hero arguably sends a problematic message to young women trying to work through their own confusion about gender roles.

Bella is so dependent on Edward that he is central to her dream world as she sleeps. Edward's lullaby for Bella, recurring throughout the series, suggests the warmth and comfort that Bella derives from the relationship.[32] But Edward enters her dreams in ways that suggest that the relationship isn't just about comfort. The first time she dreams of Edward is the day that he saves her from being crushed by her classmate's car. In her dream, Edward represents that which she longs for but which is out of reach. After that, he is in her "dreams nearly every night, but always on the periphery, never within reach" and never turning to look at her.[33] As their relationship intensifies, the heroine's dreams become likewise intense. The energy of her sleeping state now "thrill[s] with the same electricity" that had filled the day at school with Edward.[34] Like Sleeping Beauty in Bettelheim's reading of the tale, Bella appears to have experienced a sexual awakening.

In fact, Bella actually experiences many of the changes that Bettelheim discusses, but usually not for the motives that allow the adolescent in Bettelheim's model to mature in a healthy manner. Bettelheim, for instance, discusses the risk-taking that adolescents participate in once they awake from their "sleep" during the beginning stages of adolescence. Bella herself dabbles in "extreme sports" with Jacob after Edward has apparently abandoned her in *New Moon*. She decides to learn to ride a motorcycle and hears Edward's voice scolding her for risking her life.[35] After this, she goes to great lengths and willingly endangers herself to hold onto what little of Edward she has left, noting that she can cling to "his voice" but "only when he was disapproving."[36] She goes cliff-diving alone just to hear Edward's voice again. Although Bella insists later that she was not suicidal at that time, she seems very accepting of death: "I saw *him*, and I had no will to fight. [...] My subconscious had stored Edward away in flawless detail, saving him for this final moment."[37] At first, Bella may appear to be awakening from her catatonic state as she continues to bond with Jacob. As discussed earlier, Bruno Bettelheim reads the Sleeping Beauty story as a tale about adolescents gaining strength to "become themselves." Her desire for the auditory hallucinations of Edward's voice, even to the point of risking her life to hear it, suggest, however, that Bella has not experienced the strength through solitude that Bettelheim discusses.

Despite her budding sexuality, as exhibited by her intense attraction to Edward, Bella refuses to experience other rituals or acknowledge other milestones associated with growing up. Her insecurities with herself cause her to avoid any situation that would involve socializing and that would mark a transition from one stage of adolescent life to another. If Edward had not forced the issue, she would have missed her prom. She does not want the birthday party the Cullens have for her anyway.[38] Finally, she does not want a graduation party (although one is forced on her by Alice Cullen).[39] As Edward explains, the Cullens worry that she will miss important milestones associated with growing up and being "human," and they want her to experience a regular life as much as possible, despite the presence of Edward and his family.[40]

Bella, of course, does not find her humanness, with all of its faults, appealing, as her words about the threat that the dangerous Victoria poses illustrate. Bella believes that it is not safe "to be human" and that someone in her position should "be a little less helpless."[41] As a mere human teenager, she feels vulnerable, awkward, and unattractive. For Bella, facing these fears is not the answer. Instead, she wants to be transformed into what for her is an image of perfection and invulnerability: a vampire. Trying to nag and cajole Edward into changing her earlier rather than later, Bella complains that she is tired of only being "'Lois Lane'" and that she longs to adopt the role of "'Superman too.'"[42] For Bella, the vampires represent an idealized form of adulthood, one of ageless beauty, grace, strength, and wisdom, without all of the insecurities that come from adolescence or from being human. Edward, of course, is at the center of this ideal. He is described as Bella's own "personal miracle."[43] He is even like a god when he steps out into the sun.[44] But it isn't simply Edward who is idealized; the other Cullens are paragons of perfection in Bella's eyes. Rosalie, for instance, has a "glorious immortal body."[45] Even in battle, the Cullens are exemplars of beauty, grace and indomitability, as illustrated by a mock fight between Jasper and Alice. Alice is a graceful dancer "spiraling and twisting and curling" with Jasper "lunging, [...] never touching her, like every movement was choreographed."[46] Underneath the beauty and grace of this scene is the power and strength that the vampires have and for which Bella longs.

The fantasy of not being human is problematized in the series, but only briefly. Bella, who hopes to be "[s]trong and fast and, most of all, beautiful," in other words, somebody who "belonged" with Edward, also expresses fear that she could become a "monster" attacking innocent people.[47] With the discovery of her raging hormones, she even begins to wonder if there are not positive sides to being human. Her concern that her new vampire self will constantly be thirsty leads her to worry that her other drives will be muted, that even when she gains "control" again, she will never enjoy that feeling of being "[h]uman ... and passionately in love" or ever again enjoy the "complete experience" of human sexuality before her "pheromone-riddled body" is replaced by "something beautiful, strong ... and unknown."[48] The immortal vampire family to which Bella aspires is also trying to live vicariously through the human Bella, which, among other things, illustrates that what Bella is running from (a normal teenage life) is something for which these idealized immortals long. Edward explains the excitement that his family feels about her birthday, noting that "the last real birthday" that any of them had experienced was Emmett's, several decades ago.[49] Rosalie's words during her first sincere conversation with Bella are a caution about rushing away from humanity too quickly. The beautiful vampire notes that to a certain extent, Bella is more adult than she was at an equivalent age, but Rosalie also argues that Bella is "too young" to grasp what her desires might be in the future and "too young" to sacrifice all of those future possibilities without careful consideration of the consequences.[50] That the vampires, those perfect immortals who awe everyone including Bella, desire what humanity offers is an even stronger critique of Bella's idealization than her own doubts. Thus, the novels do seem to suggest that Bella's view of life as a vampire may be problematic.

This exploration of the possible sacrifices of giving up one's humanity, however, is short-lived in the novels. In the end, Bella proves to be correct about her idealization of life as a vampire, at least in relation to herself. Once she is actually transformed, she is breathtakingly beautiful, as she sees herself the first time she looks into a mirror after her transformation, an "alien creature" whose "flawless face was pale as the moon" and whose "limbs were smooth and strong, skin glistening subtly, luminous as a pearl."[51] She is unusually graceful, as she comes to understand by the reactions of others around her. Edward tells her that her first jump is "'quite graceful — even for a vampire.'"[52] She is superhumanly powerful, as she discovers during her first hunt for animal blood, her "raw, massive strength" making everything else near her "look fragile."[53] Finally, Bella's human desire and enjoyment of the physical consummation of her desire for Edward are enhanced, rather than muted. In fact, her "old mind" could not have held "this much love" while her "old heart" would not have been able to "bear it."[54] Ironically, her enjoyment of life has increased now that she is a member of the "undead."

Even more significantly, she now has a superpower all her own. What was once simply a self-protective shell that Bella could use to keep others from reading her thoughts, a trait that makes her very much like the young adolescents that Bettelheim discusses but who differ from Bella in that they wake up still human but mature, is now an active shield that protects others from the powers of the Volturi: "Fascinated, I tugged in more threads of fabric, pulling it around each glimmering shape that was a friend or ally. The shield clung to them willingly, moving as they moved."[55] This enhanced superpower may suggest that Bella has finally discovered her true self, a process that many feminist adolescent novels depict, as Roberta Trites notes, when

> the feminist protagonist learns to recognize and appreciate the power of her own voice. Her awakening is not bestowed on her by a male awakener; instead, she wakes herself and discovers herself to be a strong, independent, and articulate person. Thus, while in prefeminist novels the protagonist tends to become Sleeping Beauty in a movement from active to passive, from vocal to silent, the feminist protagonist remains active and celebrates her agency and her voice.[56]

It is important to keep in mind, however, that this new Bella only emerges once she has given up being human and is transformed by Edward. Unlike the heroines of the feminist novels Roberta Trites discusses, she still must rely on her prince to wake her. Moreover, rather than accepting her humanity with all of its limitations and possibilities, she is passively transformed by her prince into something else.

That her transformation into vampirism represents a step into an idealized fantasy adulthood rather than her growth into a mature and confident adult is indicated by the fact that the *human* adults in the novels are, quite often, ineffectual, weak, and even immature. Her relationship with her mother, while loving, is reversed: Bella has had to caution her mother about men, in essence giving the "sex talk" before having heard it herself.[57] She worries about how her mother will do without her, and her description of Renée leaves an impression of a grown woman who has trouble fending for herself, even in the simplest tasks. Bella is grateful that her mother at least has a new husband, somebody to make sure that the house will be stocked with food, that bills will be taken care of, and that the gas tank of Renée's car will always be full.[58] Moreover, in spite of the presence of a husband who will assume the adult responsibilities that Bella once had while living with her mother, Renée still seems lost without her daughter at first. During her first week in Forks, Bella receives an e-mail from her mother, who is looking for a shirt she is missing.[59]

In her relationship with her parents, Bella has never had much of chance to be an adolescent herself, a situation that she has grown accustomed to. Her mother seems aware of the difference in "maturity," laughing at her daughter's precocious adulthood. Renée, Bella explains to Edward, has always believed that Bella "'was born thirty-five years old'": "'Well, someone has to be the adult,'" she tells Edward.[60] In fact, when Bella finds that she has to play the role of teenager, it is a role that seems artificial to her. Her mother's parental concern about the intensity of the relationship between Bella and Edward confuses Bella. Unsure in her new role as "teenager" during this discussion, she struggles to find words that will placate her parent, explaining to her mother that she is "'pretty crazy about him.'" "'There,'" she thinks, "'— that sounded like something a teenager with her first boyfriend might say.'"[61] As a precocious parent to her mother Renée, Bella worries about the relationship between Renée and Renée's young, new husband, wondering if her mother can handle the new responsibility. "'You have to let them go their own way eventually,'" she reminds herself. "'You have to let them have their own life.'"[62] Even in her dreams, her parental role, not her life as a teenager, is often paramount: Edward explains that he hears her talking in her sleep, worrying about her mother.[63]

While this precocious adulthood may seem to indicate that Bella has the maturity level to choose vampirism over humanity, her insecurities, which last almost up until her transformation, suggest that she has not fully developed the inner strength that Bettelheim argues is necessary for full maturity. This in turn suggests that Bella is using the ideal of life as a vampire as an escape from those insecurities, rather than as a fulfillment of the process of maturation. On her wedding day, one of the last turning points in her human life, Bella's insecurity about her place at her beautiful bridegroom's side continues to manifest. As Alice prepares Bella for her wedding, Bella wonders why all the fuss is necessary since she will be ordinary looking compared to her bridegroom.[64] When she meets the Denali vampire clan, Bella is jealous and intimidated by the beauty of Tanya, whom she observes hugging Edward.[65] Even when she has a chance to see herself in a mirror, she has trouble reconciling the image of the beautiful bride with her usual self-image.[66] She acknowledges that the woman in the mirror is lovely, but she cannot acknowledge that woman as the person that Bella knows as herself.

The relationships that Bella has with her mother figures is important in understanding Bella as a character and the message about gender roles that her characterization might send. Unlike Renée, her human counterpart, the vampire Esme represents the ideal mother. In fact, she adopts a much more parental role in relation to Bella. Capable of deep maternal feelings and actions, Esme immediately welcomes the human Bella into the Cullen family, expressing satisfaction that Bella is the answer to the loneliness of her "son" Edward.[67] She is even kind to potential foes, as is illustrated by her welcoming of Jacob, who, as a werewolf (technically a shape-shifter), is a natural enemy of vampires. She makes a meal for Jacob (who is touched despite himself by Esme's care and unwillingly accepts it so as not to offend), and she provides extra clothing for

Leah, another member of Jacob's pack.[68] Thus, Esme performs the traditionally feminine household duties of laundry and cooking that symbolize her role as maternal caregiver. Esme's effect on others is such that Bella's human mother cannot help but respond positively to Esme. Thinking about her two mothers as she prepares for her own wedding, Bella observes that Renée "*adored* Esme" but notes that nobody could resist her "lovable almost-mother-in-law."[69] The image of Bella's human mother and vampire mother together symbolizes a transition. Having already adopted a more traditional maternal role than the childlike Renée, Esme replaces Renée as Bella's mother figure. The wedding, in fact, is the last time that Bella sees Renée.

In the adventures of many fairy tale heroines, there are also double images of motherhood: the good mother as traditional nurturer and the bad mother as a threat to the heroine's goals. The "monstrous mother" is, in fact, often a cannibal.[70] We see this, for example, in the story "Snow White," where the heroine's life is threatened by her wicked stepmother, who demands the heart of the young beauty. In its earliest forms, the "Sleeping Beauty" story also had a monstrous mother figure. In Basile's version, for instance, this ogress was the jealous wife of the heroine's lover. In Perrault, she takes the form of a monstrous mother-in-law at the end of the story: After the heroine marries the hero, the king must go off to war. Left alone with her mother-in-law, who is an ogress, she becomes the victim of the mother-in-law's desire for flesh. Her husband arrives just in time to save her and her children. (While the Grimms did not include the ogress in their version of "Brier Rose," they did include the tale "The Mother-in-Law" as a separate story in the first edition of *Household Tales.*)[71] The "divided mother," or so psychoanalytical critics often argue, provides a safe venue for expressions of emotions that would not be socially acceptable. The anger that the child may unconsciously feel towards his or her mother (who is represented by the good mother) is transferred to the evil mother figure.[72] Moreover, the presence of this powerful (if wicked) female provides a challenge to the restrictions of patriarchal codes imposed by fairy tales. Adopting a deconstructionist lens, Patricia Hannon argues that "while the nostalgia for a more stable society of orders resurfaces in the gentle demeanor of Cinderella and the obsequious inclinations of 'Sleeping Beauty,' a future encompassing women who compete with men for power creates a palpable tension that undermines longings for the past."[73] The demonization of such strong women reinforces standard gendered codes of behavior, of course, but not without raising an alternative to the passivity of the gentle heroines in the tales.

I am not suggesting that the *Twilight* series consciously alludes to the little known ending of Perrault's "Sleeping Beauty" story. However, the prevalence of the "divided mother" in many of our beloved tales suggests that the relationship between Bella and her two mothers can be read symbolically. It is often the wicked mother figure who is responsible for sending the heroine off to her adventures in the forest (as is true for Snow White), and Bella feels impelled (as a self-sacrifice) to move to the forest-covered area of Forks after the marriage of her mother. Thus, in Meyer's novels, the technically "monstrous" mother, the vampire Esme, is actually the more traditionally maternal (the good mother), while Renée, the human but less traditionally maternal figure, takes the place of the "wicked" mother figure, although she is by no means wicked. But just as the vampire Esme becomes the "good" mother, the monstrous mother (who provided a real, if brief, challenge to patriarchal codes of female behavior) has become in Renée merely irresponsible and scatterbrained, ineffectual at worst. Renée is such a nonentity, in fact, that Bella is able to dismiss her fairly easily from her life, using her mother's weaknesses as justification: she has not seen Renée since her marriage to Edward, but she is glad of that, for Renée is "too fragile" to be a part of her "world."[74] Although Bella's father Charlie will continue to be a part of the heroine's life, if in a peripheral manner, the break with Bella's biological mother represents a break with Bella's human life.[75] Roberta Trites argues that the female protagonist's relationship with her mother in current adolescent novels is a powerful symbol and can send an important message to young women about female relationships and the place of women in society:

> Mother/daughter relationships take two predominant forms in children's and adolescent novels: those traditional narratives that allow for the daughter to achieve independence from her mother in the classically Oedipal manner [...], and those less traditional and less Freudian ones that allow the daughter to mature without necessarily breaking from her mother. While the former focuses on the daughters' strength, the latter category [...] allows both mothers and daughters to be strong.[76]

Trites obviously favors the latter form, which allows for strength and mutual respect across generational lines, something lacking in the depictions of the human Bella and her relationship with her human mother.

Unlike the heroines of earlier folk tales, such as the protagonist of "The Grandmother's Tale," who come of age by saving themselves, Bella relies on her prince to save her from her humanity—to transform her. Rather than accepting her human frailties, Bella sees becoming a vampire as the answer: a form of escape. But the Cullens' longing for a human life actually suggests, although the novel does not explore this in detail, that Edward's world too has its sacrifices and compromises. Perhaps, as the "Sleeping Beauty" imagery suggests, it isn't just Bella's status as a human that is the problem, but also her status as a female. While appealing to a modern audience, Meyer's novels, through the fairy tale allusions, depict gender roles that reflect the rigid social mores of a few centuries ago. That the versions of this fairy tale lore are the ones that we favor perhaps tells us just as much about us, as Meyer's audience, as it tells us about Meyer's novels.

Notes

1. Meyer, *Eclipse* (New York: Little Brown and Company, 2006), 69.
2. Quoted in Jack Zipes, *Fairy Tales and the Art of Subversion* (New York: Routledge, 2006),

7. As Jack Zipes notes, European fairy tales, which were written down in the late eighteenth and early nineteenth centuries, contain "primal motifs" of folklore, but were transformed to reflect the values of late feudal and early capitalistic cultures: "What is interesting about the historical development of the folk tale is the manner in which it was appropriated in its entirety by the aristocratic and bourgeois writers in the sixteenth, seventeenth, and eighteenth centuries with the expansion of publishing to become the new literary genre which one could rightly call the fairy tale (*Kunstmärchen*). As a *literary* text which experimented with and expanded upon stock motifs, figures and plots of the folk tale, the fairy tale reflected a change in values and ideological conflicts in the transitional period from feudalism to early capitalism." See Jack Zipes, *Breaking the Magic Spell: Radical Theories of Folk and Fairy Tales* (Lexington: University Press of Kentucky, 2002), 10.

3. On her way to visit her grandmother, a peasant girl encounters a wolf who asks her what path she takes. (She chooses the path of needles.) Taking the shorter path, the wolf kills the grandmother and boils her flesh. The little girl arrives and is offered the flesh and blood of her grandmother, which she ingests. The heroine then gets into the bed with the "grandmother," having first removed all of her own clothing. Quickly realizing who her bed companion is, the little girl complains that she must go outside to pee. The wolf only allows her to leave after tying a string to her ankle. However, the little girl ties the string to a tree and escapes. Jack Zipes, among others, observes that there is no guilt, sexual or otherwise, in this story. The consumption of the grandmother can be read as an initiation ritual in which the young girl comes of age and replaces the earlier generation. The path of needles can be linked to the needlework apprenticeship that was so common in the life of French peasantry of the time, in which a young girl would strive to become more than just the apprentice. In fact, the heroine in this oral tale "displays a natural, relaxed attitude toward her body and sex and meets the challenge of a would-be seducer." The tale likely dates from the seventeenth century, a time in which superstitious belief in werewolves was very common and a time of the great witch hunt. See Zipes, *Art of Subversion*, 44–45.

4. The Disney animated version, for instance, is based on the Grimm version. See Jack Zipes, *The Great Fairy Tale Tradition: From Straparola and Basile to the Brothers Grimm* (New York: Norton, 2001), 696–698.

5. Stephenie Meyer, *Breaking Dawn* (New York: Little, Brown and Company, 2008), 353.

6. See, for instance, Marta Gutman and Ning de Coninck-Smith, Eds., *Designing Modern Childhoods: History, Space and the Material Culture of Childhood* (Camden: Rutgers University Press, 2008) for a recent of collection of essays that links our contemporary concept of childhood to modernity and that argues that our placing of childhood in a completely separate sphere from adulthood serves adults more than children.

7. For further discussion, see Zipes, *Art of Subversion*, 3.

8. Maria Tatar, *Off With Their Heads!: Fairy Tales and the Culture of Childhood* (Princeton, NJ: Princeton University Press, 1992), 229–230.

9. Zipes, *Art of Subversion*, 8–9. Of the appeal of folk tales, Jack Zipes argues that "the people, largely peasants" were attracted to these oral tales because "the oral folktales were those symbolic acts in which they enunciated their aspirations and projected the magic possibility in an assortment of imaginative ways so that anyone could become a knight in shining armor or a lovely princess; they also presented the stark realities of power politics without disguising the violence and brutality of everyday life." See Zipes, *Art of Subversion*, 8.

10. See Lewis Seifert, "The Marvelous in Context: The Place of the *Contes de Fées* in Late Seventeenth-Century France," in Jack Zipes, *The Great Fairy Tale Tradition: From Straparola and Basile to the Brothers Grimm* (New York: Norton, 2001), 904. Seifert discusses the role of fairy tales in *mondain* culture of seventeenth-century France. Fairy tales were associated with, among other things, the ease of artifice that hides itself ("an ease or naturalness of expression") that was embraced by so many in that society. Seifert argues that the popularity of fairy tales in seventeenth-century France can be linked to the "pietistic attacks" on polite society. These tales, Seifert believes, were a way to reaffirm *mondain* social ideals. In addition, the tales were

part of the "Battle Between the Ancients and the Moderns" going on at that time. With no apparent antecedents in classical lore (or at least, very few obvious ones in the eyes of their audience), the fairy tales represented the side of the moderns. See Seifert, "The Marvelous in Context," 902–933. For a discussion of how the gendered value of the tales ties into this debate, see also Zipes, *Art of Subversion*, 19–21.

11. Roberta Seelinger Trites, *Waking Sleeping Beauty; Feminist Voices in Children's Novels* (Iowa City: University of Iowa Press, 1997), 54.

12. Bruno Bettelheim, *The Uses of Enchantment: The Meaning and Importance of Fairy Tales* (New York: Vintage Books, 1977), 225–226.

13. Jack Zipes, *The Great Fairy Tale Tradition*, 684. See also Zipes, *Breaking the Magic Spell*, 183. For a discussion of Bettelheim's problematic methodology and the scandals in his life, see Zipes, *Breaking the Magic Spell*,179–181.

14. Maria Tatar, *The Hard Facts of the Grimms' Fairy Tales* (Princeton: Princeton Universit Press, 1987, rpt. 2003), 54. Bruno Bettelheim argues, for instance, that the pricking of the needle that occurs is symbolic of menstruation; the sleep symbolizes a state of stasis until the young girl is actually emotionally ready for sexual advances from suitors: "A natural reaction to the threat of having to grow up is to withdraw from a world and life which impose such difficulties." According to Bettelheim, "Female completeness is not achieved when falling in love, not even in intercourse, nor in childbirth, since the heroines of *Perceforest* and in Basile's story sleep all through it. These are necessary steps on the way to ultimate maturity; but complete selfhood comes only with having given life, and with nurturing the one whom one has brought into being: with the baby sucking from the mother's body." See Bettelheim, *The Uses of Enchantment*, 234–235. Tatar, however, reminds us that the existence of a Russian tale with a male Sleeping Beauty is evidence that we should not be too essentialist about the tale. See Tatar, *Hard Facts*, 47.

15. Zipes, *Breaking the Magic Spell*, 189. Jack Zipes discusses how Bettelheim's approach is self-contradictory: on the one hand, he encourages parents to allow the children to interpret the tales naturally for themselves; on the other hand, he argues for meanings in the tales that are innate, what Zipes calls the "categorical imperative": "It is the authority, Bettelheim, who claims to know how children subconsciously view the tales and who imposes this psychoanalytical mode of interpreting tales on adults. In turn, they ought to use this approach if they care for children."

16. Meyer, *New Moon*, 411.

17. Ibid., 85–93.

18. Ibid., 550.

19. Stephenie Meyer, *Twilight* (New York: Little, Brown and Company, 2005), 294.

20. Ibid., 192.

21. Meyer, *New Moon*, 233. See also *New Moon*, 235–245 for Bella's encounter with Laurent.

22. Ibid., 63.

23. Meyer, *Twilight*, 160–163.

24. Ibid., 188–189.

25. Ibid., 55.

26. Stephenie Meyer, *Eclipse* (New York: Little, Brown and Company, 2007), 68.

27. Zipes, *Art of Subversion*, 40. Patricia Hannon adds this interpretation of the "Sleeping Beauty" tale: "The needle draws blood, causing the princess to evanesce into a hundred-years' sleep, an eloquent metaphor for the feminine passivity and contained sensuality so vaunted by theorists who extolled women's chastity. Frozen in time but not lifeless, the heroine's subdued body represents those disruptive impulses to be distanced from the newly assertive rational consciousness." See Patricia Hannon, "*Corps cadavers:* Heroes and Heroines in the Tales of Perrault" in Jack Zipes, *The Great Fairy Tale Tradition*: *From Straparola and Basile to the Brothers Grimm* (New York: Norton, 2001), 937.

28. The implications of the ending with the mother-in-law as ogress will be discussed farther along in this essay.

29. See Zipes, *Art of Subversion*, 21. Patricia Hannon comments on the use of fairy tales by Perrault to control female behavior: "At a time when women's increasing prominence elicits repressive legislation and diatribes against society ladies, Perrault responds by a symbolic eradication of female sovereignty. His fairy tales mockingly yet decisively put severe limits on the reign of women. Perrault at times appears to agree with Fénelon, who asserted that women's functions should correspond to their 'natural gifts' for housewifery." See Hannon, "Heroes and Heroines," 953. Lewis Seifert discusses how "the attacks on *mondain* culture during the last decade of the seventeenth century gave particular attention to women," including attacks such as those by Madame de Mantenon and Fénelon who felt that the fallen and now immoral aristocracy were to be saved by women, who would adopt the "responsibilities of pious virtue." According to Seifert, "for women to perform this essential role, they would have to turn away from the pleasures of *mondain* life, including forms of 'worldly' *divertissements* and sociability, to take on instead the duties of domesticity." See Seifert, "The Marvelous in Context," 923.

30. Tatar, *Hard Facts*, 146.

31. Zipes, *Art of Subversion*, 27.

32. See, for instance, Meyer, *Breaking Dawn*, 649.

33. Meyer, *Twilight*, 68.

34. Ibid., 226.

35. Meyer, *New Moon*, 184–192.

36. Ibid., 358.

37. Ibid., 361.

38. Ibid., 3–29.

39. Meyer, *Eclipse*, 267–269.

40. Meyer, *Twilight*, 495.

41. Meyer, *Eclipse*, 92.

42. Meyer, *Twilight*, 474.

43 Meyer, *Eclipse*, 17.

44. Meyer, *Twilight*, 260.

45. Meyer, *Eclipse*, 153.

46. Ibid., 396.

47. Ibid., 344.

48. Meyer, *Breaking Dawn*, 22.

49. Meyer, *New Moon*, 23.

50. Meyer, *Eclipse*, 167.

51. Meyer, *Breaking Dawn*, 403.

52. Ibid., 409.

53. Ibid., 410.

54. Ibid., 426.

55. Ibid., 703.

56. Trites, *Waking*, 8. Among other feminist texts, for example, Trites discusses Cynthia Voigt's *When She Hollers* as a text that "teaches girls to overcome sexual victimization" and Beverly Cleary's *Dear Mr. Henshaw* as a text that acknowledges "that traditional gender roles have been as limiting for boys as they have for girls."

57. Meyer, *Twilight*, 468.

58. Ibid., 4.

59. Ibid., 33

60. Ibid., 106.

61. Ibid., 468.

62. Meyer, *Eclipse*, 45.

63. Meyer, *Twilight*, 294. Bella's relationship with her father is little different. While living with her father, Bella must look after a man who is unable to cook without almost setting the microwave on fire. His status as a father encourages Bella's affection but not her respect,

and his few parenting attempts are met with bemusement. These emotions do not manifest themselves as the anger and contempt of an adolescent, but of an adult humoring the whims of an overgrown child: Charlie does not parent when he shows concern about the intensity of the relationship between Bella and Edward, he "sulks." See, for instance, Meyer, *Eclipse*, 43.

64. Meyer, *Breaking Dawn*, 42.
65. Ibid., 54.
66. Ibid., 57.
67. Meyer, *Twilight*, 368.
68. Meyer, *Breaking Dawn*, 283–285.
69. Ibid., 19.
70. See Tatar, *Hard Facts*, 151–152, where she argues thus: "It may be true, as Bettelheim has asserted, that fairy tales enacting Oedipal conflicts split the mother figure in two: one mother who stands by her child and another (step)mother who stands in the way of the female child's attempts to secure the love of her father. Most fairy tales depicting the fortunes of heroines persecuted by stepmothers portray benevolent female figures in the form of wise women, or, failing that, enact a deceased mother's undying love for her child by bringing Mother Nature to the heroine's rescue." Tatar notes that the fairy tales that are the most popular today are those with the evil mother figure, rather than the threatening father figure in tales no longer in favor: "In our own culture, we find the process of selection a bias working manifestly in favor of the rags-to-riches tale that contains a powerful, wicked older woman. 'Cinderella,' 'Snow White,' and 'Sleeping Beauty' are the tales from Perrault and from the Grimms that continue to thrive even on non-native soil. [...] Of the two components that shape female Oedipal plots—the fantasy of an amorous father and the fantasy of rivalry with the mother-only the latter has become a prominent, virtually undisguised theme in popular tales depicting the marriage of female protagonists. While (step)mothers are habitually demonized as nags at home and witches in the woods, fathers qua fathers tend to fade into the background or to be absent from the tale."
71. For wicked mothers as cannibals, see Tatar, *Hard Facts*, 140.
72. Ibid., 144–145.
73. Ibid.; Hannon, "Heroes and Heroines," 956.
74. Meyer, *Breaking Dawn*, 654.
75. Maria Tatar notes that the replacement of the "bad" mother allows the heroine in fairy tales to be free to live her normal human life, now disenchanted: "Once a fairy-tale heroine succeeds in reversing the effects of her stepmother's villainy, either by completing the tasks assigned to her or by returning from the dead to broadcast the harm done to her, the process of disenchantment is complete. To emphasize the definitive end to the stepmother's reign of terror, the fairy tale describes her demise in graphic and morbid detail. Drowned, burned to ashes, torn to pieces by wild animals, or placed in a casket filled with boiling oil and poisonous snakes, she dies in both body and spirit, no longer representing a threat to the recently established royal family. And once the biological mother of that family reigns supreme, the king and even his children are destined to live happily ever after." Obviously, this is not quite the case in the *Twilight* series, where the heroine is rejecting her human life for a world that more closely resembles the "enchanted" world of fairy tales. See Tatar, *Hard Facts*, 148.
76. See Trites, *Waking*, 103.

Why We Like Our Vampires Sexy

STEPHANIE L. DOWDLE

> "If people want stories about girls who love vampires, they should have them.... It's always deeply romantic or deeply interesting or deeply scary, or all of the above."
>
> —Joss Whedon, creator of *Buffy the Vampire Slayer*[1]

It was a spring night in 2008 when I received a cryptic text message from my youngest sister: "I love my imaginary vampire boyfriend, Edward." I had no idea who or what she was talking about and chalked it up to a late night. It wasn't until we spoke some days later that she clarified her text and I was introduced to a powerful new phenomenon in young adult literature: the aloof, sophisticated, and deliciously dangerous "vegetarian vampire" Edward Cullen from Stephenie Meyer's *Twilight* series.

I had heard of these novels before but hadn't really paid them much attention—just enough to mock them, assuming that if they were *this* popular and sported such a legion of devotees, they couldn't be *that* good ... could they? After several months of constant prodding and a few more random text messages about sexy vampires and why they were better than human guys, I finally relented and picked up Meyer's novels at the library, determined to see what the fuss was all about.

While I'm not sure I will ever revel in "imaginary vampire boyfriends" to the degree that many *Twilight* readers do, I must admit that I am also a fan, if a somewhat reluctant one, of Meyer's series. I am intrigued by the popularity of these novels. Shakespeare they aren't, but good escape literature they most definitely are, and I can't help but wonder if there is something more to the almost instantaneous celebrity of the *Twilight* series than I first thought. A growing fan base among readers of all ages and the current marketable popularity of vampire lore in many facets of mainstream media has proven that this series is not strictly young adult fare. Indeed, according to the audiences' enthusiastic reactions to *The Twilight Saga: New Moon*, the film based on Meyer's second vampire novel, the *Twilight* series seems to be at the forefront of this trend. When I attended a showing of the film in late November 2009, the audience was primarily composed of middle-aged women — mothers and grandmothers, it appeared — and a few men who had visibly been dragged there by a significant other. When it came time for the now-famous scene where Jacob takes off his shirt, these women screamed the loudest, and the men slumped down in their seats, attempting to disappear.

This paper begins with an examination of the evolution of vampire lore in film and written text, and then moves on to look at some of the ways in which Meyer's novels bridge different cultural groups, primarily age groups, creating avenues for discussion (and controversy) between different discourse communities.

According to columnist Steve Wood of *The Courier-Post*, "Despite living on-and-off for centuries and sticking to an iron-rich diet, vampires— once long in the tooth, ears and fingernails— have never looked better."[2] Wood credits the Hollywood media machine with the vampires' glamorous makeover. Nina Auerbach, Professor of English at the University of Pennsylvania and author of *Our Vampires, Ourselves*, credits a more specific source with the rise of these newly glam and deliciously sexy vampires: Anne Rice.[3] According to Auerbach, Rice represents vampires as "timeless, romantic figures" and has "made them closer and closer to gods."[4] She remarks, "In earlier vampire stories they're disgusting. They're walking corpses and instinctive blood drinkers. They're close[er] to our idea of zombies."[5] It's notable, then, that from the publication of Rice's *Interview with the Vampire* in the mid 1970s, up to the more recent publication of novels like L.J. Smith's *The Vampire Diaries* trilogy (1991), Charlaine Harris' *Dead Until Dark* (2001), and Meyer's *Twilight* series (2005–2008), vampires have become increasingly more appealing and less gruesome. They still survive on blood, albeit synthetic (Harris) or animal (Meyer), and "bad vampires" still exist, yet, as Alex Remington wrote in *The Washington Post*, "[Everyone] loves a romantic lead, even if landing that hunky man means defiling the crypts of the undead. On screens big and small, vampires are increasingly becoming less demonic and more sympathetic, less evil and more nuanced — and have become the most eligible bachelors around."[6]

Vampires have not always oozed sex appeal, however, and it follows that vampire fiction was not always intended for a young adult audience. From Lord Ruthven in John William Polidori's "The Vampyre" (1819) to Bram Stoker's *Dracula* (1897), the vampire was represented as a fearsome creature, more in line with the monsters of fairy tales and folk stories recorded by Anderson, Perrault, and the Brothers Grimm. In line with these stories— the original intent of which was not merely to entertain but also to influence listeners by reaffirming established social mores— many critics have focused on the repressed (Victorian) view of sexuality inherent in Stoker's novel. According to George Stade, a retired Professor of English at Columbia and author of the forward to the 1981 Bantam edition of Stoker's *Dracula*, Count Dracula can be interpreted as "the symptom of a wish, largely sexual, that we wish we did not have," and the effect of repressing this wish "is to turn a hunger into a horror."[7] Stade continues by stating that in Stoker's day, "sex was likely to seem bestial, polluting, depleting, deathly, satanic, a fever in the blood, the theme of dreams, the motive of madness, the lurking menace in the shadow of every scene."[8] What better way to reinforce this ideology than by making sex not just dirty, but also dangerous and deadly?

Nigel Watson describes the conflict in *Dracula* as a "battle between the forces of rational civilized, good [and] instinctual, irrational, evil."[9] In Stoker's novel, Jonathan Harker, representing the rational, civilized good, offers this description of the Count, representing the instinctual, irrational evil:

> His face was ... strong ... with high bridge of the thin nose and peculiarly arched nostrils; with a lofty, domed forehead, and hair growing scantily round the temples but profusely elsewhere. His eyebrows were massive, almost meeting over the nose.... The mouth ... was fixed and rather cruel-looking, with peculiarly sharp white teeth; these protruded over the lips ... For the rest, his ears were pale, and at the tops, extremely pointed.... [His hands] were rather coarse—broad, with squat fingers.... The nails were long and fine and cut to a sharp point.... [H]is breath ... was rank.[10]

Contrast this image with Meyer's description of her heroine's first encounter with the good vegetarian vampires in *Twilight*. Though the vampire siblings are all unique in appearance, each of the five Cullen "children" is described as being some version of breathtakingly gorgeous. From the "lean" and "muscular" boys, to the "statuesque" and "pixielike" girls, the Cullens are so extraordinarily beautiful that Bella is almost certain she is looking at pieces of fine art rather than "living" creatures.[11]

It is obvious from these two descriptions that, at least physically, the members of *Twilight's* Cullen family are vastly different creatures from Stoker's Dracula. Yet, again, vampires, whether hairy and menacing like Dracula or glamorous and sexy like Edward, have always tempted audiences with their frightening ability to seduce us (see, for example, the scenes at the Theater of the Vampires in Anne Rice's *Interview with the Vampire*) and they continue to hold a powerful place in our literary and cultural fabric.

One only has to perform a basic search for the word "vampire" at imdb.com to reveal over 1,300 entries, with production dates ranging from 1896 to the present day.[12] A select sampling of the entries includes the following:

- 1922 = Max Schreck as Count Orlock in *Nosferatu*
- 1931 = Bela Lugosi as Count Dracula in *Dracula*
- 1958 = Christopher Lee as Count Dracula in *Dracula*
- 1967–1971 = Jonathan Frid as Barnabas Collins in *Dark Shadows*
- 1979 = Klaus Kinski as Count Dracula in *Nosferatu*

- 1987 = Kiefer Sutherland, et al. in *The Lost Boys*
- 1992 = Gary Oldman as Count Dracula in *Bram Stoker's Dracula*
- 1994 = Brad Pitt as Louis and Tom Cruise as Lestat in *Interview with the Vampire*
- 1998 = Wesley Snipes as Eric Brooks/Blade, the dhampir in *Blade*
- 2002 = Aaliyah as Queen Akasha and Stuart Townsend as Lestat de Lioncort in *Queen of the Damned*
- 2008 = Stephen Moyer as Bill Compton in HBO's *True Blood*
- 2008 = Robert Pattinson, et al. as the Cullens in *Twilight*
- 2009 = Robert Pattinson, et al. as the Cullens in *New Moon*

Notice the slow but sure transition from gruesome creature to sex symbol here. The "fear factor" is still there, but, at least physically, the vampires themselves have changed dramatically. Now, we like our vampires sexy. This sex appeal is manifest in the number of shows currently identified as being "in production" and slated for release in 2010–2011, and beyond. This list includes film adaptations of the last two novels in Meyer's *Twilight* series—*Eclipse* (2010), and *Breaking Dawn* (2011)—as well as Elizabeth Kostova's *The Historian* (2010) and a (rumored) version of *Dark Shadows* starring Johnny Depp as Barnabas Collins (2011).[13]

Clearly, vampires are big business, and the demand for all things vampiric continues to grow. A quick search at amazon.com using the term "vampire" revealed over 28,300 separate links, broken down by department (Books, Movies & TV, MP3 Downloads, and so on). One of the most surprising revelations here came in the form of 2,477 hits in the area of Home/Garden.[14] These products ranged from TSL Vampire ATV/UTV Tires, to Balkan Vampire Blood Cross Statues, Vegetarian Vampire Aprons, and beyond. Today's vampires are crossing all sorts of boundaries.

Focusing an amazon.com search specifically on "Stephenie Meyer" yielded everything from movie posters, to baby onesies, t-shirts, refrigerator magnets, key chains, buttons, trading cards, bookmarks, window clings for the car, Edward Cullen body shimmer, and, of course, the novels themselves.[15]

A big draw for *Twilight* fans of all ages has been the launch parties held at bookstores worldwide before the publication of most of Meyer's novels. Additionally, the "Twilight Proms" which were held at some theaters for the opening nights of *Twilight*, the first film based on one of Meyer's novels which opened nationwide on November 20–21, 2008, drew enthusiastic, costumed fans of all ages. One devotee of the novels, a clerk at my local Barnes & Noble store made up a "wedding announcement" (in red and black, of course) to advertise the store's release party for the final novel in the series, *Breaking Dawn*. Yours truly attended an opening night gala of sorts where a friend had rented out an entire theater for a showing of *Twilight*. While I was not decked out in my best vampire gear or a "Bite Me!" t-shirt, it was not hard to pick out those fans who were caught up in the fervor of *Twilight* mania that permeated the theater lobby that evening.

While I waited to enter the theater that night, I noted the variety of people in attendance; surprisingly, these were mostly women from their mid 20s up through their early 60s. Tweens and teens were there in force too, along with a handful of men and boys who looked like they had been dragged along on the night's outing. As we sat in the theater with our popcorn and sodas waiting for the movie to begin, the group I was with played a variety of *Twilight*-themed games and contests, complete with *Twilight*-themed prizes, all designed to hype-up the already raging anticipation for the screen adaptation of the novel.

Anticipation for the November 2009 film debut of *The Twilight Saga: New* Moon, reached the same fever-pitch as that of its predecessor. The trailer for *New Moon* premiered at Comic-Con International 2009, and according to George Roush, a writer for *LatinoReview.com*, the "biggest craze ... [at the conference was] not the comic, that's for sure. The *Twilight* fans came out in droves and even camped out overnight just to make sure they got a glimpse of New Moon footage."[16] Footage of the event was leaked to the *Twilight* fans worldwide via an illegal video-phone recording that was quickly posted online. At times, it's difficult to hear the actors speaking because of all the screaming fans.[17] At the live *New Moon* actors' panel at Comic-Con 2009, the response was similar.[18] From these two events, it's easy to surmise that the public's lust for vampires is not merely a passing trend. Vampires, and *Twilight's* Cullen family in particular, are here to stay.

Vampire proms, fake wedding announcements, and mass movie hysteria aside, it is obvious that vampires are popular figures now more than ever. As a fairly recent "fan" of the horror genre, I find myself asking the following questions: What is so captivating about a creature that, for all intents and purposes, is a lethal being? Moreover, how and why did vampires transition from the creatures found in Bram Stoker's novel *Dracula* and early films like *Nosferatu* and *Dracula* to the still lethal, but infinitely more appealing, creatures such as Louis, Lestat, Bill Compton, and Edward Cullen?

According to George Stade, "People [once] read horror fiction as they used to read pornography, on the sly. Reviewers with intellectual pretensions titter in print."[19] Indeed, the original lure of vampire fiction was nothing like the sparkly, youthful, sex gods that draw so many diverse readers to the *Twilight* series. From the introduction of her first novel, *Twilight*, in 2005 until the publication of the series' capstone novel, *Breaking Dawn*, in August of 2008, Stephenie Meyer's writing has brought together readers from across the globe. According to an online source, her books have been translated into "37 different languages."[20] Her rise to fame has been dramatic, calling for the writer to be compared by many to J.K. Rowling.

In an article published in early August 2009, Carol Memmott and Mary Cadden of *USA Today* write that Meyer's *Twilight* series has effectively eclipsed records previously set by Rowlings' *Harry Potter* series on *USA Today*'s Best-Selling Books list.[21] Memmott and Cadden inform us that "Rowling, overall, has sold more books than Meyer—her seven-book series about boy wizard Harry Potter has 143 million copies in print in the U.S.A., while Meyer has sold 40 million copies of her four books." The *Twilight* books, however, "have stayed in the list's top 10 for 52 consecutive weeks," whereas "Rowling's first four *Potter* books were top 10 for 13 consecutive weeks, 24 weeks total."[22] The *Twilight*-based graphic novels are likely to drive the popularity of Meyer's work even higher.[23]

In a further comparison to J.K. Rowling, since first emerging onto the literary scene, Stephenie Meyer has also been both lauded and criticized for her success. While the sales numbers for her novels and *Twilight* merchandise continue to grow, critiques of Meyer's writing and even of Meyer herself continue to cover quite a broad range. Respondents to an online survey I conducted said that Meyer's novels were either too sexy, not sexy enough (one respondent called *Twilight* a Harlequin romance without any of the good bits), anti-feminist, pro-female, too Mormon, and even Mormon-apostate.[24]

Even the reigning "king" of horror fiction, Stephen King himself, has weighed in on Meyer's popularity and skills as a writer. In December 2008, Lorrie Lynch of *USA Weekend* flew to Maine to interview King for a forthcoming cover story. During their interview, Lynch asked him what influence his success in the horror genre might have had on "the massive careers of *Harry Potter* creator J.K. Rowling and *Twilight* author Stephenie Meyer."[25] He responded by saying, "I think that I serve that purpose for some writers, and that's a good thing. Both Rowling and Meyer, they're speaking directly to young people. ... The real difference is that Jo Rowling is a terrific writer and Stephenie Meyer can't write worth a darn. She's not very good."[26]

The criticisms of Meyer's literary topics, prowess, and merit do not stop with Stephen King. While some readers criticize Meyer for the pseudo-sexual nature of Bella and Edward's relationship, others criticize her for creating an anti-feminist heroine and a chauvinistic hero. Danielle Douvikas, writer for *the Contra Costa Times*, had this to say:

> I do not even know why I read this series. I guess I just read them to try to convince teens that they are not the greatest novels ever created.... The "Harry Potter" novels suggest that love drives people to do extraordinary things. "Twilight," on the other hand, is merely an interesting story about a whiny, hormone-driven teenager.[27]

Douvikas is joined in her critique of *Twilight* by Christine Siefert, Assistant Professor of Communications at Westminster College in Salt Lake City, Utah. In an article published in the e-zine *bitch: Feminist Response to Pop Culture*, Siefert categorizes Meyer's writing as "abstinence porn, sensational, erotic, and titillating."[28] Despite such criticism, the fan base for Meyer's novels, and for vampire lore in general, continues to grow. Indeed, though these books were initially touted as "adolescent literature," the immense popularity of *Twilight* series (*Twilight*, 2005; *New Moon*, 2006; *Eclipse*, 2007; *Breaking Dawn*, 2008) among readers of all ages, and in some instances, genders, has proven that they are not strictly young adult—or even female—fare. This ability to bridge different cultural groups, creating crossroads for discussion among a variety of discourse communities, is one of the most powerful aspects of Meyer's writing ... despite what Stephen King may think about her style.

As I gathered information for this essay, one of my students, a twenty-something mother of two, was kind enough to send me four pages of single-spaced notes detailing her unabashed enthusiasm for *Twilight*. In her notes, Jen wrote specifically about her affection for Meyer's fourth novel, *Breaking Dawn*, and her belief that the "happily ever after ending" was not a sappy cliché, but rather something readers should take comfort in:

> When Bella first becomes a vampire the one thing that I was concerned about was the fact that she was changing her looks, she was becoming more beautiful. This was a concern because I wondered what the lesson was supposed to be, is it that you have to be unbelievably gorgeous in order to live happily ever after? It bothered me at first because I kept thinking does Edward like her better now? I didn't want him to suddenly love her more just because she looked better; in fact I found it crucial that he didn't.[29]

In early January 2010, Jen stopped by my office for an impromptu chat about the second film based on one of Meyer's novels: *The Twilight Saga: New Moon*. As we discussed the film and whether or not women over 20 should find Jacob Black (Taylor Lautner) attractive, it was easy to see that Jen's enthusiasm for Meyer's characters has not waned; if anything, she is *more* enthusiastic than ever and looks forward to the final films based on the *Twilight* series.

Echoing Jen's passionate defense of Meyers' novels and the first film, many responses to a blog posting on www.parentdish.com entitled "Does *Twilight* Send Teen Girls a Bad Message" emphasize the positive qualities of Meyer's novels and their power to transcend different cultural and age groups. One respondent to the blog prompt writes:

> [T]his story digs deep into the soul of many women (many, not all).... It's just a fantasy after all, not like a lot of us actually want that in our everyday lives so much, but the idea of it isn't so bad. Everyone needs saving once in a while, even men.... Some people ... need to grow up and remember that dreams and fantasies are good for the soul."[30]

Another respondent comments that when her eleven-year-old daughter suddenly announced she loved reading and dove into the *Twilight* series, she decided Meyer's novels were a "positive influence."[31] Yet another blogger "salute[s] Stephenie Meyer for her work,"[32] and one respondent, an educator in a junior high school, found it "refreshing that an author chose to have the romance [that] ... didn't push sex and all the other things teens have to deal with constantly."[33]

As these responses illustrate, although it is touted as young adult fiction, Meyer's *Twilight* series is more than this. One of the largest fan bases for the novels is comprised of twenty and thirty-something moms, like Jen. This is demonstrated by the popular blog site *TwilightMOMS.com: The Hand That Rocks the Cradle is the Hand That Rules the World.*[34] It is advertised as a place "for fans of Stephenie Meyer to gather and discuss our love of her writing and characters while balancing family, work, home, children and marriage."[35] You are allowed to join the site if you meet the following criteria: you are at least 25 years old, you are a mom, or you are married.[36]

An über-specialized networking site (think an extended Facebook group with a really tight focus), *TwilightMOMS* encourages members to choose their own vampire name as they participate in discussion boards, online contests, games, and the like. One member identifies herself as "Coven Mother Lisa." *TwilightMOMS* even has an official charity, the details of which I was not allowed to view since I am not a "Twilight Mom."

TwilightTeens.com is a sister site to *TwilightMOMS.com*, allowing teens to participate in many of the same activities, focused specifically towards their age group. As on *TwilightMOMS*, users at this teen site are also encouraged to pick a vampire name, some being Firstsight, EdwardLover, and CullenLover. The forum link on this site is a multi-layered text, with no fewer than thirty-nine separate discussion links. They include links for participants to vote on the now inevitable debate over which series is better, *Twilight* or *Harry Potter*, and discussion spaces for each of the four novels in Meyer's series. Additionally, you can find links to a discussion space devoted solely to the musings of "*Twilight* guys," as well as places to submit fan fiction and pointers for creating your very own vampire apparel and decor.[37] Here we are back to Home&Garden again!

Websites like *TwilightMOMS* and *TwilightTeens* would certainly support the ideas expressed by journalist Sydney Ang in "Undead Evermore: Vampire Mythology in the 21st century." Here, Ang comments that it is specifically Edward's sex appeal that has helped the *Twilight* series add "to the underground romanticism of vampire culture that has started ever since Dracula was published."[38] Ang continues:

> While there have been others before *Twilight*, no book or movie has generated such a frenzied and rabid response from young adults, with hordes of fans around the world swearing undying love and devotion to Cullen. And this is not a bad thing, despite what most puritan parents and clergies said. Ultimately it is no different than having a crush on a movie star and utterances of "I want to be vampire" are no different from "I want to be a wizard" when Mr. Potter was the current favorite.[39]

Indeed, it is this ability to create such strong emotional connections with readers of all ages and backgrounds that continues to popularize vampires and make the *Twilight* series such a phenomenon. Perhaps in homage to the dangerous vampires of earlier days, even the baddies are sexy, as we see with the characters of Damon in the CW's *The Vampire* Diaries, Eric in HBO's *True Blood*, and James, Laurent, and Victoria in the film adaptation of Meyer's *Twilight*.

For Alex Remington of *The Washington Post*:

> No matter how mundane their politics or morals, vampires will always be cool, because sex and death never go out of style. More and more, vampires are not hard to sympathize with: They eternally have to choose between loving us and feeding on us. Given that rapacious dilemma, Hollywood can't help but to keep feeding us the ... vampire. And evermore, we'll keep biting.[40]

Remington's article goes on to quote Alan Ball, the creator of HBO's *True Blood*: "Vampires are just like humans. Nobody's a hundred percent good, nobody's a hundred percent bad."[41] After reading the *Twilight* series, I must conclude that Stephenie Meyer would agree with Ball's assessment. The vampires in her novels, whether seen as good or evil, all retain the power of choice.[42] Perhaps it is precisely this humanizing characteristic which accounts for the widespread popularity of the *Twilight* series, and reveals just why we like our vampires sexy.

Notes

1. Jennifer Vineyard. "Sinking Our Teeth into Modern Vampires: How Do 'Twilight,' 'Buffy,' and Others Compare?" 29 October 2008, http://www.mtv.com/movies/news/articles/1598112/story.jhtml.

2. Steve Wood. "Vampires Better Looking, Thanks to Hollywood," *Deseret News Online*, 31 October 2008, http://deseretnews.com/article/705259221/Vampires-better-looking-thanks-to-Hollywood.html.

3. Ibid.

4. Auerbach, qtd. in Wood, http://deseretnews.com/article/1%2C5143%2C705259221%2C00.html.

5. Ibid.

6. Ibid.

7. Alex Remington, "Vampires Stake a Claim on Audience's Hearts," *Washington Post*, 7 September 2008. M03. http://www.washingtonpost.com/wpdyn/content/article/2008/09/05/AR2008090501418.html.

8. "Introduction," Bram Stoker, *Dracula* (New York: Bantam, 1981), vi.

9. Ibid., vii.

10. "Nosferatu," *Talking Pictures*, 2001, http://tinyurl.com/cyrkhf.

11. Stoker, *Dracula*, 18–19.

12. Stephenie Meyer, *Twilight* (New York: Little, Brown and Company, 2005), 18–19.

13. See http://www.imdb.com/find?s=all&q=vampire.

14. See http://www.imdb.com/keyword/vampire/?sort=release_date&start=1201.

15. See http://www.amazon.com/s/ref=nb_sb_noss?url=search-alias%3Daps&field-keywords=vampire.

16. See http://www.amazon.com/s/ref=nb_sb_ss_i_0_8?url=search-alias%3Daps&field-keywords=stephenie+meyer&sprefix=stepheni.

17. "Comic-Con 2009! New Moon Interview with Kristin Stewart & Taylor Lautner," July 24, 2009, http://www.latinoreview.com/news/comic-con-2009-new-moon-interview-with-kristen-stewart-taylor-lautner-7485.

18. *New Moon* trailer from Comic-Con International 2009, http://www.youtube.com/watch?v=ACaSD_pGVdw.

19. *New Moon* panel at Comic-Con International 2009, http://www.youtube.com/watch?v=C5zyPFr-CQY.

20. "The Apparitions of Horror," excerpted from "Literature as Equipage," delivered at Columbia College Dean's Day on April 17, 1999, http://www.college.columbia.edu/cct_archive/sep99/25a.html.

21. "Exploring Twilight," http://www.juggle.com/info/book/twilight-5/.

22. Carol Memmott and Mary Cadder, "Twilight Series Eclipse Potter Records on Best-selling List," *USA Today*, August 3, 2009, http://www.usatoday.com/life/books/news/2009–08–03-twilight-series_N.htm.

23. Ibid.

24. Ibid.

25. Online *Twilight* Survey, Surveymonkey.com, November 2008–January 2009.

26. "Exclusive ..." February 2, 2009, http://blogs.usaweekend.com/whos_news/2009/02/exclusive-steph.html.

27. Ibid.

28. Danielle Douvikas. "*Twilight* Series Sends Girls a Wrong Message," *The Herald*, November 28, 2008, http://www.heraldonline.com/107/story/985071.html.

29. Christine Siefert, "Bite Me! (or, Don't)," *bitch: Feminist Response to Pop Culture*, 2008, http://bitchmagazine.org/article/bite-me-or-dont.

30. Email from Jen Javier to Stephanie Dowdle, November 26, 2008. Jen was such a fan of the series that she saw the film version of *Twilight* four times during its opening weekend in November 2008.

31. See c_rousseau05, blog response, *parentdish.com*, November 25, 2008, http://www.parentdish.com/2008/11/25/does-twilight-send-teen-girls-a-bad-message/.

32. stephanie, blog response, parentdish.com, November 30, 2008, http://www.parentdish.com/2008/11/25/does-twilight-send-teen-girls-a-bad-message/

33. ALAN, blog response, parentdish.com, December 3, 2008, http://www.parentdish.com/2008/11/25/does-twilight-send-teen-girls-a-bad-message/.

34. aoknal, blog response, parentdish.com, November 25, 2008, http://www.parentdish.com/2008/11/25/does-twilight-send-teen-girls-a-bad-message/.

35. http://twilightmomsforums.freeforums.org/twilight-sales-vs-harry-potter-sales-t14761.html

36. Ibid.

37. Ibid.

38. *Twilight Teens*, February 24 2009, http://www.twilightteens.com/twilight-forum/.

39. Sydney Ang, "Undead Evermore: Vampire Mythology in the 21st Century," *The Manila Times*, October 30, 2008. http://www.manilatimes.net/national/2008/oct/30/yehey/life/20081030lif1.html [italics added].

40. Ibid.

41. "Vampires Stake a Claim on Audience's Hearts," *Washington Post*, September 7, 2008, M03, http://www.washingtonpost.com/wp-dyn/content/article/2008/09/05/AR2008090501418.html.

42. Ibid.

43. Ibid.

Forks, Washington: From Farms to Forests to Fans

CHRISTINE M. MITCHELL

My introduction to the *Twilight* phenomenon came in a class I teach for English education majors at Southeastern Louisiana University. As fall semester 2006 began, I mentioned that my family and I had spent a lovely summer in the cool Northwest air of Forks, Washington. One young woman's ears pricked up. "Forks? Washington? Are you serious?" she asked.

"Yeaaaah. Do you know it?" I was surprised that she had ever heard of Forks, Washington, small town that it is.

"Oh, my god! That's where *Twilight* is set! Is that a real place!?" At this point, I was sure that she had taken leave of her senses, but a quick explanation reminded me that I'd heard something about a young adult novel set in Forks because the author was looking for the darkest, rainiest place in the country. I had no plans to read the book, and I didn't think much more about it.

However, by the next summer, when we returned to Forks, *Twilight* could not be ignored. Forks had been invaded by the group of fans known as "Twi-hards," those (mainly) adolescent girls and their mothers on the hunt for anything and everything *Twilight*.

History of Forks

SETTLEMENT

Long before it was overrun by Twi-hards, the Forks Prairie, some twelve to fifteen miles inland from La Push at the mouth of the Quillayute River, was the hunting grounds of the Quileute (the same tribe from which Jacob, Bella's werewolf friend, hails). Quileute hunters burned the prairie to encourage vegetation growth. The ferns were eaten by herds of elk and deer which in turn were killed by the hunters. Life was good for the natives, as is so often the case, until the settlers arrived.

Julie Van Pelt gives an excellent overview of Forks' development in her essay for the *Free Online Encyclopedia of Washington State History* at http://www.historylink.org. In "Forks—Thumbnail History," Van Pelt describes how Scandinavian pioneers came by boat and trail to the area in the latter half of the nineteenth century: "Eli Peterson, Ole Nelson, and Peter Fisher were trappers living on the prairie when Luther and Esther Ford arrived by way of La Push with their family in January 1878 and claimed a 160-acre homestead a mile east of Forks' present-day town center."

Settlement of the town site followed, if not steadily, then by fits and starts. "A post office was established in 1884 in Nelson's cabin,"[1] and Forks was named for its location at the confluence of three rivers, the Calawah, Bogachiel, and Sol Duc.

Farming and dairying provided occupations, if not a thriving livelihood, for the first settlers. Grains, vegetables, and hops grew well in the area, but farmers had a difficult time getting their crops to markets, some 60 to 100 miles away. Dense forests hindered road building, and shipment by water was prohibitively slow and expensive. The Forks Cooperative Creamery, established in the early 1900s, was a success for some 70 years, even though initially butter had to be transported to Clallam Bay for placement on steamships to Seattle.[2]

Throughout this time, the town grew slowly. Buildings, a bank, and a newspaper were established. Electricity arrived in 1923, and the town was incorporated in 1945, amid some debate. Citizens feared the effect incorporation would have on taxes and governance. However, by a vote of 129 to 99, the measure to incorporate passed,[3] and the 1950 census showed the population to be 1,120, a figure that held steady until the 1970s.

Development

As might be expected, logging and forestry were important industries in Forks throughout the early twentieth century. Again, limited access to transportation for the timber slowed progress somewhat. However, completion of the Olympic Loop Highway in 1931[4] and various rail lines afforded the town opportunities to move logs to market. In the 1930s, "Bloedel-Donovan's Beaver Camp employed about 300" loggers,[5] and a number of other logging companies, cedar shingle mills, and related businesses grew thereafter, so that by the 1970s Forks billed itself as the "Logging Capital of the World." At that time, there was "plenty of money and big, burly loggers looking for a place to spend it. The dozen saloons in town were known both for two-fisted drinking and two-fisted fighting."[6] Bill Brager, quoted in Van Pelt's "Thumbnail History," recalls that in the 1970s a bolt cutter (one who cuts sections from logs) "could make $25,000 to $30,000 a year."

As the highway opened up Forks and the west end of the Olympic Peninsula to the rest of the state, tourists also started arriving. Some residents capitalized on the public's interest in exploring the great out of outdoors by becoming hunting, fishing, and trekking guides. Minnie Nelson Peterson, daughter of Nels Nelson, was one of the first guides, male or female, to take visitors to the Olympic Mountain glaciers. She led her first pack trip to the meadows and glaciers in 1927 and her last in 1978 at the age of 80. Since those early days, the town has been closely tied to the environment, and many more amateur "naturalists"—fishermen, hunters, and packers—have offered tours to visitors wanting an insider's view of the forest. By the 1970s, the population doubled to over 3,000 as tourism and logging provided a reasonably good living for the inhabitants of the small Olympic peninsula town.

Environmental Crisis and Recession

What goes up must come down, though, and the popularity of nature was, in some sense, Forks' undoing. A national recession in the 1980s was part of the problem, but the town's real collapse came with the Endangered Species Act of 1990 which mandated protection for the Northern Spotted Owl. The bird nested in old-growth forests, the very trees that Northwest logging companies had clear-cut. Homes and businesses around the peninsula posted signs in windows reading, "This family supported by timber dollars," and "Support your local logger." According to Don C. Brunell, current president of the Association of Washington Business, "Timber harvests in the Pacific Northwest dropped by 80 percent" in the 1980s, while forest-related jobs in Forks fell by almost 25 percent after 1990.[7] "The state estimated that Forks experienced as high as 19 percent unemployment in 1991, and U.S. Census data from 1999 put the Forks poverty rate for families at 14.6 percent, double that of the state."[8] The 1990 census listed the population of Forks as 2,862, down nearly 200 people from a decade before.[9]

A New Economy

Forks, 1990s

For more than a decade, Forks languished as it sought new ways to support its economy. Some people moved away, some took jobs in the two peninsula prisons, while others returned to a diminished logging industry. Tourism continued to attract visitors to the town, as it was the only one on the 150-mile stretch between Aberdeen to the south and Port Angeles to the north. Between the two towns are areas of intense natural beauty, including the Olympic

National Forest and National Park. The park is designated as a wilderness area, so its interior is closed to all motor traffic, with most of it accessible by trail only. Hikers to the interior and upper reaches discover icy glaciers, hot springs, and towering trees. The Hoh Rain Forest, one of the few temperate rainforests remaining in North America and a popular tourist destination in the park, is located only about 30 miles from Forks. Beautiful beaches hug the coastline. Among them are Ruby Beach, with its wide sand and rock shelf, tide pools, and sea stacks; Kalaloch, where a person can hike for several hours north or south; and First Beach at La Push, noted for its sea stacks, drift trees, and, of course, the cliffs from which Jacob, his friends, and Bella leap. (A word of warning from one who has been there: *do not* attempt this stunt. The cliffs are much higher and more dangerous than described in the novels!) From the 1990s, eco-tourists coming to the peninsula have needed gear, food, and provisions, and shops in Forks have been ready and able to supply them.

The first time I saw Forks was at the height — or depth, as it were — of the great Spotted Owl calamity. My family and I had camped our way up the Pacific coast in August 1991, slogging through sand dunes and sleeping under cedar and spruce trees. After about two weeks on the trail, some minor ailments led us to urgent care at the Forks Community Hospital. The doctor was a southern California transplant who claimed that he loved his new town — rain, unemployment, and all — and that he had no thoughts of returning to the rat-race of the south. He bandaged us up and then sent us to the Forks Coffee Shop for sustenance.

The smoky restaurant (this was *way* before smoke-free anything!) was full of tourists in hiking boots and shorts and loggers in blue-and-white striped railroad work shirts and Carhartt jeans held up with red logger's suspenders. These men were eating hearty plates of burgers and omelets heaped with French fries and drinking endless cups of coffee. Although the restaurant seemed to be doing a good business, the rest of the town looked a bit down on its luck. "Supported by Timber Dollars" signs dotted windows all over town, but the shops behind many of the windows were closed, and it seemed as if those dollars were too few and far between.

The grocery store adjacent to the coffee shop was none too prosperous; however, we were able to buy necessities for another week of camping. My husband was elated to be able to purchase his very own "Logger's World" suspenders, although the clerk gave him a sideways glance, as if to say, "Why would anyone want those?" We loaded groceries into coolers, pushed our teenaged girls into the backseat, and headed north on Highway 101 to Port Angeles and back to civilization (i.e., shopping malls).

The next time I saw Forks was six years later, on the Fourth of July. We were camping again and needed to do laundry. As we drove into town, we met a crowd of people celebrating freedom at the Forks Old-Fashioned Fourth of July. The town has had a parade for many years in the best small-town tradition: kids with wagons, folks with old cars, Native Americans in costume, pioneer descendents and honored tourists waving from convertibles. Afterwards, we went to the logging competition, demolition derby, and fireworks display—quite a show, considering that the town still exhibited signs of a weak economy: closed store fronts and few restaurants.

Still, it was a beautiful area, and for us children of the '60s, raised on Thoreau, nature, and a desire for open spaces, my husband and I thought it could offer great opportunities for summer retreats and potential retirement. Thus, in 2003, we sought out a realtor and found some land where we promptly put a small cabin.

The economy in Forks was looking up. By the 2000 census, the population had rebounded, reaching 3,120, its pre–Spotted Owl level. Van Pelt reports that between 1995 and 2005, "two new motels and nine bed-and-breakfasts opened,"[10] and West End Surf, opened in 2007 by Darren Greeno and Leah Hornaday of Kauai, was the "coolest place" around.[11] But the sparkling, luminous, unlikely ray of hope for the economy came in the form of a novel, or a series of them, from Phoenix author Stephenie Meyer: the *Twilight* series.

Twi-hards Unite!

By summer 2007, *Twilight* had become a tourist draw and marketing success, as the townspeople found ways to incorporate it into all of their advertising. Marcia Bingham, Forks Chamber of Commerce Executive Director says, "In the summer and fall of 2007 momentum was picking up; it was like something got shot out of a cannon, it mushroomed. We realized we needed to do something ... for the growing number of *Twilight* fans traveling hundreds, sometimes thousands, of miles to visit locations central to the books."[12]

Among the "somethings" the Chamber of Commerce initially devised to attract tourists were themed dishes at a few local restaurants and maps to locations mentioned in the books (Forks High School, Forks Police Station, the reservation at La Push). Mike Gurling, Visitor Center Manager, had read the books and suggested that the Chamber have a cake for visitors to celebrate Bella's birthday, September 13. As Bingham remarks, "Forks folks are receptive of the wave of fans arriving and *Twilight* is becoming more and more of an attraction in the town."[13] These small gestures were just the beginning, however.

Bella and Edward and Jacob, Oh My!

By summer 2008, Twi-hards were the new wave of immigrants to Forks. An article in the July 23, 2008 *Forks Forum* reported that "*Twilight* fans by the hundreds are flocking to Forks."[14] This figure was no exaggeration. The most important aspect of this invasion was the influx of dollars the tourists were bringing:

> [R]etailers up and down Forks Avenue are benefiting from the attention the book series has brought to the rural town. Bruce Paul of Forks Outfitters said his family's store is seeing a lot of *Twilight* visitors, and that other retailers are reporting similar boosts to their businesses.... [F]orks High School Spartan gear is selling well, as well as *Twilight*-themed T-shirts that store has created. The Thriftway side of Forks Outfitters is prominently mentioned in the book series as the grocery store where main characters shop.[15]

Capitalizing on Twi-hards' insatiable thirst for all things *Twilight*, the Chamber of Commerce began offering *Twilight* tours on June 7, 2008. Gurling drove fans to the City Hall where Police Chief Charlie Swan works, to Forks High School where Bella, Edward, and the rest of the gang go to school, and to First Beach near La Push, where Jacob and the werewolf clan live and shape-shift. Since then, the demand for tours has become so great that another business, Dazzled by Twilight, now gives tourists the full Bella/Edward/Jacob experience.

Twilight-themed dishes appeared on menus at every restaurant in town. Fans could get Bella Burgers at Sully's Drive-In, Bella Berry Smoothies at Café Paix, Jacob's Blackberry Cobbler at the Forks Coffee Shop, and Bellasagne at Pacific Pizza, among others. Not to be outdone, Three Rivers Resort on the "treaty line" between vampires and werewolves offered the following menu: Swan Sandwich, Werewolf Burger, Cullen's Clam Chowder, Jacob Black's Shake, Bella Banana Split, and Edward Sundae.[16]

In addition, collectibles, books, posters, and shirts of all types filled the shops. Chinooks Pharmacy, the town's only drug store and variety store sold—or should I say "sold *out*"?—custom-made tee-shirts with phrases such as "My last *Twilight* I was bitten in Forks" emblazoned across the chest. Leppell's Flowers and Gifts (aka "Twilight Central") sold postcards, photos, baby onesies, and scrapbooking supplies. JT's Sweet Stuffs enticed visitors and locals alike with ice creams named Edward's Hugs and Smooches and Jacob's Beach Comber as well as wax vampire fangs. Even Jerry's Lock and Key got into the act with Forks High School "ID" key rings and a display of Forks High School varsity jackets (that are also for sale).

To accommodate Twi-hards who want to prove that they've been to the mystical town, the "Welcome to Forks" signs on both ends of the town have been more conveniently located. According to Bill Sperry, a member of the Revitalization Committee, the south side sign was moved on December 9, 2009 because it "was formerly located in a marshy area which lacked safe parking for fans to pull over. The new location ... is adjacent to the Forks Timber Museum and near the Forks Chamber of Commerce's Visitor Center."[17] The north side sign presented an even more dangerous predicament for devotees wanting to document their visit. Until summer 2009, it was located just yards off Highway 101 on a hill with a slippery slope and no steps or ramp for access. It was not unusual to see eight to ten cars, most with out-of-state license plates, stopped at the side of the road. Twi-hards slipped and clawed their way to the top, where they then smiled broadly, pointing at the sign for the camera. Sometimes, cars even parked on the other side of the road while fans scampered across armed with cameras, often not noticing the logging trucks barreling down the road. In late summer, crews finally moved the sign to a safer spot with better parking.

Locals have tried to welcome visitors in many ways. In 2007, the Chamber of Commerce selected homes for the Swans and the Cullens. The Swans "live" in a modest home on K Street, identified only by a "Home of the Swans" sign in the yard. The Cullens, on the other hand, spend their time at the Miller Tree Inn, a bed and breakfast that originally was home to pioneer packer Minnie Peterson. While the Swan home remains a private residence, the B&B, like other lodging establishments in the area, is happy to benefit from its association with the novels. Innkeepers Bill and Susan Brager commented in an email message to me on December 30, 2009 that "the advent of *Twilight* on the Forks scene has been a great boost. We have seen our occupancy go up for the years 2008 and 2009." Other motels and B&B's have embraced the wave of tourists as well. Many advertise at least one *Twilight*-themed room, such as the Bella Suite at the Dew Drop Inn, the Twilight/Eclipse Cabin, and the New Moon/Breaking Dawn Cottage.

Forks residents have a sense of humor, and they extend it to their newfound celebrity. The Olympic Suites Inn plays on the idea that the *Twilight* vampires do not sleep with a sign reading, "Edward Cullen Didn't Sleep Here!" The Miller Tree Inn keeps Twi-hards current on Edward's activities by posting a daily note. Dr. Cullen has a "Reserved Parking" spot at the Forks Community Hospital, and at the Three Rivers Resort, the "treaty line," a sign reading "No Vampires Beyond This Point" points south, and "No Werewolves Beyond This Point" points north.

While most Twi-hards come and go, a few come to stay a while. One is Styna Whatman, a young woman from Belleville, Ohio. In April 2009, Whatman cut her hair, sprinkled it with glitter, and made the trek cross country to present herself in Forks as Alice Cullen, Edward's "sister." She does, in fact, look very much like Ashley Greene, the actress who portrays Alice in the films. According to her *I'm Not Obsessed* website, upon arriving in Forks, Whatman found a job at Leppell's Flowers and Gifts where she "dresse[s] up as Alice Cullen, down to the fine details like sparkly makeup, just the right hair cut and golden brown eyes thanks to a pair of contact lenses" and poses as Alice for pictures with fans.[18]

Perhaps the most noticeable and controversial émigré benefiting from the *Twilight* phenomenon is Annette Root, who, with her husband Tim, came to Forks in November 2008 to open Dazzled by Twilight, a shop devoted entirely to Meyer's books and the fans they have engendered. Root sells licensed books, posters, tee-shirts, jewelry, mugs, life-sized cutouts, magnets, stickers, candy, tea, coffee — the list goes on — at her stores in Forks and Port Angeles (the town some 60 miles north where Bella and Edward have their first date). Root opened a third business, known familiarly as the "Twilight Experience," in late summer 2009. Described as a "Disneyland-like experience for Twilight fans,"[19] the "experience" is an interactive multi-media encounter, complete with fake grass, trees, and other aspects of nature intended to simulate the experience of being in one of Meyer's novels.

In addition, Dazzled by Twilight now offers three tours daily, loading breathless teenaged girls, their friends, sisters, and mothers into black-and-gray fifteen-passenger shuttles and taking them on a three-hour tour of the "World of Twilight" where they can snap photos of homes where characters never lived, creep through forests where vampires and werewolves never roamed, and eat snacks that vampires never ate.[20] Root's business, while obviously successful and a huge draw for the town, is nonetheless controversial. Root and her family are transplants from Vancouver, Washington, and some locals question the allegiance of such newcomers to the town. One businesswoman remarked that new businesses are certainly good for the town's economy, but it remains to be seen whether they are in it for the long haul or just taking advantage of the moment. Another businessman observed that some newcomers see Forks only as a business opportunity, with actual land ownership separating those passing through from real residents.

Several stores, including Forks Outfitters and Chinook Pharmacy, staged book release parties at midnight on August 2, 2008, just like Barnes & Noble, Borders, and other major booksellers across the country. The pharmacy set up a buffet of "La Push scones" and "Twilight punch" for fans as they stalked the aisles, snatching up anything with the word *Forks* or *Twilight* on it, waiting for 12:01 A.M. when they could purchase *Breaking Dawn*, the last installment in the series. Anyone who waited in line got a copy with "Chinook Pharmacy and Variety ... Home of the *Twilight* Series" stamped in the cover. (I know this because I dragged my husband down there to buy one.)

Stan Peterson, pharmacist, former owner of Chinook Pharmacy and Variety, and my neighbor, takes a keen interest in visiting Twi-hards. He is both amused and puzzled by their devotion, observing that he cannot fathom a father's driving across the country to visit a town where fictional characters "lived." Since 2008, Stan has placed composition books in the variety store where fans can record their comments. (They're up to the fifteenth notebook!) He was surprised to see that they included poems, illustrations, and oaths of undying love to the *Twilight* characters, especially Edward. Visitors have come from all states in the country and many nations, including England, Germany, Japan, and Australia. Among the most interesting notes, he says, was one from a Scottish grandmother who told Stan that this was her last trip to the United States. She had offered to take her granddaughters anywhere they wanted and where did they pick? Forks, Washington.

Even academia has discovered Forks. In June 2008, a company called Literature-Inspired Fandom Events, Inc. hosted a symposium in Forks on "any topic relating to the Twilight Series novels and/or the fan community."[21] The program included lectures, roundtables, workshops, and fan fiction, and culminated in a *Twilight* prom, the proceeds of which went to Forks High School. The event was wildly popular, as Twi-hards and academics alike converged on Forks to discuss the series and such topics as religion in the novels. Larry Carroll, senior writer for MTV News, was the invited "graduation speaker" and wrote that visiting Forks for this occasion was "a truly once-in-a-lifetime experience."[22]

Newspapers from Forks to Seattle to New York to London and beyond publish stories on *Twilight*, if not on Forks, almost daily, feeding the need-to-know frenzy of die-hard Twi-hards, while reporters, bloggers, and media outlets from around the globe conduct interviews in Forks. The *Today Show* on NBC sent Lee Cowan to interview Marcia Bingham and the Chamber of Commerce, while ABC's *Nightline* visited in November 2009. York Baur, producer of *Twilight in Forks: The Series of the Real Town*, claims a connection to the area—"I actually grew up partially in the Forks area. My family's had a summer cabin since I was 3 years old out there"—and wanted to "expose this really cool and unique area to the world."[23] Zig Gauthier, Los Angeles producer and founder of Red Varden Studios, came to Forks on December 22, 2009, to interview "outgoing personalities who can represent the real Forks" for a reality show based there. His take on the show? "If we can get this on the air, it is a whole [new] level of exposure for Forks."[24]

In addition, a Showtime cable TV channel crew was in Forks the weekend of December 11, 2009. "The scenes of Forks will be used as short segments accompanying the first television broadcast of the film *Twilight* ... set to air beginning in mid–January [2010]." The crew interviewed Marcia Bingham of the Chamber of Commerce and students at the high school who told "what it is like to be a 'real' Spartan student."[25]

The Next Chapter

So now that Forks is a town *célèbre*, what do residents think about their newfound notoriety? Some express concern about the usual issues that plague tourist attractions: not enough parking or restroom facilities, more traffic than the one-light town is accustomed to. Sometimes, when Twi-hards are driving through, searching for the sites or stores, they don't pay attention to where they are driving, and more than one local has had to avoid cars or people stopping at the northern Forks sign. But as Bingham observes, "It's a pretty minor price to pay."[26]

Most residents think *Twilight* is just great. Forks typically has a fairly brisk tourist trade during the summer, when the weather is conducive to hiking, fishing, surfing, camping, and other outdoors activities. However, winter business is generally on the slow side, with only the hardiest hunters coming to town. The past couple of years, however, have been growth times for Forks. In 2008, although summer gas prices topped $4.00 a gallon across the Northwest, and many families took "stay-cations," visitors continued to come to Forks. The lodging tax revenue in Forks from January through September was "$85,159, a 48 percent increase" over the same period in 2007.[27] Miller Tree innkeepers Bill and Susan Brager tell me that "since the *Twilight* phenomena our summer is longer and our off season is busier.... We are very thankful to Stephenie Meyer."[28] Other businesses have encountered similar successes.

Charlene Cross, owner of Leppell's Flowers, reports that "business is three times what it normally would be,"[29] while Janet Hughes, owner of JT's Sweet Stuffs, told me over the phone that *Twilight* has been a "fabulous thing for Forks." Mark Rahner from the *Seattle Times* reports that "more than 5,000 people from around the world have taken the $39 Twilight bus tour of the area."[30]

Stan Peterson has lived through the ups and downs of Forks' economic situations, and he is happy to see that good times are here again. The great-grandson of Nels Nelson and grandson of Minnie Peterson, Stan tells me that on a typical pre–*Twilight* summer day, the variety store took in $500–800; in summer 2009, that figure was $5,000–6,000 a day. The store sold 80 to 100 shirts a day: tee-shirts, sweatshirts, anything that bore the words *Forks, Twilight, Bella, Edward,* or *Jacob.* Pura Carlson, co-owner of the store with her husband Chuck, could barely keep items in stock.

The Visitor Center keeps count of the number of visitors who sign in (of course, not everyone does so), and Mike Gurling provided me with some significant statistics. The annual number of visitors to the town has more than quadrupled. A more telling statistic is the monthly number of tourists who have signed the book. Forks has a fairly strong tourist trade during summer months, but even those numbers are rather surprising. In July 2009, a record 16,186 sightseers signed the book; the previous July record was 3,546, with August 2008 having the previous monthly high of 4,186. A look at winter figures substantiates innkeepers' observations. In January 2008, there were 2,003 visitors; the previous record was 225 ten years earlier, with lows of 80 and 78 in 2004 and 2005, respectively. Decembers fared even better: only 74 visitors registered in 2005, while 2540 registered in 2009.[31]

Year-end figures also show Forks' economy looking very good, as the following two charts on taxes received by the City of Forks reveal:

Hotel-Motel Taxes	***Sales Taxes***
2003 — $84,000	1995 — $295,000
2006 — $88,471	2000 — $321,067
2008 — $105,879	2006 — $353,837
2009 — $133,585	2009 — $405,195[32]

The town had a tremendously profitable 2009 and anticipates profits continuing into 2010. Perhaps most noteworthy is this information from Don C. Brunell: Forks was "one of the few communities in the entire state to report a steady increase in tax revenues. Last year [2008] sales tax collections increased 7.46 percent."[33]

It seems as if the obsession with *Twilight*, and thus with Forks, is not over yet. In early 2010, two movies remain to be made; maybe one of the production companies will film in the *real* Forks. Even if they do not, the town is on the map with Twi-hards. A look at only two blogs shows a love affair between the aficionados and the town. Several visitors commented on www.MTV.com about the friendliness of the residents and the astounding natural beauty of the Olympic peninsula. A common refrain was voiced by a blogger on *ForksGift-Shop.com*:

> While Stephenie's *Twilight* was what initially brought me to the town it is the town and the area that keep me coming back. It is some of the most beautiful landscapes [sic] you'll ever see in your life. Words and pictures can not do it justice. First Beach, Second Beach, Third Beach, the Hoh, Hurricane Ridge, etc. are all breathtaking.

Forks inhabitants by and large return the compliments. On the same site, embarrassedbyignorance writes:

> I am from Forks and would like to have it known that there are many people in our small town who are so happy for the *Twilight* phenomenon. It has helped to shelter our businesses from the economic downturn happening in so many other small towns. It has also been a great feeling to drive down our main street and see so many tourists with smiles on their faces who are so happy to be in our town.

And while some naysayers express skepticism that anyone would travel to the site of an imaginary tale, "Cassandra" perhaps expressed it best when she blogged on *I'mNotObsessed.com*:

> The description of the little town in the story made me want to see it for myself. And it was unbelievable. And I'll go back — not because of the book or the movie, but because of the true "small town" feel of Forks, and all the great people I met when I was there. The town didn't ask for this to happen to them, but in this unbalanced economy, they should take advantage of it. I came from Missouri, cabined next to two sisters from Canada, and we met a family all the way from GERMANY because of a BOOK.

Conclusion

One day, the *Twilight* phenomenon will come to an end. Twi-hards will find a new heartthrob to fall in love with, a new book to read, a new city to explore. The girls who held their breath until their parents drove them across the country to stand in the rain in Forks will be driving their own daughters to another destination, unknown to us now. When that happens, Forks will still be there, as it has been for many years: a small town where people know each other and are friendly to newcomers; a hometown where everyone lines the highway to honor a young Marine killed in battle; a place with a pioneer spirit and rugged surroundings to match; a center of natural splendor and breathtaking scenery. Forks will welcome the visitors who initially came to see vampires, but who returned because something touched them while they were there.

Local businessman Carroll Lunsford probably sums up the changes in Forks in this philosophical way:

> Every action has the possibility to bring change to any community.... Over the years we have seen opportunities come and go.... As we adapt and welcome new gifts such as *Twilight* we are reminded to look at all changes as new opportunities and make the best of them no matter how long the impact.[34]

By the way, at last count: "City of Forks, Population 3175, 8.5 vampires."

Notes

1. Julie Van Pelt, "Forks— Thumbnail History," *Free Online Encyclopedia of Washington State History*, December 10, 2007, www.historylink.org.
2. Van Pelt, "Forks."
3. Julie Van Pelt, "Town of Forks Incorporates on August 7, 1945," 2007, *Free Online Encyclopedia of Washington State History*, December 4, www.historylink.org.
4. Lonnie Archibald, *There Was a Day: Stories of the Pioneers* (Forks, WA: Olympic Graphic Arts, 1999), 14.
5. Archibald, 51.
6. Ron Dalby, "Community Profile — Forks: Logging Town at a Crossroads," *Washington Business*, July/August 2005, http://www.awb.org/articles/magazine.
7. Don C. Brunell, "When Opportunity Knocked, Forks Answered," Association of Washington Business, May 15, 2009, www.awb.org/articles/presidentscolumn2009.
8. Van Pelt, "Forks."
9. W. J. McGinnis et al., "Clallam County, Washington, Population," *County Portraits of Washington State*, 1997, www.pcouncil.org/communities/comdoc/apdxa3.pdf.
10. Van Pelt, "Forks."
11. Jonathan Raban, "Surf's Up, Hopes Are Too," *New York Times*, November 25, 2007, www.nytimes.com.
12. Chris Cook, *Forks Forum: Twilight Territory* (Sequim, WA: Olympic View Publishing, 2009), 13.
13. Cook, *Twilight Territory*, 16.
14. Chris Cook, "*Twilight* Mania Building in Forks, Across the World," *Forks Forum*, July 23, 2008, 1.
15. Cook, "*Twilight* Mania," 1–2.
16. "Three Rivers Resort," Forks Chamber of Commerce, www.forkswa.com/details/three-rivers-resort.html.
17. Chris Cook, "Forks South Side Welcome Sign Moved," *Forks Forum*, December 30, 2009, www.forksforum.com.
18. "Vampire Look Alike Settles Down in Forks, Loves the Attention," *I'm Not Obsessed*, June 16, 2009, www.imnotobsessed.com.
19. "Locations," *Dazzled by Twilight*, http://dazzledbytwilight.com/locations.
20. "Tours," *Dazzled by Twilight*, http://dazzledbytwilight.rezgo.com/tour.

21. "*Twilight* Saga Symposium," Humanities and Social Sciences Net Online, www.h-net.org/announce.

22. Larry Carroll, "*Twilight* World Comes to Life in Forks, Washington," MTV, June 29, 2009, http://www.mtv.com/movies/news/articles.

23. Larry Carroll, "*Twilight* Documentary Sheds Light on the Real Forks," MTV, August 25 2009, http://www.mtv.com/movies/news/articles.

24. Paige Dickerson, "Made Famous by *Twilight*, Forks Could Get Reality Show; Casting Call Slated Next Week," *Peninsula Daily News*, December 19, 2009, www.peninsuladailynews.com.

25. Chris Cook, "Showtime in Forks," *Forks Forum*, December 30, 2009, www.forksforum.com. 26. Mark Rahner, "*Twilight* Phenomenon Both Blessing, Curse for Forks," *Seattle Times*, October 27, 2009, http://seattletimes.nwsource.com.

27. Tom Callis, "A Novel Idea—*Twilight*— Helps Boost Peninsula Tourism Revenue," *Peninsula Daily News*, October 12, 2008, www.peninsuladailynews.com.

28. Bill and Susan Brager, email message to author, December 30, 2009.

29. Carroll, "*Twilight* World."

30. Rahner, "*Twilight* Phenomenon."

31. Mike Gurling, email message to author, February 6, 2010.

32. Gurling, email.

33. Brunell, "Opportunity."

34. Carroll Lunsford, email message to author, January 5, 2010.

The Pleasures of Adapting: Reading, Viewing, Logging On

PAMELA H. DEMORY

Prologue

Stephenie Meyer's *Twilight* opens with a one-page Preface, the narrator telling us "I'd never given much thought to how I would die...." She describes being in "a long room," facing death in the form of a "hunter," who, we're told, "smiled in a friendly way as he sauntered forward to kill me."[1] The film begins with the same line, spoken in voiceover against a black screen, so that for just a moment we might think we're simply seeing a representation of the scene from the novel. But then the black screen gives way to a shot of a deep green mossy forest floor. We move up over a slight rise and then look down to see a fawn, facing away from us, drinking water out of a shallow forest pool. "But dying in the place of someone I love," continues the voiceover, "seems like a good way to go."[2] A series of cuts brings us closer to the fawn, to its face, but still we seem to be observing through the forest greenery—it's more of a psychological than physical move forward. It hears something, and now we do, too—a low roaring that builds—as we watch the fawn begin to run—to an urgent orchestral accompaniment. We also hear brush rustling—the fawn is being chased through the forest by a predator who we see, barely, at the end of the sequence—jumping, blurred, catching the fawn in mid-air—so fast we can't make out who he is. Disconcertingly, we find ourselves observing this entire sequence from the point of view of the predator, as if we ourselves are chasing the fawn. The shot ends in freeze-frame, immediately fading to a blinding white light that turns out to be a shot of the Phoenix sky and our introduction to Bella.

This opening illustrates, in a number of interesting ways, how the *Twilight* adaptation works. For one thing, the scene is both completely different from the original and eerily parallel, complicating our notion of what "fidelity" to a source text might mean. The voiced lines are almost word for word from the book, but the images are completely different. Instead of a room, we have a forest; instead of Bella and her killer, we have a fawn and unseen predator; instead of a conversation and a slow saunter, we have a chase through the forest. When, in the next sequence, we see Bella and realize that she is the speaker, we can't help but associate the fawn with her and to understand that she is in danger of being menaced by a predator, and that the entire scene functions as metaphor, countering arguments by some critics that cinema is inherently too literal a medium to convey figurative meanings. What complicates the sequence even more is the point of view. While in the next sequence we are encouraged to identify with Bella as the protagonist of the narrative, and to understand that we will be journeying through the story in her company, the opening places us squarely in the point of view of the predator. At this point we can't tell what this might mean — are we to sympathize with the predator point of view? or at least to realize that the relationship between predator and prey might be more complex than we might ordinarily expect? Or are we instead being offered an even more complex viewpoint — are we tracking the predator as well as the prey?

Further, this quick analysis shows how *much* information film can convey in a very short sequence — much more, arguably, than the book can in its Preface. Film must show as well as tell, and it has multiple registers from which to draw — graphic, aural, and kinetic — as well as verbal. As we watch the opening, we take in literal story information from the voiceover narration and from the actions of the figures in the scene. Simultaneously, we take in abstract ideas — about innocence, nature, fertility, the cycle of life — from the verdant forest mise-en-scène, and our emotions — the fear of being hunted; the excitement of the chase — are engaged by shot composition, camera movement, and sound.

And finally, the opening shows us how important *readers* are to the adaptation, for many viewers of the film will be intimately familiar with the novel, and for them, the registers are even more complex. They will know how the book opens, so as they're watching the film, they will already know the story: they'll know that the book's opening refers to the scene at the end of the novel when James (not Edward) moves to kill Bella, and that the "someone" is a reference to her mother. They'll also recognize the scenario as representing how Edward hunts. So for the reader, this opening suggests intriguing parallels — not only between the fawn and Bella — but also between Bella and her mother, and between the good vampire (Edward) and the bad vampire (James). The reader's pleasure in the text is thus enhanced by viewing the film. As one fan writes, "I loved how it was so similar to the book. But what i loved the most was how different it was. I thought i would be upset that it wasn't Twilight the Book: The Movie. They had alot of the same diolouge but went about it in a completely new, different, cool way. It's the differences that make the movie that much better.[3]

Although Stephenie Meyer has said that both book and film are about "innocence" and "self-denial,"[4] I argue that both book and film attract adoring fans largely because they offer pleasure to their female fans. The book and the film each offer a particular kind of pleasure — one slow, private, and intensely personal; the other fast, communal, and graphic. But this is not an essay about which kind of pleasure might be better or more effective or more significant — because the real point is that adaptation means you don't have to choose just one form of pleasure — you can have them all. Critics of the book and film may argue that such pleasures are superficial, reactionary, even dangerous, but I argue that it's also possible to see *Twilight* positively.[5]

The Pleasures of the Book

> Reading for pleasure is an extraordinary activity. The black squiggles on the white page are still as the grave, colorless as the moonlit desert but they give the skilled reader a pleasure as acute as the touch of a loved body, as rousing, colorful and transfiguring as anything out there in the real world. And yet, the more stirring the book the quieter the reader; pleasure reading breeds a concentration so effortless that the absorbed reader of fiction (transported by the book to some other place, and shielded by it from distractions), who is so often reviled as an escapist and denounced as the victim of a vice as pernicious as tippling in the morning should instead be the envy of every student and every teacher.[6]

This description of the pleasures of reading from Victor Nell's analysis of the psychology of reading, *Lost in a Book*, seems particularly appropriate for the reader of *Twilight*, tying together as it does images of death and barrenness ("still as the grave," "colorless as the moonlit desert") with those of eroticism and fertility ("the touch of a loved body," "rousing," "breeds a concentration"). The reader is able to experience vicariously the thrill of becoming close to a dangerous predator — but the primary pleasure of *Twilight* is the romance.

As Stephenie Meyer explains in an interview on the DVD, "the story of *Twilight* is really the story of falling in love for the first time."[7] And it repeats the familiar generic narrative pattern: he and she meet, but obstacles stand in their way. The narrative develops through the tension of desire and delay — with the certain knowledge that eventually the two erstwhile lovers will overcome the obstacles and be united. What's compelling about the genre is that though it relies on the certainty of the happy ending, the delay of that ending is where the greatest pleasure lies. As soon as the ending arrives, desire is fulfilled, the tension is over — the story is over. The general pattern, of course, is common to both the books and the movies, but the particular pleasure of *reading* the story is the length of time it takes. The movie is over in a couple of hours, but it takes many hours to get through the 500 or so pages of each of the four *Twilight* novels, allowing the reader to immerse herself in that world. Comments by fans illustrate the power of that delay: "I Adore the books ... adore ... is that the right word? Addicted is more like it.... When I finished Breaking dawn it was Sunday 12am. I was up till 2am THINKING about the book and sighing my head off."[8] Another fan writes: "The thing in the book that makes their love story real is how it develops over time."[9]

Stephenie Meyer's novels draw out the story partly through a long-winded prose style that some critics have faulted her for. But arguably, critics of Meyer's prose style are working within long-entrenched, gendered, assumptions about how a "good" narrative ought to be written. Susan Winnett argues that although theories of narrative have concerned themselves "with the relation between narrative and pleasure," theorists "have largely neglected to raise the issue of the difference between women's and men's reading pleasure."[10] Narrative theory, she argues, has been dominated by a male metaphor of sexual tension and release; but a woman "can begin and end her pleasure according to a logic of fantasy and arousal that is totally unrelated to the functioning and representation of the 'conventional' heterosexual act. Moreover, she can do so again. Immediately. And, we are told, again after that."[11] She goes on to point out that if we were to examine narrative structure using a female sexual metaphor, our expectations for what that structure would look like would be quite different. As an example of such a narrative, she points to Mary Shelley's *Frankenstein*, which raises a number of major questions and then doesn't resolve them. "This lack of resolution," she goes on, "is often attributed to the young author's lack of skill, her inability, for all her imagination, to write a coherent plot,"[12] but perhaps it can instead be explained by a different narrative logic, one that finds pleasure in those very "detours and repetitions" themselves.[13] Perhaps such a narrative logic might also describe Meyer's novels: drawn-out, somewhat rambling, repetitive, but appealing to a desire for multiplicity and delay rather than for climax and resolution.

The novels draw out the story partly through extended conversations—conversations reminiscent of the almost endless phone conversations (or internet chats) that teenage girls have with their friends and boyfriends. Every word and gesture of every encounter must be examined, analyzed, and challenged, from a variety of perspectives. In the *Twilight* books, the extended time that readers spend with the characters and the narrative allows them to imagine themselves in that world, to imagine not only the romantic encounter itself but also talking about it. For part of the pleasure offered to the young female reader is the opportunity to identify with Bella and to negotiate the real demands of adolescence and young adulthood through her experiences, fictional and fantastic though they may be. As one reader writes: "I can relate to Bella, it almost seems to me like Stephenie has told us a little about herself as well ... she told it so well.... I had a best friend I fell in love with, but I also loved another man. Just like Bella, I had to make a choice. But in real life, my best friend didn't get to imprint on another woman, no, he's still in love with me and we don't talk at all. No happy ending there."[14] The books offer the reader a way to re-write the endings of unhappy experiences and thus are therapeutic as well as entertaining.

The Pleasures of the Film

The film offers its own particular pleasures, distinct from the reading experience. One of those pleasures is experiencing the story in a community of like-minded people. As Peter Brooker points out, reading novels and viewing films are "differently situated experiences."[15] Reading is a solitary experience; film-going is (or can be) a group experience. For the target audience — teenage girls— the way that the film fosters a community experience may be part of the attraction; even though many of the discussions on the fan sites center on anxieties about whether or not the film will live up to their expectations, there is almost uniform excitement at the prospect. One fan writes, "I was trembling before the movie began and hyperventilating (it was the first time I went to watch any movie with such anticipation. I thought I would pass out!)"[16]

Another pleasure of the film is in the way it complicates point of view. The book's narrative is controlled entirely by Bella's first-person narration. We have no entry into the story without her, and part of the pleasure of the narrative is that intimate one-on-one storytelling situation. In film, first-person narration is usually simulated through a combination of shots *from* the protagonist's point of view (literally, a first-person point of view) with shots *of* the protagonist. Having the protagonist narrate the story in voice-over can enhance our sense of the narrative as being parallel to literary first-person. And it would be possible to restrict the film's narrative just to what the protagonist knows.

Twilight does employ voiceover narration to unify the narrative and preserve that illusion of first-person narrative, and to remind the reader of the book, and it does preserve Bella's image and her point of view throughout most of the story, but the first-person perspective is violated in several places. Partly these shifts are simply a necessary trade-off to create a more streamlined narrative for a two-hour version of the story. The objective point of view used for the two murder scenes, for example, and for the sequences towards the end of the film showing Edward and his family tracking the nomads while Bella is in Phoenix, both work to efficiently move the plot forward. Partly, the shifts allow us to share the point of view of Edward or of one or another of the nomad vampires. As in the Prologue, we occasionally find ourselves occupying, briefly, the position of predator. This enhances our fear for and protectiveness of Bella, but it also, in a way, makes us complicit in the devouring gaze of those who menace her. Overall, these shifts are interesting psychologically, because of the way they wrest control of the narrative away from Bella. The film knows more than Bella knows—and that means that *we* know more than Bella knows. So while we are likely to share Bella's experience in the film narrative, in much the same way we do in the novel, we are *also* provided a more general, more distanced perspective that allows us to be both outside and inside the narrative at the same time.

The one element of the film that would at first seem *not* to be particularly pleasurable for fans of the books is its pacing: One fan complains, for example, that "The love story felt extremely rushed.... It almost felt like the love happened over night."[17] Rosenberg's script does cut a few scenes entirely, notably the scene early in the novel where Bella faints in biology class when the students are asked to draw blood for a blood-typing exercise, and it cuts or makes more concise many of the extended conversations and much of the backstory of the Cullen family history, particularly that of Dr. Cullen. The entire middle part of the book is shortened by rearranging the narrative so that it moves in a more linear way. But surprisingly little narrative action is cut, and the relative speed of the film narrative is balanced by moments of stillness. The first kiss, for example, occurs a full hour and 15 minutes into the film, and a half-hour *after* Bella and Edward have their conversation in the woods where he acknowledges what he is (a delay that in itself illustrates restraint). Bella and Edward are in her bedroom, talking, and he says: "I just want to try one thing."[18] With the close-up framing, dim lighting, absence of music, and lips centered in the frame, time seems suspended. He moves toward her, agonizingly slowly, and finally their lips touch. A full 30 seconds—an eternity in screen time!—elapses from the moment he speaks, to the moment they actually kiss. So while the developing relationship may proceed more efficiently in the film, it still captures the requisite sense of delay.

Further, the streamlined plot of the narrative has its own pleasures, in the way it conforms to the familiar patterns of classical Hollywood narrative. By introducing three sequences—the murder at the warehouse, the second murder of Charlie's friend on the boat, and the encounter at the Police Station where Bella and Edward learn of the investigation into the murders—Rosenberg creates a linear cause-effect organizational structure, with public (crime) and private (romance) plots that develop simultaneously and come together in the climax. The first sequence is introduced by a scene in the school parking lot, with Bella telling us in voiceover that she plans to confront Edward and demand to know what his problem with her is. We see other people arrive, the other Cullens and the group of kids she knows, and we see Bella standing by the truck, waiting. A brief montage follows, of scenes in biology class, the cafeteria, and back to the parking lot, while Bella's voiceover tells us that "things were getting a little ... strange."[19] And then there's a sudden cut to the murder sequence. Later, Edward shows up, "better," having taken some personal days. The juxtaposition of Edward's puzzling absence from school with the sequence of the man being attacked sets up the possibility that Edward is somehow involved in that murder, adding an element of tension to the narrative that the novel lacks.

Film adaptations are often discussed in terms of what they *lack* in relation to a novel: that they can't convey dreams, interior lives, moods, abstractions, etc., or that they have to cut too much detail, description, and plot, in order to fit within the standard two-hour feature film length. But film also adds. Visual images can convey multiple meanings very concisely.

Consider, for example, the scene where Bella accidentally knocks an apple off the counter, it drops, and Edward neatly kicks it up with his foot so that it lands perfectly in his hands.[20] The book narrative makes occasional references to apples, but the phrase "I picked up an apple, turning it around in my hands" has little, if any, symbolic resonance. The cinematic image, in contrast, resonates on several levels: it is, after all, just an apple, one of a number of pieces of fruit on offer at the cafeteria; it is also an index of (a) Bella's clumsiness and (b) Edward's more-than-human reflexes; but it also of course has symbolic overtones: it calls to mind the biblical apple of the Garden of Eden, the fruit of the tree of good and evil — the embodiment of forbidden knowledge. So when Edward seems to offer it to Bella, we may think of Satan, in the guise of a snake, offering the apple to Eve. This may, in turn, complicate our feelings about Edward and about Bella's quest to understand Edward and his family. The shot also mimics the image on the original book cover of the red apple being proffered. And so for book lovers, the image is yet another reminder of the text.

Or consider the scene when Edward comes to pick Bella up for the baseball game.[21] Charlie is cleaning his shotgun, and then he cocks it, menacingly, just as Edward comes in. No words need to be exchanged for us to understand that Charlie will protect his little girl, with violence if necessary, from any unwanted male attention; and we probably also will think of the "shotgun wedding" trope.

And then there's the cross— the image that symbolizes, for Christians, Jesus' death and the power of faith, and in traditional vampire lore the holy symbol that has the power to repel vampires. In the book, Bella notices the large old wooden cross on the wall, and is shocked. She and Edward stop and discuss it. In the film, the cross is on the wall, but goes unremarked by the characters.[22] But we undoubtedly see it and will understand its meanings. Not only does it lack any power to repel vampires, it's placed at an angle on the wall, just a decorative object, completely ineffectual, with no spiritual power whatsoever.

Because film operates on multiple registers, it has the capacity to be richer in meaning, moment to moment, than a page of text. Robert Stam points out that "although filmic characters in adaptations lose some of the slowly evolving textured verbal complexity developed in a novel, they also gain an automatic 'thickness' on the screen through bodily presence, posture, dress, and facial expression."[23] The scene where we are first introduced to the Cullens illustrates the power of film to convey the "same" textual information more concisely and to provide that pleasurable "thickness." In the book, we first "see" the Cullens when Bella relates her first sight of them on page 18. Most of the next two pages are devoted to describing them — a paragraph on the group as a whole, a paragraph on the boys, a paragraph on the girls, a paragraph on their inhuman beauty, and a paragraph describing Alice as she walks away. There is a delay between the announcement that Bella sees them, and the actual description of the people. We know as we're reading that Bella and Edward are in the room together, but we have to wait a little to "see" exactly what he looks like. "Who are *they*?"[24] asks Bella, and the ensuing conversation about the Cullens takes up most of the next three pages, interspersed with descriptions of the glances back and forth between Bella and Edward.

In the film, as in the book, we first see the Cullens in the lunchroom. But instead of having all the characters *in* the room together at the outset of the scene, the script has them enter the room after Bella and her friends are already seated. This mimics the delay in the book between Bella's general reference to the Cullens and her description of them. So we get to see them make an entrance — and we get to see them *move* as well as *be*. Shot composition and editing emphasize their *difference:* they're shot in slow motion; the camera tracks right; they walk left. Horizontal blinds cut across and partially obscure their figures. And they enter in three groups: in one shot, Emmet and Rosalie; in a second shot, Jasper and Alice; and then — after cutting back to the girls who are talking about them, and back to the door — we finally see Edward, who opens the door and thus appears clearly in the doorway: we, like Bella, get the full force of his ethereal beauty.

This scene illustrates what is perhaps the most obvious difference between the movie and book version of the narrative: the embodiment of the characters. Fans respond viscerally to the physicality of the actors. When I asked my 13-year-old niece, a fan of the books, what she liked most about the movie, she immediately said (as if it were obvious): "Edward's face!" One on-line fan writes: "The actors did a phenomenal job. Rob is an excellent Edward. The initial haters should really feel ashamed of themselves. He was just.... Delicious."[25] Even critics who are not overly fond of the movie appreciate Pattinson's embodiment of Edward: "The film may not be high art, but it knows how to entertain. Just look at Robert Pattinson's facial expressions."[26]

These examples of fans' reactions to "Edward's face" illustrate how the traditional theory of spectatorship is challenged in the *Twilight* films. Based in Laura Mulvey's 1975 essay, "Visual Pleasure and Narrative Cinema,"[27] the theory argues that Hollywood film is produced for male consumption, to satisfy male desires. Essentially, it argues that desire in film operates in two ways: objectification and narcissistic identification. The male spectator is encouraged to identify with the male protagonist who is depicted whole and in command, and to objectify the female body, depicted as a collection of appealing parts and at the mercy of the male viewer. Further, the theory goes that the female spectator, in order to enjoy the film, is forced to adopt the male position and thus to become complicit in her own subjugation. The monolithic nature of this theory is now largely contested. Theorists are more inclined to notice a range of possible spectator positions, and to acknowledge the possibility of an active audience that could mediate or invalidate the film's subject positioning. In the *Twilight* films certainly it's the girls who seem to own the gaze. It's Bella whose position controls most of the narrative and the point of view and whom the spectator is encouraged to identify with, and it's Edward (in *Twilight*) and Jacob (in *New Moon,* particularly) who are objectified by the camera and offered up to the admiring gaze of the spectator.

The Pleasures of Transtextuality

> I honestly couldn't find anything I didn't like about it [*Twilight*, the book]. My husband thought I was nuts, I always had this goofy grin on my face reading it. Sometimes I just start laughing and that was it. Poor guy, he got NO attention those four days. Monday rolled around I was at work, I didn't want to work, I was thinking about the books and nothing more. I found I wanted more.... I got on Meyer's website to find just that. I read all the quotes, I read all the extras, I even read all the stuff she took out. I still wanted more.
>
> Addicted? I was beyond all help. Then I found the draft to Edwards twilight. Let's just say my monday was booked. I finished that monday night at around 10.30pm.
>
> After reading it, I wanted MORE. Ugh, will this ever end?!?! So here I am, tuesday morning, reading twilight AGAIN![28]

* * *

> I didn't want [*New Moon,* the movie] to end at all! There is still this saddness that I won't see it again in an amount of time (hope the local theatre will bring it sometime in the next two months, too). I so didn't want it to end , that when we we leaving the theatre, I was turning back to watch the credits (yeah, I'm such a nerd!).[29]

What's interesting about these fan postings is the paradox they reveal: on the one hand, both people clearly derive a great deal of pleasure from reading *Twilight* and seeing the movie. On the other hand, neither finds either text completely satisfying. Instead of sating their desire, the books and films only increase their desire for more. They each seek out supplemental texts, but each new text only partially fulfills the desire, sending people back to the book, or forward to the next book, to the next film, and to all the seemingly endless supplemental materials available on-line, in magazines, on DVDs, in radio and television interviews, all of which can be defined as "paratexts"—"all the accessory messages and commentaries which come to surround the text and which at times become virtually indistinguishable from it."[30]

One way of explaining this paradox is to turn to the post-structuralist concept of the "supplement." As explained by Jonathan Culler,[31] a "supplemental" text calls into question, by its very existence, the completeness of the original text. For if the original, "the thing itself," were complete, it would need no further elaboration or interpretation. A film adaptation is a kind of supplement in this sense. It fleshes out and interprets the source text, revealing a kind of absence, or hole, in that source text. Yet the adaptation is also only a partial fulfillment of some *idea* of the original text; so it, too, requires supplementation. "'Through this series of supplements,' writes Jacques Derrida, 'there emerges a law: that of an endless linked series, ineluctably multiplying the supplementary mediations that produce the sense of the very thing that they defer: the impression of the thing itself, of immediate presence, or originary perception.... The more these texts want to tell us of the importance of the presence of the thing itself, the more they show the necessity of intermediaries.... What we learn from these texts is that the idea of the original is created by the copies, and that the original is always deferred—never to be grasped.'"[32] In this case, the "thing itself" turns out NOT to be *Twilight*, Stephenie Meyer's novel, but the *idea* of *Twilight*—the story, the characters, the imagery, the mythology—that is represented in the book *and* in the film *and* in all the paratextual elements, but which is always partial, incomplete, in any one textual incarnation. The relation among all these texts can be termed, in narrative theorist Gerard Genette's term, "transtextuality," referring to "all that which puts one text in relation, whether manifest or secret, with other texts."[33]

The pleasure of transtextuality, then, is that the story never ends. In Robert Stam's image, adaptations "are caught up in the ongoing whirl of intertextual reference and transformation, of texts generating other texts in an endless process of recycling, transformation, and transmutation, with no clear point of origin."[34] Because of the films and Meyer's other series of books (Edward's story), and all the other paratexts, in some ways the central romantic convention of "the end" is both fulfilled *and* delayed. The story ends, desire is fulfilled, tension is resolved, but it is then reawakened in each new iteration, in each "Making of ..." featurette on a DVD, and then again in each new message string on a fan website, on and on. And on.

Pleasures: Perverse and Otherwise

Twilight, in all its forms, offers pleasures to its fans. But pleasure is a vexed concept. And there is no shortage of critics who argue that in spite of (or even *because of*) the pleasures offered its consumers, *Twilight* lacks value. One line of argument would have it that mass culture, in general, offers a "false pleasure," that unlike the satisfying and "perverse" pleasure, or "jouissance," in Roland Barthes' terms, of authentic literature, mass culture lures its audience to a false complacency with the promise of equally false and insipid pleasures."[35] According to this line of thinking, any mass-produced product of popular culture must confirm the values of the dominant ideology. Hollywood film, in particular, is a commercial enterprise. If producers of a mainstream Hollywood film want to turn a profit, they cannot afford to alienate their audience and so will tend to reinforce conservative, middle-class values, so as to appeal to as large an audience as possible. And this leads, as Sarah Hentges in her analysis of teen coming-of-age films points out, to "a narrow range of plot lines" available to girls and women.[36] Thus *Twilight,* by its very popularity, must necessarily be shallow and conservative.

Further, some criticize the films as being "just chick flicks"—that is, as silly, overly-emotional films that only girls would want to see. And while the assumption that chick flicks (or, in fact, "chick" culture items in general) are superficial and trashy has been challenged by a substantive body of scholarly analysis in recent years,[37] the *Twilight* films are chick flicks in only "the simplest, broadest sense," as "commercial films that appeal to a female audience."[38] They lack the qualities that rescue chick lit/film for post-feminist scholars, that is, postmodern irony and a straightforward unapologetic engagement with female sexuality. Instead, *Twilight* sublimates sex in what Christine Seifert, in an article in the on-line magazine, *Bitch*, calls "abstinence porn."[39] Arguably, it conforms to the formulas of traditional romance: Bella needs Edward to rescue her, from the careening truck in the icy parking lot and from the bad vampires; and, indeed, the entire narrative trajectory is arguably centered on her goal to capture the man of her dreams. According to Seifert, "the sexual politics of Meyer's abstinence message" suggest that "when it comes to a woman's virtue, sex, identity, or her existence itself, it's all in the man's hands."[40]

Twilight also seems conservative in its relation to the horror genre. A number of theorists have demonstrated the progressive potential of horror films, particularly slasher films such as *Texas Chainsaw Massacre.*[41] While *Twilight* superficially has characteristics of the horror film — it has vampires, werewolves, and people dying in gruesome ways— it has none of the anarchic energy of the slasher films. And in its revision of vampire mythology, the film is divested of moral force. *San Francisco Chronicle* columnist Mark Morford snarkily points out that "even the original 'Dracula' served as wicked social commentary on everything from women's roles in society to conservative sexuality to colonialism. Now all we get is, what, a pack of emo boys in hair gel and sallow cheekbones whose last names just happen to rhyme with 'sullen'?"[42]

On the other hand, we can perhaps detect a few fissures in these critical assessments of *Twilight*'s value (or lack thereof). For one thing, although popular texts tend to work to re-establish dominant cultural values, that doesn't mean they are always successful at doing so, or that savvy consumers cannot "read against the grain" of such texts. As Nickianne Moody points out in her review of feminism and popular culture in *The Cambridge Companion to Feminist Literary Theory*, "consumers of popular culture need not be considered as passive. Rather, they are active participants in the creation of meaning, and their activity includes resistance to their subordination."[43] And Sarah Hentges argues that though "it is often assumed that popular culture is a shallow substitute for more meaningful rites of passage, ... [it] absolutely acts as a set of myths and markers for adolescence.... When considered as a mass media vehicle of cultural meaning, [film] is, at least potentially, a powerful determinant of social, cultural, and economic realities."[44] So, for example, while *Twilight* may conform, in a general way, to one characteristic of "chick" culture — its reliance on formulaic romance — it reacts against some of its more superficial and consumerist characteristics, such as easy, explicit sex and endless shopping. Bella is a resolutely anti-girly girl: she doesn't want to go to her high school dances, doesn't want to buy a prom dress, isn't interested in shopping for clothes, and prefers to drive an old truck. In the books, she cooks and keeps house for her father — traditional feminine tasks— but in the movies she has jettisoned even this.

Twilight also offers its female audience a welcome alternative to the reign of post-classical fantasy cinema, the tradition that began with *Star Wars* and has continued with the *Harry Potter* franchise and *The Lord of the Rings* series. *Twilight* has much in common with these series: the elements of fantasy (or at least an alternative reality), the appeal to a youthful audience, the avid fan base, and the development of the story over the course of several films.[45] But instead of the male-centered action-adventure story, *Twilight* is a girl-centered *Bildungsroman*. In fact, in many ways it has more in common with teen coming-of-age films than it does with postmodern chick flicks, vampire films, or fantasy adventure flicks. As with other examples of the teen film genre, *Twilight* offers a model of the female adolescent struggle to negotiate love and sex, family and career, dependence and independence. And if it doesn't suggest that young women should pursue sexual relationships as freely as celluloid men have done in the past, it does provide (as Stephen King has pointed out about Meyer's series) a "kind of a safe joining of love and sex in those books. It's exciting and it's thrilling and it's not particularly threatening because they're not overtly sexual. A lot of the physical side of it is conveyed in things like the vampire will touch her forearm or run a hand over skin, and she just flushes all hot and cold. And for girls, that's a shorthand for all the feelings that they're not ready to deal with yet."[46] *Twilight* also presents us with a young woman who chooses her own destiny: Bella is the one who decides to move to Forks— not her mother, not her father. She is the one who pursues Edward, who decides that she wants him, at all costs. She is the one who insists on being responsible for her life, and death, over the objections of everyone around her. Even if we disagree with her decisions, her determination to control her own destiny is admirable.

Twilight's most significant cultural contribution may lie in its success at the box office. As of this writing, both *Twilight* and *New Moon* are among the top 110 all-time U.S. box office earners (*Twilight* at #109 with over $191 million, and *New Moon* at #33 with over $293 million).[47] While this success says nothing about the films' quality or their worthiness, it may indicate that Hollywood will finally take note of the powerful potential of its young female audience and shift its programming strategy accordingly. A decade ago such a shift seemed in the offing, with the astounding success of *Titanic* (1997), a success widely attributed to female moviegoers. Until quite recently *Titanic* was the top U.S. box office earner of all time.[48] In an article published a year after its release, Peter Krämer notes that commentators at the time believed that the film could signal a return to female-centered Hollywood, "by returning female characters and romantic love to the centre of the industry's big releases and also by returning female audiences to the central place in Hollywood's thinking that they had once occupied in its golden age but which they lost to the young male audience in the late 1960s."[49] Krämer himself remained somewhat skeptical that the film would have the momentum to force such a shift: "Early indications are that, much like the Titanic, Hollywood's inertia may well be too big for the industry to be able to change course. Already executives say that the film's success will only lead to ever-more expensive action-adventure films, not to more female-oriented films."[50] Overall, Krämer's skepticism has proven accurate. Most of the top box office earners in the last decade have been male-oriented action-adventure flicks: *The Dark Knight, Pirates of the Caribbean, Spiderman, Transformers,* and *Avatar*. Still, *Twilight*, in all its transtextual whirl of proliferating texts—films (two of which have yet to be released), books, websites, DVDs, blogs, forthcoming graphic novels, and more — is arguably a more significant cultural, and economic, force than *Titanic*, and so perhaps it will be able to accomplish what *Titanic* could not. After all, while Rose may survive the sinking of the *Titanic* and live just long enough to see it resurrected, Bella not only survives, she becomes a superhero— and lives forever.

Notes

1. Stephenie Meyer, *Twilight* (New York: Little, Brown, 2005), 1.
2. "Welcome to Forks, Population 3120," *Twilight*, DVD, Three-Disc Deluxe Edition, directed by Catherine Hardwicke (2008; Universal City, CA: Summit Entertainment, 2009).
3. colegurl, posting to "Twilight Movie — Fan Reactions," Twilight Lexicon Discussion Forums, November 22, 2008, http://forum.twilightlexicon.com. Here and throughout the paper I have quoted discussion forum entries verbatim, complete with grammatical errors, typographical errors, and misspellings.
4. Stephenie Meyer, "Stephenie Meyer Answers Questions from TwilightMOMS Members, Part 2," *Twilight Moms*, www.twilightmoms.com.
5. Because at the time of writing only the first *Twilight* film was available on DVD, I decided to limit my discussion to the relationship between the first film and the first book — with a few brief references to *New Moon*. I leave it to others to test my conclusions about the first book/film pair against the other three pairs of texts.
6. Victor Nell, *Lost in a Book: The Psychology of Reading for Pleasure* (New Haven: Yale University Press, 1988), 1.
7. Stephenie Meyer, "A Conversation with Stephenie Meyer," Bonus Features Disc, *Twilight*, DVD, Three-Disc Deluxe Edition.
8. Precious, posting to "Addicted to Books," *Twilight Lexicon Discussion Forums*, October 7, 2008, 6:38 P.M.
9. Apparition, "Critical of Twilight Movie," *Twilight Lexicon Discussion Forums*, November 23, 2008, http://forum.twilightlexicon.com.

10. Susan Winnett, "Coming Unstrung: Women, Men, Narrative, and Principles of Pleasure," *PMLA* 105.3 (May 1990): 505.
11. Ibid., 507.
12. Ibid., 508.
13. Ibid.
14. Precious, posting to "Addicted to Books."
15. "Postmodern Adaptation: Pastiche, Intertextuality and Re-functioning," in *The Cambridge Companion to Literature on Screen,* Deborah Cartmell and Imelda Whelehan, eds. (Cambridge, UK: Cambridge University Press, 2007), 108.
16. despoina92, posting to "On New Moon," Twilight Lexicon Discussion Forums, November 22, 2008, http://forum.twilightlexicon.com
17. Apparition, posting to "Critical of Twilight Movie."
18. "I Like Watching You Sleep," *Twilight*, DVD.
19. "First Day of School," *Twilight*, DVD.
20. "La Push, Baby," *Twilight*, DVD.
21. "I Like Watching You Sleep," *Twilight,* DVD.
22. "An Excuse to Use the Kitchen," *Twilight,* DVD.
23. Robert Stam, "Introduction: The Theory and Practice of Adaptation," in *Literature and Film: A Guide to the Theory and Practice of Film Adaptation,* Stam and Alessandra Raengo, eds. (Malden, MA: Blackwell, 2005), 22.
24. Meyer, *Twilight*, 18.
25. KaGe, posting to "Twilight Movie — Fan Reactions," Twilight Lexicon Discussion Forums, November 22, 2008, http://forum.twilightlexicon.com.
26. Louis Peitzman, "11 Things: The Movie Was Better Than the Book," *San Francisco Chronicle,* November 19, 2009.
27. Laura Mulvey, "Visual Pleasure and Narrative Cinema," in *Visual and Other Pleasures* (Basingstoke, UK: Macmillan, 1989), 14–26.
28. Precious, posting to "Addicted to Books."
29. despoina92, "New Moon."
30. Stam, "Introduction," 8.
31. *Literary Theory: A Very Short Introduction* (New York: Oxford University Press, 1997), 9–12.
32. Quoted in Culler, *Literary Theory*, 11.
33. Quoted in Stam, "Introduction," 27.
34. Stam, "Introduction," 31.
35. Tania Modleski, "The Terror of Pleasure: The Contemporary Horror Film and Postmodern Theory," in *The Film Cultures Reader,* Graeme Turner, ed. (London: Routledge, 2002), 270.
36. Sarah Hentges, *Pictures of Girlhood: Modern Female Adolescence on Film* (Jefferson, NC: McFarland, 2006), 1.
37. See, for example, Suzanne Ferriss and Mallory Young, eds., *Chick Lit: The New Woman's Fiction* (New York: Routledge, 2006); Ferriss and Young, *Chick Flicks: Contemporary Women at the Movies* (New York: Routledge, 2008); Roberta Garrett, *Postmodern Chick Flicks* (Basingstoke, UK: Palgrave Macmillan, 2007); and Nickianne Moody, "Feminism and Popular Culture," in *The Cambridge Companion to Feminist Literary Theory*, Ellen Rooney, ed. (Cambridge, UK: Cambridge University Press, 2006), 172–189.
38. Moody, "Feminism," 185.
39. "Bite Me! (or Don't)," *BitchMedia,* December 12, 2008, http://bitchmagazine.org/article/bite-me-or-don't.
40. Ibid.
41. See, for example, Robin Wood, "An Introduction to the American Horror Film," in *Movies and Methods vol. II,* Bill Nichols, ed. (Berkeley: University of California Press, 1985) and Modleski, "The Terror of Pleasure."

42. "Let the Vampire Backlash Begin! Why Do We Keep Regurgitating the Same Old Bloodsuckers?" *SFGate.com*, October 30, 2009.

43. Moody, "Feminism," 173.

44. Sarah Hentges, *Pictures of Girlhood: Modern Female Adolescence on Film* (Jefferson, NC: McFarland, 2006).

45. For interesting analyses of the *Harry Potter* and *Lord of the Rings* adaptations, see, respectively, Deborah Cartmell and Imelda Whelehan, "Harry Potter and the Fidelity Debate," in *Books in Motion: Adaptation, Intertextuality, Authorship*, Mireia Aragay, ed., and I.Q. Hunter, "Post-Classical Fantasy Cinema: *The Lord of the Rings*," in *The Cambridge Companion to Literature on Screen*, Cartmell and Whelehan, eds., 154–166.

46. Casey Shaw, "Exclusive: Stephen King on J.K. Rowling, Stephenie Meyer," *USA Weekend Who's News Blog*, February 2, 2009, http://whosnews.usaweekend.com/2009/02/exclusive-stephen-king-on-jk-rowling-stephenie-meyer/.

47. "All-Time Box Office: U.S.A.," The Internet Movie Database, http://www.imdb.com/boxoffice/alltimegross.

48. Ibid.

49. "Women First: 'Titanic' (1997), Action-Adventure Films and Hollywood's Female Audience," *Historical Journal of Film, Radio, and Television* 18:4 (1998): 600.

50. Ibid., 614.

About the Contributors

Ann V. Bliss is an assistant professor at Texas A&M University, San Antonio. Her research explores how the practices and ideology of domestic photography established in the nineteenth century have endured and have become a part of the cultural subtext of the photograph, continuing not only to inform how we read photographs, but also defining the social structure of the family while disguising and exposing trauma within the family.

Lori Branch is an associate professor of English at the University of Iowa, where she teaches and writes about secularism, subjectivity, and the transformation of Christianity in modernity. Her first book, *Rituals of Spontaneity: Sentiment and Secularism from Free Prayer to Wordsworth,* was named 2007 Book of the Year by the MLA affiliate Conference on Christianity and Literature. Her second book, currently in progress, is *The Violation of God: Masculinity and Secularism in Enlightenment.* She lives in Iowa City with her husband and three-year-old twin daughters.

Amy M. Clarke is a continuing lecturer in the University Writing Program at the University of California, Davis. She teaches courses in science fiction and fantasy, including seminars on both the Harry Potter series and the *Twilight* phenomenon. She has published work on a number of science fiction writers, most recently a book titled *Ursula K. Le Guin's Journey to Post-Feminism* (McFarland, 2010).

Pamela H. Demory is a continuing lecturer in the University Writing Program at the University of California, Davis. She specializes in film adaptations, and her most recent publications include "Apocalypse Now Redux: *Heart of Darkness* Moves into New Territory," *Literature/Film Quarterly* (January 2007); "'It's About Seeing ...': Representations of the Female Body in Robert Altman's *Short Cuts* and Raymond Carver's Stories," reprinted in *Short Story Criticism* (2007 edition); and "Jane Austen and the Chick Flick in the 21st Century" in *Adaptation Studies: New Approaches* (2010).

Stephanie L. Dowdle is an associate professor of English at Salt Lake Community College in Salt Lake City, where she teaches courses ranging from composition and research, to cultural studies, critical theory, women writers, and Shakespeare. Her research interests include online/distance education, reality television, food, travel, and literature.

Janice Hawes is an assistant professor of English at South Carolina State University, Orangeburg, with research interests in Old Norse studies, Old English studies, medievalisms, and folklore. Her publications include "The Monstrosity of Heroism:

Grettir Ásmundarson as an Outsider," *Scandinavian Studies* 80:1 (2007), and "The Land Spirit's Rebellion: Independence and Religious Conflict in *Bárðar saga*," in *Translatio or the Transmission of Culture in the Middle Ages and Renaissance*, ed. Laura H. Hollengreen (Brepols, 2008).

Susan Jeffers has degrees from Brigham Young University and Abilene Christian University. Her thesis work at ACU was an ecocritical reading of *The Lord of the Rings*. She has presented at many different conferences on a variety of topics, including a consideration of patriarchal violence and female agency in *The Canterbury Tales*, presented at the International Congress on Medieval Studies at Kalamazoo. She has taught introductory composition courses and early American literature at ACU and is an active member of the Church of Jesus Christ of Latter-day Saints.

Kristian Jensen teaches literature and Native American studies at the University of California, Davis. He has also taught American literature and Native American studies at Johannes-Gutenberg Universität in Mainz, Germany. His dissertation research focuses on the impact of early anthropology on nineteenth-century American and Native American writers, and in it he explores how ethnography has influenced narrative in American literature. His recent publications include encyclopedia entries for the *Greenwood Encyclopedia of American Poetry* and some of his own poetry.

Yvette Kisor is an associate professor of literature at Ramapo College of New Jersey. She has various publications on Tolkien, *Beowulf*, and medieval literature more generally. Among her recent publications are "'Elves (and Hobbits) Always Refer to the Sun as She': Some Notes on a Note in Tolkien's *The Lord of the Rings*," *Tolkien Studies* 4 (2007); "Moments of Silence, Acts of Speech: Uncovering the Incest Motif in the Man of Law's Tale," *The Chaucer Review* 40 (2005); and "Numerical Composition and *Beowulf*: A Reconsideration," *Anglo-Saxon England* 38 (2009).

Emma Catherine Mc Elroy is a specialist in *Twilight* studies. She studies American literature and French — as well as rhythm tap — in both Davis and Berkeley, California. In addition to varied dance performances at such venues as the University of California, Davis, Mc Elroy is also an active ornithologist who is engaged in examining seasonal waterfowl patterns at the Vic Fazio Yolo Wildlife Area and Sacramento National Wildlife Refuge.

James Mc Elroy, a graduate of Trinity College and University College, Dublin, currently teaches at the University of California, Davis. His articles and reviews have appeared in *The New York Times*, *The Los Angeles Times*, and *The American Poetry Review*. His book *James Joyce: Ecological Perspectives* will be published by the Edwin Mellen Press (New York) in 2010.

Christine M. Mitchell is an associate professor at Southeastern Louisiana University in Hammond with a doctorate in English rhetoric and composition from the University of Southwestern Louisiana in Lafayette. Among her areas of research and instruction are rhetoric (focusing on history and gender issues), American literature, popular culture, and English language arts pedagogy. The summer heat in Louisiana brought her and her husband to Forks, Washington, and thus to a study of *Twilight*.

Marijane Osborn is an emeritus professor at the University of California, Davis, who publishes mainly on Old and Middle English poetry. She has written or been a major contributor to several books on *Beowulf*, has published three books on Middle English topics, and has written reams of articles on various subjects including C.S. Lewis. Her current book is *Nine Medieval Romances of Magic* (Broadview Press, 2010).

Sarah Schwartzman earned her master's degree in religious studies from the University of California, Riverside. Her research area is religion in the secular public sphere, focusing specifically on how religious identities are cultivated and expressed in relation to secular politics, literature, and popular culture.

Keri Wolf holds a Ph.D. from the University of California, Davis and researches the intersections between space, place, and identity in Old English heroic poetry. Her most recent publication is "Enacting the Ties That Bind: Oath-Making vs Oath-Taking in the Finnsburg Episode," *Comitatus: A Journal of Medieval and Renaissance Studies* 40 (2009).

Bibliography

Primary

Meyer, Stephenie. *Breaking Dawn*. New York: Little, Brown, 2008.

_____. *Eclipse*. New York: Little, Brown, 2007.

_____. *The Host*. New York: Little, Brown, 2008.

_____. "Jacob." "*New Moon* Outtakes." *The Official Website of Stephenie Meyer*. http://www.stepheniemeyer.com/pdf/nm_outtakes_jacob.pdf.

_____. *Midnight Sun. The Official Website of Stephenie Meyer*. http://www.stepheniemeyer.com/pdf/midnightsun_partial_draft4.pdf.

_____. *New Moon*. New York: Little, Brown, 2006.

_____. "Scholarship." "*New Moon* Outtakes." *The Official Website of Stephenie Meyer*. http://www.stepheniemeyer.com/pdf/nm_outtakes_scholarship.pdf.

_____. *Twilight*. New York: Little, Brown, 2005.

Online Sources

"The *Breaking Dawn* Concert Tour — Seattle Q&A." *Twilight Lexicon*. http://www.twilightlexicon.com/?page_id=1323.

"Frequently Asked Questions: *Breaking Dawn*." *The Official Website of Stephenie Meyer*. http://www.stepheniemeyer.com/bd_faq.html.

Hatchette Book Group. "Interview." http://www.hachettebookgroup.com/9FA6868D6CC441738975A4C8D11EA37A.aspx.

"Interview: *Twilight* Author Stephenie Meyer." Interview by William Morris. *A Motley Vision*, October 26, 2005. http://www.motleyvision.org/2005/interview-twilight-author-stephanie-meyer/.

Irwin, Megan. "Charmed: Stephenie Meyer's Vampire Romance Novels Made a Mormon Mom an International Success." *Phoenix New Times News*, July 12, 2007. http://www.phoenixnewtimes.com/2007-07-12/news/charmed/.

"*New Moon*: The Movie. *TheTwilightSaga.com's* Q and A with Stephenie Meyer." *Stephenie Meyer Official Website*. http://www.stepheniemeyer.com/nm_movie_qanda.html.

"Personal Correspondence #7." *Twilight Lexicon*. http://www.twilightlexicon.com/?p=62.

"Personal Correspondence #12." *Twilight Lexicon*. http://www.twilightlexicon.com/?p=360.

"Q&A at Fairless Hills." *Stephenie Says*. http://stepheniesays.livejournal.com/20266.html.

"Stephenie Meyer's 'Twilight' Zone." Interview with Gregory Kirschling. *Entertainment Weekly*, July 5, 2008. http://www.ew.com/ew/article/0,,20049578,00.html.

Sullivan, Robert. "Dreamcatcher." *Vogue*, March 2009. http://www.vogue.com/feature/2009_March_Stephenie_Meyer/.

"10 Second Interview: A Few Words with Stephenie Meyer." *Amazon.com*. http://www.amazon.com/Twilight-Book-1-Stephenie-Meyer/dp/0316160172.

"*Twilight* author Stephenie Meyer Unfazed as Fame Dawns." Interview with Carol Memmott. *USA Today*, July 30, 2008. http://www.usatoday.com/life/books/

news/2008-07-30-stephenie-meyer-main_N.htm.

"*Twilight* Tuesday: Stephenie Meyer Says She May Revisit 'Twilight' Universe Someday." Interview by Larry Carroll. *MTV.com*, August 5, 2008. http://www.mtv.com/movies/news/articles/1592141/story.jhtml. 3.

"*TheTwilightSaga.com*'s Q and A with Stephenie." *The Official Website of Stephenie Meyer*. http://www.stepheniemeyer.com.

Valy, Karen. "Stephenie Meyer: 12 of My 'Twilight' Inspirations." *Entertainment Weekly*, September 29, 2009. http://www.ew.com/ew/gallery/0,,20308569 20308554,00.html.

"Video & Transcript: Q+A at Vroman's, Pasadena, CA." *Stephenie Says*, August 25, 2007. http://stepheniesays.livejournal.com/3221.html.

Secondary Sources

Andrade, Manuel, and Leo Frachtenberg, eds. *Quileute Texts*. New York: Columbia University Press, 1931.

Ang, Sydney. "Undead Evermore: Vampire Mythology in the 21st Century." *The Manila Times*, October 30, 2008. http://www.manilatimes.net/national/2008/oct/30/yehey/life/20081030lif1.html.

Bancroft-Hunt, Norman, and Werner Forman. *People of the Totem: The Indians of the Pacific Northwest*. New York: G. P. Putnam's Sons, 1979.

Bayer-Berenbaum, Linda. *The Gothic Imagination: Expansion in Gothic Literature and Art*. East Brunswick, NJ: Associated University Presses, 1982.

Beahm, George. *Bedazzled: Stephenie Meyer and the Twilight Phenomenon*. Nevada City, CA: Underwood Books, 2009.

Bettelheim, Bruno. *The Uses of Enchantment: The Meaning and Importance of Fairy Tales*. New York: Vintage Books, 1977.

Bordo, Susan. *Unbearable Weight: Feminism, Western Culture, and the Body*. Berkeley and Los Angeles, CA: University of California Press, 1993.

Botting, Fred. *Limits of Horror: Technology, Bodies, Gothic*. Manchester: Manchester University Press, 2008.

Butler, Judith. *Bodies that Matter: On the Discursive Limits of "Sex."* New York: Routledge, 1993.

Campbell, Joseph. *The Hero with a Thousand Faces*. Princeton, NJ: Princeton University Press, 1968.

The Church of Jesus Christ of Latter-day Saints. "The Family: A Proclamation to the World. " http://www.lds.org/library/display/0,4945,161-1-11-1,00.html.

The Church of Jesus Christ of Latter-day Saints. *Gospel Principles*. Salt Lake City, Utah: The Church of Jesus Christ of Latter-day Saints, 1988.

Clark, Ella E. *Indian Legends of the Pacific Northwest*. Berkeley: University of California Press, 1953.

Collins, Gail. "A Virginal Goth Girl." *The New York Times*, July 12, 2008. http://www.nytimes.com/2008/07/12/opinion/12colllins.html.

"A Conversation with Stephenie Meyer." *Twilight*, DVD, Three-Disc Deluxe Edition, directed by Catherine Hardwicke. 2008. Universal City, CA: Summit Entertainment, 2009.

Cook, Chris. *Forks Forum: Twilight Territory*. Sequim, WA: Olympic View Publishing, 2009.

Coudray, Chantel Bourgault du. *The Curse of the Werewolf: Fantasy, Horror, and the Beast Within*. London: I.B. Tauris, 2006.

Dennison, Michael J. *Vampirism: Literary Tropes of Decadence and Entropy*. New York: Peter Lang Publishing, 2001.

Douvikas, Danielle. "*Twilight* Series Sends Girls a Wrong Message." *The Herald*, November 28, 2008. http://www.heraldonline.com/107/story/985071.html.

Ernst, Alice Henson. *The Wolf Ritual of the Northwest Coast*. Eugene: University of Oregon Press, 1952.

Fosl, Peter S., and Eli Fosl. "*Vampire-Dämmerung:* What Can *Twilight* Tell Us about God?" Twilight *and Philosophy: Vampires, Vegetarians, and the Pursuit of Immortality*, edited by Rebecca Housel and J. Jeremy Wisnewski, 63-77. Hoboken, NJ: John Wiley & Sons, 2009.

Frost, Brian J. *The Monster with a Thousand Faces: Guises of the Vampire in Myth and Literature*. Bowling Green, OH: Bowling Green State University Popular Press, 1989.

Glosecki, Stephen. "Wolf." In *Medieval Folklore: An Encyclopedia of Myths, Legends, Tales, Beliefs, and Customs*, ed. Carl Lindahl, John McNamara, and John Lindow, Vol. 2, 1057–1061. Oxford: Oxford University Press, 2002.

Granger, John. "Mormon Vampires in the Garden of Eden: What the Bestselling *Twilight* Series Has in Store for Young Readers." *Touchstone* 22.8 (2009): 24–29.

Grossman, Lev. "It's Twilight in American." *Time Magazine*, November 23, 2009. www.time.com/time/magazine/article/0,9171,1938712,00.html.

_____. "Stephenie Meyer: A New J.K. Rowling?" *Time*, April 24, 2008. http://www.time.com/time/magazine/article/0,9171,1734838–1,00.html.

Grosz, Elizabeth. *Volatile Bodies: Towards a Corporeal Feminism*. Indianapolis: Indiana University Press, 1994.

Haraway, Donna J. "Universal Donors in a Vampire Culture: It's All in the Family: Biological Kinship Categories in the Twentieth-Century United States." In *Uncommon Ground: Rethinking the Human Place in Nature*, edited by William Cronin, 321–378. New York: W.W. Norton, 1996.

_____. *When Species Meet*. Minneapolis: University of Minneapolis Press, 2008.

Hentges, Sarah. *Pictures of Girlhood: Modern Female Adolescence on Film*. Jefferson, NC: McFarland, 2006.

Higley, Sarah. "Finding the Man under the Skin: Identity, Monstrosity, Expulsion, and the Werewolf." In *The Shadow-Walkers: Jacob Grimm's Mythology of the Monstrous*, edited by T. A. Shippey. Tempe: Arizona Center for Medieval and Renaissance Studies, 2005.

Holman, Thomas B. "Commitment Making Mate Selection Processes among Active Mormon American Couples." In *Mormon Identities in Transition*, edited by Douglas J. Davies, 129–130. London: Cassell, 1996.

Hopkins, Ellen, ed. *A New Dawn: Your Favorite Authors on Stephenie Meyer's* Twilight *Series*. Borders, 2008

Housel, Rebecca J., Jeremy Wisnewski, and William Irwin, eds. Twilight *and Philosophy: Vampires, Vegetarians, and the Pursuit of Immortality*. Hoboken, NJ: John Wiley and Sons, 2009.

Jenkins, Henry. "Why Heather Can Write." *Digital Renaissance*, February 6, 2004. http://www.southernct.edu/~hochman/Whyheathercanwrite.htm.

Jepson, Eric W. "Saturday's Werewolf: Vestiges of the Premortal Romance in Stephenie Meyer's *Twilight* Novels." *Reading Until Dawn* 1, no. 2 (2009).

Kapralos, Krista. "Birth of the Bloggernacle." *Religion Dispatches*, February 24, 2009. http://www.religiondispatches.org/archive/mediaculture/1148/.

_____. "Mormon Bloggernacle is No Choir." *Religion Dispatches*, March 4, 2009. http://www.religiondispatches.org/archive/mediaculture/1179/.

Kazez, Jean. "Dying to Eat: The Vegetarian Ethics of *Twilight*." In Twilight *and Philosophy: Vampires, Vegetarians, and the Pursuit of Immortality*, edited by Rebecca Housel and J. Jeremy Wisnewski, 25–38. Hoboken, NJ: John Wiley, 2009.

Kinney, Shirley, and Wallis Kinney. "The Jane Austen—*Twilight* Zone." *Jane Austen Society of North America*. http://www.jasna.org/film/twilight.html.

Klockars, Donna. *Wolf Family*. Chemanius Tribal Council, Nanaimo, B.C.: Pacific Edge Publishing Ltd., 1992.

Kristeva, Julia. *Powers of Horror: An Essay on Abjection*. 1980. Translated by Leon S. Roudiez. New York: Columbia University Press, 1982.

Lewis, C. S. *The Discarded Image: An Introduction to Medieval and Renaissance Literature*. Cambridge: Cambridge University Press, 1964.

May, Dean L. "Mormons." In *Mormons and Mormonism*, edited by Eric A. Eliason, 72–74. Urbana: University of Illinois Press, 2001.

McMillan, Alan D. *Since the Time of the Transformers: the Ancient Heritage of the Nuu-chah-nulth, Ditidaht, and Makah.*

Vancouver: University of British Colombia Press, 1999.

Modleski, Tania. "The Terror of Pleasure: The Contemporary Horror Film and Postmodern Theory." In *The Film Cultures Reader*. Edited by Graeme Turner, 270. London: Routledge, 2002.

Mogen, David, Scott P. Sanders, and Joanne B. Karpinski, eds. *Frontier Gothic: Terror and Wonder at the Frontier in American Literature*. Rutherford, NJ: Fairleigh Dickinson University Press; London: Associated University Presses, 1993.

Mullaney, Jamie L. *Everyone Is NOT Doing It: Abstinence and Personal Identity*. Chicago: University of Chicago Press, 2006.

Mulvey, Laura. "Visual Pleasure and Narrative Cinema." In *Visual and Other Pleasures*, 14–26. Basingstoke, UK: Macmillan, 1989.

Myers-Smith, Isla. "The Ecological Consequences of Vampirism: AKA, Wherein an Ecologist Takes Down *New Moon*." *Inkling Magazine*, November 30, 2009. http://www.inklingmagazine.com/articles/the-ecological-consequences-of-vampirism/.

Nell, Victor. *Lost in a Book: The Psychology of Reading for Pleasure*. New Haven: Yale University Press, 1988.

Norman, Tony. "The Twilight of the Monsters Has Arrived." *Pittsburgh Post-Gazette*, November 27, 2009. http://www.post-gazette.com/pg/09331/1016613–153.stm.

Offenbacher, Matthew. "Green Gothic." *Arts Journal*. http://www.artsjournal.com/anotherbb/2009/08/green-gothic-by-matthew-offenb.html.

Ostling, Richard N., and Joan K. Ostling. *Mormon America*. New York: HarperOne, 2007.

Pearson, Carol, and Katherine Pope. *The Female Hero in American and British Literature*. New York: R.R. Bowker Company, 1981.

Powell, Jay, and Vickie Jensen. *Quileute: An Introduction to the Indians of La Push*. Seattle: University of Washington Press, 1976.

Reynolds, John Mark. "*Twilight*'s Flawed Faith." *The Scriptorium*, July 31, 2009. http://www.scriptoriumdaily.com/2009/07/31/twilights-flawed-faith/.

Robisch, S.K. *Wolves and the Wolf Myth in American Literature*. Reno: University of Nevada Press, 2009.

Rosenbloom, Stephanie. "A Ring That Says No, Not Yet." *The New York Times*, Dec 14, 2005.

Shaw, Casey. "Exclusive: Stephen King on J. K. Rowling, Stephenie Meyer." *USA Weekend Who's News Blog*, Feb. 2, 2009. http://whosnews.usaweekend.com/2009/02/exclusive-stephen-king-on-jk-rowling-stephenie-meyer/.

Siefert, Christine. "Bite Me! (or, Don't)." *bitch: Feminist Response to Pop Culture*, December 12, 2008. http://bitchmagazine.org/article/bite-me-or-dont.

Smallwood, Christine. "Vampire Studies: What is *Twilight Really* About?" *n+1*, November 29, 2009. http://www.nplusonemag.com/vampire-studies.

Stacey, Judith. *In the Name of the Family: Rethinking Family Values in the Postmodern Age*. Boston: Beacon Press, 1996.

Tatar, Maria. *The Hard Facts of the Grimms' Fairy Tales*. 1987. Princeton: Princeton University Press, 2003.

_____. *Off With Their Heads!: Fairy Tales and the Culture of Childhood*. Princeton, NJ: Princeton University Press, 1992.

Thomas, Ethan "'Twilight' Loses Luster with Deseret Books." *Deseret News*, April 23, 2009. http://www.deseretnews.com/article/705299108/Twilight-loses-luster-with-Deseret-Book.html.

Trites, Roberta Seelinger. *Waking Sleeping Beauty; Feminist Voices in Children's Novels*. Iowa City: University of Iowa Press, 1997.

Vineyard, Jennifer. "Sinking Our Teeth into Modern Vampires: How Do 'Twilight,' 'Buffy,' and Others Compare?" *MTV*, October 29, 2008. http://www.mtv.com/movies/news/articles/1598112/story.jhtml.

Walker, Michael. "A Teenage Tale with Bite." *BYU Magazine*, Winter 2007. http://magazine.byu.edu/?act=view&a=1972.

Warner, Jessica. *The Day George Bush Stopped Drinking: Why Abstinence Matters to the Religious Right.* Ontario: McClelland & Stewart, 2008.

"Welcome to Forks, Population 3120." *Twilight*, DVD, Three-Disc Deluxe Edition, directed by Catherine Hardwicke. 2008. Universal City, CA: Summit Entertainment, 2009.

Winnett, Susan. "Coming Unstrung: Women, Men, Narrative, and Principles of Pleasure." *PMLA* 105.3 (May 1990): 505.

Wolcott, James. "The *Twilight* Zone." *Vanity Fair*, December 2008. http://www.vanityfair.com/culture/features/2008/12/twilight200812.

Zipes, Jack. *Breaking the Magic Spell: Radical Theories of Folk and Fairy Tales.* Lexington: University Press of Kentucky, 2002.

_____. *Fairy Tales and the Art of Subversion.* New York: Routledge, 2006.

_____. *The Great Fairy Tale Tradition: From Straparola and Basile to the Brothers Grimm.* New York: Norton, 2001.

Index